£55,00
1989

THE LAW OF
MARITIME DELIMITATION
—REFLECTIONS

THE LAW OF
MARITIME DELIMITATION
—REFLECTIONS

by

PROSPER WEIL

Professor of International Law, University of Paris

Translated from the French by
MAUREEN MACGLASHAN
Assistant Director of the
Research Centre for International Law
University of Cambridge

CAMBRIDGE

GROTIUS PUBLICATIONS LIMITED

1989

SALES &　　　　　　GROTIUS PUBLICATIONS LTD.
ADMINISTRATION　　PO BOX 115, CAMBRIDGE CB3 9BP, UK

British Library Cataloguing in Publication Data

Weil, Prosper
　　The law of maritime delimitation—reflections.
　　1. Territorial waters. Boundaries. International legal aspects
　　I. Title　II. Perspectives du droit de la
　　　　　　　delimitation maritime. *English*
　　341.4'48

ISBN 0-949009-40-7

Printed in Great Britain by
Gomer Press, Llandysul, Dyfed

PREFACE

This volume is a translation of *Perspectives du Droit de la Délimitation Maritime* published in French in 1988 by Editions A. Pedone of Paris (ISBN 2-233-00183-4). I am grateful to the original publishers for their agreement to the appearance of the present translation.

The translation, and the index to it, have been made by Miss Maureen MacGlashan, the Assistant Director of the Research Centre for International Law in the University of Cambridge. Miss MacGlashan has brought a skill, dedication and patience to this task for which I thank her warmly. The initiative in proposing and arranging the translation was taken by Mr E. Lauterpacht, CBE, QC, the Director of the same Centre. I am glad that it has been possible to publish the volume under the auspices of the Centre.

I also extend my appreciation to Mr John Adlam of Grotius Publications Limited for his assistance in seeing the text through the press.

Prosper Weil

Paris, May 1989

TABLE OF CONTENTS

CONCLUSION

TABLE OF CASES

Listed below are the full titles of cases cited in the text, together with references to where they may be found. Those cases marked with an asterisk will also be found in a collection of maritime boundary cases in preparation by the Research Centre for International Law in the University of Cambridge and shortly to be published by Grotius Publications Limited.

ABBREVIATIONS

AFDI	Annuaire Français de Droit International
AJIL	American Journal of International Law
BYIL	British Year Book of International Law
CLJ	Cambridge Law Journal
CYIL	Canadian Yearbook of International Law
EEZ	Exclusive Economic Zone
ICJ	International Court of Justice
ICLQ	International and Comparative Law Quarterly
ILC	International Law Commission
ILCYB	International Law Commission Yearbook
ILM	International Legal Materials
ILR	International Law Reports
IRAN-U.S. C.T.R.	Iran-United States Claims Tribunal Reports
JDI	Journal de Droit International
NTIR	Nordisk Tidsskrift for International Ret
PCIJ	Permanent Court of International Justice
RGDIP	Revue générale de droit international public
UNCLOS I/III	United Nations Conference on the Law of the Sea I/III
UNRIAA	United Nations Reports of International Arbitral Awards
Virg. J	Virginia Journal of International Law
ZaöRV	Zeitschrift für Ausländisches Öffentliches Recht und Völkerrecht

The footnote references to 'CR' and 'C 1/CR' are to the *comptes rendus* (verbatim records) of the hearings in the International Court of Justice produced daily during the hearing of cases. In due course these appear in printed form in the series *ICJ Pleadings, Oral Arguments, Documents*.

The full title of all articles and books not cited *in extenso* in the text will be found in the Bibliography on page 291. A figure in square brackets after an author's name identifies which of his several works, as listed in the Bibliography, is intended.

INTRODUCTION

INTRODUCTION

A T a time when, with only a few exceptions, States have at last stabilized the contours of their territorial sovereignties, the determination of the limits of their maritime rights and jurisdictions has become one of the principal concerns of international relations and, therefore, of the international law of the second half of the twentieth century. The limits in question are, in the first place, the outer seaward limits, with the enormous extension of maritime rights of coastal States and the economic appropriation of the oceans to a distance of 200 miles or more from the coast; and in the second place, the limits between the jurisdictions and maritime rights of neighbouring States with opposite or adjacent coasts. Every time the maritime projections of two States meet and overlap, each of them must inevitably forego the full enjoyment of the maritime jurisdictions it could have claimed had it not had the geographical misfortune to find its appropriation in conflict with that of its neighbour. A line of separation then has to be drawn, which is exactly what maritime delimitation is all about. The need for delimitation has existed ever since the territorial sovereignty of the coastal State was extended, beyond its land territory and so-called internal waters, over an area of adjacent sea known, significantly, as the territorial sea. But the maritime projections of three, six or twelve miles thus generated collided less often—and the difficulty caused by such a collision was easier to resolve—than maritime projections extending great distances from the coasts. This means that maritime delimitation today is of a magnitude previously unknown.

The problems arise in stages of varying intensity. The delimitation of the territorial sea rarely gave rise to major difficulties, even when its breadth went beyond the modest three miles of tradition. But it was obvious from the beginning that the problems of continental shelf delimitation would be difficult, and matters quickly reached crisis level. The critical phase seems now to have passed as far as the delimitation of the continental shelf is concerned, but it may still lie ahead in respect of the exclusive economic zone.

At first sight, the economic stakes seem always to occupy first place in these difficulties, in that States are thirsty for energy and anxious to obtain exclusive rights to marine and submarine resources over as large an area as possible. But the problems of delimitation would not have loomed so large if behind the economic preoccupations did not lurk political concerns. In theory, maritime jurisdictions are limited to sovereign rights of a functional nature, but who can be confident that, one day, these modest rights will not be transformed into a separate, fully-fledged sovereignty, as some States have already said they hope will happen? The delimitation cases which have so far come before international tribunals leave little room for doubt: when a State claims a particular line for the delimitation of its continental shelf or exclusive economic zone, or refuses to accept another which would allow a neighbouring State to come and explore or exploit marine resources at a few cable-lengths from its shores, its immediate preoccupation may well be economic. However, considerations of security and sovereignty almost always show through, are even sometimes openly declared. The courts find themselves faced by a difficult question: how far are considerations of a political nature relevant for the delimitation of maritime areas over which, in principle, States exercise only narrowly defined, essentially economic, rights, and, again in principle, have no sovereignty properly speaking? Although their answer to this question has varied a little, their most recent decisions show no hesitation in acknowledging the legitimacy of these political preoccupations. Indeed, they go so far as to say that a delimitation must avoid causing either of the parties to find itself faced with the exercise of rights, off its coasts and in their immediate vicinity, which could compromise not only its economic interests but also its security in the broadest sense.

The problems of maritime delimitation are both qualitatively important and numerous. A glance at the map shows that there are several hundred delimitations of the territorial sea, the continental shelf and the exclusive economic zone still to be made. As new exclusive economic zones are proclaimed, so the number of problem situations is bound inexorably to increase. Just imagine, for example, the difficulties which would arise if the States around the Mediterranean were to claim exclusive economic zones in a sea so narrow that none of the States bordering it could possibly project 200 miles from its shoreline.

Some of the problems of delimitation are practically insoluble in the present state of political relations—it would be wrong to pretend otherwise. Others have been resolved by agreement at the end of sometimes long and difficult negotiations; it is estimated that there are about a hundred agreements defining either a line of delimitation for a specific maritime jurisdiction (for the continental shelf, for example), or a single boundary separating all maritime jurisdictions between the two States. Finally, half-a-dozen problems have been resolved through judicial or arbitral settlement. This shows the size of the task which still awaits governments and international tribunals. The International Court of Justice has observed that, after concentrating for many years on "the seaward limit of the area in respect of which the coastal State could claim exclusive rights of exploitation", that is to say, on "the legal basis on which any rights at all . . . could be claimed", attention has now turned to "the main issue . . . of boundaries between States".[1] The problem of seaward *limits* is now enjoying a respite, to be replaced by that of the *delimitation* of the maritime spaces between neighbouring States, in other words, the establishment of maritime boundaries.

THE LEGAL CONQUEST OF MARITIME DELIMITATION

Maritime delimitation must, inevitably, be a painful process since, by its very definition, it implies an amputation of the area which each of the States involved could hope to appropriate if it faced the oceans on its own. Unless one appropriation is to be completely sacrificed to the other—and this would conflict not only with the demands of justice and good sense but also with the principle of the equality of States—the sacrifices must be shared equally. Any number of approaches can be imagined: equality of sacrifice, quantitative or proportional; equality of resultant areas; the allocation of surface areas or the division of resources. More space or resources might be given to the State whose land territory was the greater, or coastal facade the longer, or wealth the greater; or the opposite would be possible, with an attempt to correct natural inequalities by according more sea to the State with less territory, or less coastline, or less wealth. And what method is to be used to achieve the desired goal? A perpendicular to the shoreline? A line at an equal distance from the two coasts? Or some other method?

Rules of the game are clearly needed, in other words, a law of delimitation. When two governments try to reach agreement through negotiation on a line of separation, this need is not imperative, since States are free to decide whatever solution seems to them appropriate. Nonetheless, it is useful for them to have guide-lines, so as to put the brake on excessive claims, discourage extreme

---

[1] *North Sea*, para. 48.

positions and keep the discussion within reasonable limits. But it is when governments, unable to reach agreement, seek a third-party settlement that a law of maritime delimitation becomes indispensable, for how is the judge or arbitrator to avoid deciding *ex aequo et bono*—which States generally do not want—if he does not have a body of rules on the basis of which to settle the disputes submitted to him?

Experience shows that a new activity rarely acquires legal rules straight away. It is only after a process, sometimes long, sometimes short, that the law manages to master a new domain and give it predictability, accompanied by that subtle mixture of reassuring stability and openness to change peculiar to the law. Scarcely thirty years ago, when the International Law Commission began to study the problems of maritime delimitation, there was hardly a single rule of law to regulate this new chapter in international relations. States had an obligation to delimit their maritime jurisdictions—at that time it was a question of the territorial sea and the continental shelf—by means of agreement with a view to reaching an equitable result. That was all. This, under the guise of a legal obligation to negotiate, was a barely disguised admission that there were no substantive norms governing maritime delimitation. There was also reluctance to contemplate a judicial or arbitral settlement in the absence, it was said, of rules of law which could be applied by the judge or arbitrator. An *ex aequo et bono* solution seemed to some the only way out. Only slowly was the challenge taken up and legal norms developed which can now be called, without exaggeration, a law of maritime delimitation.

Essentially judge-made law

This production of norms, started in the 1950s and still incomplete, was fed from several quarters. There is often a multiplicity of formal sources in international law. What is less usual is the relative importance these various sources assume in the law of maritime delimitation.

Contrary to what normally happens in new chapters of international law, the treaty source took off rapidly. The work of the International Law Commission gave birth to the provisions of the 1958 Geneva Conventions relating to the delimitation of the territorial sea and the continental shelf. And the Third United Nations Conference on the Law of the Sea produced the provisions of the Convention on the Law of the Sea, signed at Montego Bay in 1982, relating to the delimitation of the territorial sea, the continental shelf and the exclusive economic zone.[2] Although this body of treaty provisions relating to such a new matter may seem impressive, it has to be recognized that its contribution to the law of maritime delimitation has been relatively modest. The limited place the courts accorded the 1958 provision on the delimitation of the continental shelf and their minimalist interpretation of it has prevented its playing the dynamic and creative role it might have. As for the 1982 provisions on the delimitation of the continental shelf and exclusive economic zone—not yet in force—their lack of precision has limited them to the minor role of vague and general guidelines, incapable of leading to a precise normative content.

Bilateral agreements, on the other hand, could have developed into a practice generating customary law, but they too have been abandoned by the wayside, so much so that the law of maritime delimitation has been built up on the fringe of bilateral treaty practice just as it has developed in the margin of the provisions of multilateral conventions.

Since treaty sources have played such a restricted role, it is customary law which has been called to fill the front rank; nowadays, the law of maritime delimitation usually means the customary law. This is surprising, to say the least. Here we are, with a new field of international law which has had the rare good fortune, after only a few years, to enjoy a flurry of agreements, both bilateral and multilateral, and yet it is not these agreements which have produced the normative corpus governing this new field and ensured its development, but a customary law which looks elsewhere for inspiration.

This reversal of the respective roles of treaty and customary law can be easily explained. International tribunals, and in particular the International Court of Justice, in half-a-dozen *causes célèbres*, have made a *capitis deminutio* of the treaty source and themselves undertaken the direct definition of the law of maritime delimitation, giving it the appearance and name of general or customary international law. There is probably no other chapter of international law which has been written so exclusively and rapidly by the international courts. In scarcely fifteen years, the International Court of Justice, through its *North Sea* (1969), *Tunisia/Libya* (1982), *Gulf of Maine* (1984), and *Libya/Malta*(1985) judgments, and arbitral tribunals in the *Anglo-French* (1977) and *Guinea/Guinea-Bissau* (1985)

---

[2] For convenience, the texts of the articles relating to delimitation in the 1958 and 1982 Conventions are set out at p. 289 below.

cases,[3] have managed to build up a normative system sufficiently comprehensive to govern all maritime delimitations, whether of the territorial sea, the continental shelf or the exclusive economic zone, so much so that it is possible today to speak of a *single* law—a common law—and not of the *laws* of maritime delimitation.

In the final analysis, the legal conquest of maritime delimitation is not the work of either treaty or custom but of the courts which, far from being a subsidiary source of international law, here play the role of a primary and direct source of law, even if they have chosen modestly to ascribe the credit to customary law.

A suppletive law

The collection of rules thus built up by the courts has, however, only a limited field of application: it governs delimitations which States have submitted to judicial or arbitral settlement, but not those decided by governments themselves by agreement. The rules which make up the law of maritime delimitation do not have the character of *jus cogens*, binding on States, and allowing them no scope for derogation. In a word, although it binds the international judge or arbitrator, the law of maritime delimitation, as far as States are concerned, is no more than suppletive.

This observation is, however, only theoretically correct. In practice, the impact of the rules forming the law of maritime delimitation goes beyond those cases, inevitably few in number, where the delimitation has been entrusted to an international court. Although in principle at liberty to free themselves from the law, States negotiating a delimitation agreement almost always try to base their claims on legal precedent and rarely fail to take the law as a

---

[3] These cases have all been submitted to judicial or arbitral settlement by means of a *compromis*. In addition, the International Court of Justice was seised of the question of the delimitation of the continental shelf in the Aegean between Greece and Turkey at the unilateral request of Greece, but it decided that it had no jurisdiction (Judgment of 19 December 1978, ICJ *Reports*, 1978, p. 3). To the cases quoted in the text, which relate exclusively to maritime delimitations, there should be added two arbitral awards covering wider ground. The *Beagle Channel* arbitral award of 18 February 1977 between Argentina and Chile (*ILM*, vol. 17, 1978, p. 632; *ILR*, vol. 52, p. 93), in order, as required by the *compromis*, to decide sovereignty over the small islands in this narrow waterway, effected a delimitation of territorial waters within the Channel. There is a short passage in the award on this question (paras. 103-10). The arbitral award of 19 October 1981 between the Emirates of Dubai and Sharjah (unpublished) simultaneously determined the land and maritime (territorial waters and continental shelf) boundaries between the parties. Mention should also be made of *Jan Mayen*, the subject of a conciliation procedure between Iceland and Norway; for this case, see p. 29 n. 26 below.

point of reference in their discussions and sometimes even in their agreements. And each judicial or arbitral decision is gone through by interested government departments with a fine tooth-comb, since they know what effect this case-law can have on their bargaining power in negotiations with their neighbours for the delimitation of their own maritime areas, and what weight it will carry should they decide to submit a problem to judicial or arbitral settlement.

Nor, in evaluating the importance of this legal corpus, should one overlook the considerable impact of each new legal contribution on the doctrine. One only has to flick over the pages of legal reviews throughout the world to be persuaded of the keen attention lawyers devote to each stage in the development of this judicial and arbitral edifice.

THE LONG MARCH OF THE LAW OF MARITIME DELIMITATION

The development of the case-law has not gone entirely smoothly. It would be surprising had it done so, given that thirty years ago the page was still almost a blank. This new chapter of international law was written with pain, traces of which show themselves in various ways, giving the matter both its intellectual attraction and, in some respects, its somewhat disappointing character.

Development by fits and starts

One has the impression, reading the decisions of the courts, that the development has been in a straight line. On the face of it, there is nothing abnormal: the judgments and awards rely on those which have gone before, quoting their findings as if the decisions formed an uninterrupted chain the links of which would succeed one another, without break. To see, for example, *Libya/Malta* refer to the *North Sea* case, *Tunisia/Libya*, or *Gulf of Maine*, one would assume that the case-law was moving steadily forward, without pause or break of rhythm.

Even if this impression were well-founded, the law of maritime delimitation would not, of course, present itself as a monolithic block of case-law, for, like all case-law, there are various factors bound to affect its development, but it would at least be a structured whole in which each constituent part would relate to the others in a logical and coherent fashion. With this horizontal concept, the findings of one judgment would have as much normative value as those of another, and the various judicial contributions, although staggered over time, would be regarded as constituting the elements of the legal corpus of maritime delimitation, on the same level.

This approach is all the more attractive in that it is, to a large extent, that adopted by the courts themselves. Recent judgments do not hesitate to rely on previous judgments, as if these decisions were all based on the same philosophy and it was a matter each time of simply applying and developing a position of essentially unchanging principle. As we shall see, it is only on the subject of the abandonment of natural prolongation in favour of distance that the International Court of Justice has plainly acknowledged a volte-face.

The linear approach is inevitable for the courts who naturally seek, as is the case in any Praetorian activity, to avoid the appearance of breaks or U-turns. But it is also understandable on the part of States who have to argue before international courts. Anxious not to set the judges of today against those of yesterday, governments and counsel do not venture to distinguish between those positions in the judgments which are out of date, and those which are still valid, preferring to stick to the reassuring image of a case-law which is comprehensive and coherent: the judicial continuum is, for them, part of the rules of the game.

This way of looking at things gives the scholar a precious moment of comfort: what he seems to be dealing with is a single body of case-law, from which he is free to glean where he will the elements of his description and analysis, his telling quotations. Not all scholars resist the temptations of this optimistic and self-fulfilling fiction.

For it is, of course, a fiction we are talking about, and one which will not stand the test of a really scholarly approach. The truth is that the development of the law of maritime delimitation has not been continuous. There are differences between judgments which cannot be hidden by quoting from them approvingly. On the role of equity, for example, and its relations with the law, on the legal nature of equitable principles and methods of delimitation, on the structure of the process of delimitation, there is a great gulf between the theory of one judgment and that of another, even though the more recent wants to hide the change by referring to previous decisions. No: despite appearances, *Libya/Malta* is not in the direct line of succession to *Tunisia/Libya* or *Gulf of Maine*, any more than *Tunisia/Libya* or *Gulf of Maine* are to the *North Sea* and *Anglo-French* cases. The scholar must look at the judicial solutions as creatures of their time, rather than as contemporaneous elements on the same level and part of the same ensemble; what was the law of maritime delimitation yesterday need not still be so today. The linear and horizontal conception must be replaced with a vertical one, which will give pride of place to the most recent decision and examine the case-law in terms of development and reversal.

To complicate matters still further, it should be added that incongruities are also common currency within the same decision: two legal truths are sometimes to be found just a few pages apart, and it is not unusual for a judgment to adopt one legal position at a general level and to proceed quite differently when it comes to apply it to the concrete situation. The need to get a majority of judges to agree on a given text is not the whole story: account must also be taken of the extreme complexity of a subject which is still young and on the boil, where black can so easily seem white and white black.

This means that the cases are far from being a regular series, the elements of which the lawyer can exploit indiscriminately. They have gone in fits and starts, with contradictions, and steps forward followed by steps backward. The judicial fluctuations are an unavoidable fact of life, bearing witness to the vitality of the subject-matter.

A piece-meal and multipolar approach

It will be seen from this that it will not be easy to describe the law of maritime delimitation in a systematic manner. In contrast to other normative systems, which appear as coherent constructions governed by principles from which it is possible to draw logical conclusions, the law of maritime delimitation is resistant to the deductive approach. It is a discontinuous ensemble, in which various principles and rules of law coexist, with no hierarchy between them, and without its always being possible to determine their mutual relations with precision: correlation and complementariness; or synonymy, with different formulations for the same concept or principle; or, again, inconsistency and incompatibility. One is dealing not with a logically articulated legal system but a ballet of concepts. These concepts often take the shape of key words, the connotations of which—the subject of frequent controversy—go beyond the ordinary, everyday meaning of the word in question. Examples rush to mind: law and equity; special circumstances and relevant circumstances; adjacency; geography; proportionality; or the famous trilogy of equity/equitable principles/equitable solution. Some of these terms are so heavily charged with polemic—one thinks for example, of equity and equidistance—as to have been the cause of veritable legal wars of religion.

The coded words can turn into slogans, legal assumptions expressing verities all the less discussed because they are sufficiently flexible to tolerate a wide variety of interpretations. Here again, examples abound: "the land dominates the sea"; "it is not a question of completely refashioning geography or rectifying nature"; "equity does not imply equality"; "each case is *sui generis*"; "the law must lead to a solution which is equitable taking into account all the relevant circumstances".

In addition to codewords and legal slogans, the loosely woven fabric which still makes up the law of maritime delimitation encompasses a series of contrasts, both real and artificial, constituting lines of cleavage around which this normative system has crystallized and made what progress it could: title and delimitation; equitable principles and equitable solution; general configuration of the coasts and exceptional configurations; opposite and adjacent coasts; principles and methods, etc.

This shows how difficult it is to present an orderly account of the law of maritime delimitation, beginning at the beginning and progressing step by step. Every question, every problem, involves all the others, and it is impossible to avoid repeating the same story over and over again from different angles: a Holy Trinity where the parts are the whole and the whole the parts.

An inherent contradiction

The main reason the law of maritime delimitation has made such slow progress is fundamental. In defining the legal rules governing maritime delimitation the courts have always been faced with the formidable challenge of striking a balance between two contradictory requirements. On the one hand is the necessity, inherent in the law, of defining rules which are sufficiently general in character to cover all individual situations of like character, for, without a minimum of generality, the rule of law will not fulfil the functions of predictability and certainty expected of it. On the other hand, too general a rule risks being inappropriate in some cases, and applying it may lead to unreasonable or inequitable results. True enough, the need for a balance between the generality of the legal norm and its necessary individualization appears in every section of the law. It is particularly difficult to meet it, however, in the area of maritime delimitation, because of the great variety of geographical and other conditions. Here, more than elsewhere, it is hard to keep one's balance between the Scylla of the blind automatism of the general and the Charybdis of the irreducibly unique, and the risk of falling to one or other of them is considerable.

The courts are sometimes accused of having weighted the scales in favour of the particular to the detriment of the generality of the rule of law. The judges' task would certainly have been a great deal easier if they had stuck to general norms, applying them automatically. It is to their credit that they have chosen the harder path of tailor-made equity. But what is equity? Does it consist in "respecting nature", or correcting its whims? Reinforcing the inequalities of States, or reducing them? Giving more to the richer State, or to the poorer? Or sharing out resources? These are only a few of the fundamental options courts have to face when they embark on this obstacle-strewn path. Should one be surprised if their pace has been slow, that they have felt their way forward, and not found the perfect solution at their first attempt?

It should be added that, every time the opportunity is presented of translating certain concepts of law or equity into scientific terms, or putting them on a mathematical basis, the courts have turned a deaf ear. They have been decidedly cautious about allowing technique too large a place in the law, preferring to stick to a pragmatic and intuitive approach which leaves them a greater margin of appreciation, but also gives the jurisprudence a nebulous character, overstretched and ill-defined.

Having chosen the praiseworthy but difficult route of seeking to strike a balance between the general, automatically applicable norm, and the equitable norm of variable application, and having refused to accept any technical diktat, the courts have been unable to avoid a certain dissonance between those arguments in their decisions which are truly legal, and therefore general in nature, and the actual solution reached for the specific problem in each case. The logical link between the first part of a judgment, which sets out the applicable principles and rules of international law, and the second, which has a statement, generally rather brief, of the delimitation decided for that particular case, is not always very obvious, and it is sometimes hard to avoid the impression of a non-sequitur. Members of the Court have themselves made no secret of the matter. "The reasonings put forward do not invariably and automatically 'produce' a delimitation line", and "the reasoning does not necessarily, mathematically, 'issue' in the conclusion adopted". There is often "a regrettable but doubtless inevitable gap" to be observed between the legal arguments and the actual line.[4]

---

[4] Ruda, Bedjaoui and Jiménez de Aréchaga, *Libya/Malta*, Joint Separate Opinion, p. 90, para. 37.

An incomplete law

These features are so many symptoms of the courts' uneasiness in working out the law of maritime delimitation. In many respects, the conceptual framework remains fragile and uncertain, and the concrete solutions adopted have not always been convincing. The fear has even been expressed that these waverings may dissuade governments from resorting to judicial or arbitral settlement and that the law of maritime delimitation will prove incapable of fulfilling its primary responsibility to ensure regulation and certainty.

These fears should not be exaggerated. From all the evidence, the law of maritime delimitation has not yet reached its maturity. It is a law in the making, and far from complete. A crucially important staging-post has been reached with the *Libya/Malta* judgment, delivered by the International Court of Justice in 1985, but there is no reason to suppose that the position has yet stabilized. Trends are emerging which permit a glimpse of future developments. The precariousness of the law of maritime delimitation, so often denounced, is but a childhood illness, and the progress we have seen in the past gives us cause to hope for more in the future.

TAKING STOCK, THE PAST AND FUTURE

This book looks at the development of the law of maritime delimitation.

It is not a treatise on maritime delimitation. It does not describe the technical and cartographic processes in delimitation. It does not analyse those delimitation agreements already concluded.[5] Even less does it undertake an examination of those problems which are in the course of negotiation or *sub judice*.

The book is concerned with the law. For all that, however, it is, equally, not a treatise on the law of maritime delimitation. It does not set out to study all the legal problems posed, nor all the solutions already reached or still being worked out. Nor does it seek to retrace in detail the history of this law. More modestly, its ambition is to take stock of certain key aspects, in the hope of discerning the most likely paths of future development. Taking as its basis what already exists, together with the trends and counter-trends of the law of maritime

---

[5] Several studies relating to technical aspects of delimitation and State practice are listed in the bibliography. Cf. p. 69 n. 160 and p. 153 n. 148 below.

delimitation today, it tries to identify the directions it will take tomorrow.[6]

---

[6] The author had the opportunity to argue some of the theses in this book in his pleadings before the International Court of Justice, for Canada in *Gulf of Maine* and, in greater depth, for Malta in the *Libya/Malta* case.

PART I

THE CONCEPT OF MARITIME DELIMITATION

PART I

THE CONCEPT OF MARITIME DELIMITATION

Paradoxically, of the many aspects of the law of maritime delimitation it is the concept itself which has attracted the least attention in the case-law and legal theory. It is not that the question is unimportant. There is no problem of the law of maritime delimitation which does not make an assumption about its nature. But, despite the fact that it underlies the whole subject, discussion on the notion of maritime delimitation remains largely inchoate, buried, indeed, in the legal subconscious. It is essential to bring it to the light of day since, at each turn in the examination, many difficulties will evaporate if only proper account is taken of the profound and original nature of maritime delimitation.

I

DELIMITATION: FROM THE DECLARATORY
TO THE MAN-MADE

As long as maritime delimitation was concerned only with territorial waters, that is to say, roughly speaking, until about 1950, a pragmatic approach sufficed. The discussion was about appropriate methods of delimitation; no questions were asked about the fundamental nature of the exercise.[1] The International Court of Justice raised the problem in 1969, in the *North Sea Continental Shelf* case, its first judgment dealing with maritime delimitation. This is the only time it has done so explicitly; since then the question has only been broached by implication.

In fact, what the Court considered in the *North Sea* case was not the general concept of maritime delimitation but simply the delimitation of the continental shelf. This limited approach is one reason why the development of an overall concept, valid for all maritime areas, has been so slow and difficult. Another is that, perhaps without the Court's fully realizing it, the declaratory concept of continental shelf delimitation which it adopted in 1969 was in reality a denial of the whole idea of delimitation. It is not surprising that it took many years for this self-destructive approach to be abandoned in favour of a constitutive, man-determined, concept. Although it happened almost silently and certainly discreetly, and without attracting any real comment, this evolution—nay, revolution—is one of the most fundamental and important in the law of maritime delimitation.

1. DECLARATORY DELIMITATION: A NON-EVENT

The declaratory theory in the 1969 North Sea *case*

The idea which prevailed in 1969 in respect of the delimitation of the continental shelf is best explained by the Court's approach to the

---

[1] See, for example, discussion of territorial sea delimitation in Gidel, vol. III, pp. 746ff and 765ff.

notion of the shelf itself. This was dominated by the idea of a natural prolongation, a phrase not used by either the International Law Commission or the 1958 Convention but introduced into the vocabulary of the international law of the sea (as it later observed)[2] by the Court itself. Starting from the proposition that "[t]he institution of the continental shelf has arisen out of the recognition of a *physical fact*", i.e., that "[t]he continental shelf is . . . an area *physically* extending the territory of most coastal States into a species of platform which has attracted the attention first of geographers and hydrographers and then of jurists",[3] the Court declared, in formulae which are still cited, that a State's continental shelf constitutes "a natural prolongation of its land territory into and under the sea" and that the rights of the State in respect of this shelf "exist *ipso facto* and *ab initio*, by virtue of its sovereignty over the land, and as an extension of it".[4] As a result, the jurisdiction of the coastal State over the continental shelf was seen not so much as having a specifically maritime nature but rather in the form of rights over a piece of submerged territory which was the prolongation of land which had emerged from the water. As the judgment puts it, the underwater areas in question "although covered with water . . . are a prolongation or continuation of that territory, an extension of it under the sea". They are not "areas of sea, such as the contiguous zone" but "stretches of submerged land" and the legal regime applicable to them is "that of a soil and a subsoil, two words evocative of the land and not of the sea".[5]

Against the background of this natural, physical, conception of the continental shelf the Court was drawn irresistibly into adopting a view of its delimitation equally natural and physical. The language of the judgment is famous:

> Delimitation is a process which involves establishing the boundaries of an area already, in principle, appertaining to the coastal State and not the determination *de novo* of such an area . . . [T]he process of delimitation is essentially one of drawing a boundary line between areas which already appertain to one or other of the States affected.[6]

---

[2] *Tunisia/Libya*, para. 43. Already in 1945 the Truman Proclamation saw the continental shelf as "an extension of the land mass of the coastal nation . . . thus naturally appurtenant to it".

[3] *North Sea*, para. 95.

[4] *Ibid.*, para. 19.

[5] *Ibid.*, paras. 43 and 96.

[6] *Ibid.*, paras. 18 and 20.

The delimitation exercise is therefore not a matter of dividing, according to legally-determined criteria, an underwater area over which the two States can establish rights one against the other; there is no "apportionment of something that previously consisted of an integral, still less an undivided whole".[7] The delimitation exercise is limited to discovering how far the natural prolongation of each of the two States extends under the sea, in other words, to determining the extent of the underwater platform which "already" belongs to them. In a sense, the demarcation line predates the delimitation, the sole purpose of which is to establish where exactly it lies. In truth, there is nothing to delimit; it is a matter simply of establishing the title of each, *suum cuique tribuere*. Delimitation is declaratory, an act of recognition: there is nothing about it man-made or constitutive.

This concept of delimitation—or, to put it more accurately, non-delimitation—gave rise to two principles which were to acquire the status of more or less indestructible dogmas. Because it was not a question of sharing but simply of allocating to each what nature had given it, the demarcation line was not drawn in such a way as to effect an "apportionment"[8] of the areas concerned and to award "just and equitable shares to each State in a common, as yet undelimited area of shelf".[9] The resources are where they are, and so much the better (or worse) if nature has put them here rather than there. This declaratory concept was also responsible for the legal rejection of the idea of equidistance. The moment delimiting the continental shelf was seen as nothing more than noting the limits of the natural prolongation of each, proximity, the keystone of equidistance, lost any decisive value it might have had. As the Court put it, "equidistance . . . clearly cannot be identified with the notion of natural prolongation or extension".[10] There is a clear and close link in the 1969 judgment between the declaratory concept and the Court's negative attitude towards the equidistance concept.[11]

An exact but partial reading of the North Sea *judgment*

Although the judgment in the *North Sea* case is dominated by the physical concept of natural prolongation and the declaratory view of continental shelf delimitation, this is not to the exclusion of all else. Alongside these two physical themes, the judgment sounds another,

[7] *Ibid.*, para. 20.
[8] *Ibid.*, para. 18.
[9] *Anglo-French* award, para. 78.
[10] *North Sea*, para. 44.
[11] *Ibid.*, paras. 39-43.

more juridical note. This is already to some extent the case at the level of title to the continental shelf, that is to say, in the very notion of the continental shelf,[12] but it becomes even more noticeable at the level of delimitation. The judgment recognizes that States are free to agree on a line which does not reflect the limits nature has assigned to them. In particular, it allows them to reach agreement on an equidistance line which, by definition, takes no account of the configuration of the seabed. This is what was done, even before the judgment was given, in the delimitation agreements between Norway and other countries bordering on the North Sea, agreements which took no account of the Norwegian Trough. The Court made no objection.[13] But it went further. The idea appeared in the 1969 judgment that, in exceptional cases, where there was a single shelf which could be seen as the natural prolongation of one State just as much as of the other, the idea of delimitation confined to allocating to each party what "already" belonged to it would be unworkable. Nature being silent, it is necessary to make the delimitation on the basis of a man-made rule of law. Hence the Court's cautious language: delimitation must take account of the physical and geological structure "so far as known or readily ascertainable". It must be effected in such a way as to "leave as much as possible to each Party all those parts of the continental shelf that constitute a natural prolongation of its land territory into and under the sea . . ."[14] If this objective cannot be achieved because "the claims of several States converge, meet and intercross" and cause "overlapping", then it is a question of "division" of these "overlapping areas".[15]

However, this tentative appearance of the constitutive idea, in the *North Sea* case, did not prevent the recognitive interpretation prevailing over many years. As proof, one need only look to the enormous efforts made since then by one or perhaps both the parties in

---

[12] In *Tunisia/Libya* (paras. 42 and 44), the Court was to try to distance itself from a purely physical reading of the concept of natural prolongation as set out in the *North Sea* judgment.

[13] *North Sea*, para. 45. Cf. Jiménez de Aréchaga, *Tunisia/Libya*, Separate Opinion, pp. 111-12, paras. 43-4 and 46.

[14] *North Sea*, para. 101. In *Tunisia/Libya* (para. 44), the Court relied on these formulae to show that even in 1969 it had not established any identity of meaning between the concept of delimitation and the "determination of the limits of 'natural prolongation' ".

[15] *North Sea*, paras. 89 and 99. Since, according to the Court (paras. 4, 89 and 99), it was a question in the North Sea of a single continental shelf (in its view, the exceptional situation), so that there were no "natural" limits, one wonders what point there could be in such radical and solemn statements of principle about the declaratory nature of continental shelf delimitation.

contentious cases to persuade the judges to resolve the difference on the basis of a boundary allegedly dictated by nature. In the end, it is of little interest whether the declaratory concept of delimitation is rightly or wrongly laid at the door of the *North Sea* case, but the fact is that it has seriously unsettled the subsequent development of the law of maritime delimitation.

2. THE INEXORABLE DECLINE OF THE DECLARATORY PRINCIPLE

It was only at a later stage that maritime delimitation managed to acquire its proper character. The development took place slowly, almost unnoticeably and without sudden changes. The declaratory idea which predominated in the *North Sea* case, while not being completely brushed aside, underwent a gradual erosion before being abandoned in 1985 in *Libya/Malta*, a case which marked the end of this evolution. At the same time, the idea, originally a minor one, of delimitation as a distributive process, came to occupy an increasingly important place until it finally carried the day in 1985. This co-existence of two conflicting concepts, with fluctuating nuances in the weight accorded them, makes the judgments sometimes difficult to understand and explains why, in subsequent disputes, those for and against the declaratory theory have both been able to find precedents apparently supporting their current thesis.

Somewhat simplifying the story, one could say that the declaratory concept has given way under the assaults of two distinct phenomena. One is intrinsic: the inherent obstacles which confront the underlying myth of a natural maritime boundary. The other is external: the considerable changes to continental shelf theory caused by developments in the law of the sea generally, title sliding away from the physical concept of natural prolongation towards the legal concept of distance. It was inevitable that this development in respect of title would bring delimitation in its wake.

Even if it is now a matter of history, it is not without interest to retrace in detail this long agony, its ups and downs, and the reasons for it.

A. *The Impossible Theory of Natural Maritime Boundaries*

As we have just seen, the declaratory concept is based on the idea that, since the legal solution is to be found in the facts of nature, the act of delimitation is limited to listening carefully to what nature has to say. Once the natural limits have been discovered by means of an appropriate scientific investigation, there remains nothing more to be done except to draw the demarcation line between the continental shelves of the two countries at the point where nature has placed the limits of their respective natural prolongations. In the end, the only rule of law governing delimitation is that which requires it to conform with nature. Facts dictate the law. The maritime boundary is a natural boundary.

Despite its apparent simplicity and undeniable attractiveness, this idea of the natural maritime boundary has been found, in a series of cases, to be full of holes.

Already in 1969, as noted above, it proved inapplicable whenever it was a case of a single, continuous shelf on which nature had not drawn any precise line of separation. In such a situation it was necessary to turn to a legal test. Experience has shown that, far from being exceptional, this situation crops up frequently. It was the case in the North Sea, where the seabed has no natural divisions. It was also the case in the Channel and in the Atlantic region, where delimitation had to be effected "in the marginal areas where their respective continental shelves converge".[16] In such a situation, the Court of Arbitration noted, delimitation cannot be determined "exclusively by the physical facts of geography" but "also by legal rules".[17] In 1982, in *Tunisia/Libya*, the International Court of Justice found itself once more faced with "a natural prolongation common to both territories" and again drew the conclusion that in such a situation delimitation "must be governed by criteria of international law other than those taken from physical features".[18] In 1984, in the *Gulf of Maine* case, the Chamber again had to draw the boundary "without reference to any real factor of natural separation of the continental shelf of the two countries, because no such factors are discernible".[19] The same situation in 1985, in the *Guinea/Guinea-Bissau* case, drew the same answer: "the rule of natural prolongation can be effectively invoked for purposes of delimitation only where there is a separation of continental shelves".[20]

But the fragility of the theory of the natural submarine boundary was to show itself far beyond those cases where nature has not provided any seabed boundary. The interminable arguments to which the determination of the natural prolongation of the parties

[16] *Anglo-French* award, para. 78.
[17] *Ibid.*, para. 191.
[18] *Tunisia/Libya*, para. 67.
[19] *Gulf of Maine*, para. 47.
[20] *Guinea/Guinea-Bissau*, para. 116.

has given rise in various cases have laid bare the intrinsic weaknesses of this approach.

Nature: a false friend

The natural concept is more ambivalent than it seems.

First, what nature do we mean? *Tunisia/Libya* has shown that very different concepts are possible. Should one stick, as Tunisia asked, to the facts of geomorphology, that is, the discontinuities in the surface or relief, the depressions and escarpments of the seabed? Or is it more appropriate, as Libya suggested, to look to the geology, i.e., the underlying structure of the marine depths? And in the latter case, is it the historic geology which matters, or the contemporaneous geological situation?[21] ''Complying with the dictates of nature'', as Libya wanted,[22] required the Court to choose which facet of nature was meant, and this choice nature itself did not dictate.

Libya/Malta raised an even more formidable problem. The natural delimitation Libya asked the Court to make was along a ''rift zone'' said either to mark geologically the boundary between two tectonic plates or to be an important geomorphological feature, in any case a clear physical separation between Libya's natural prolongation and that of Malta. However, it was difficult to see whether, in the Libyan view, the natural boundary followed a line of the rift zone, or whether this whole zone, about a hundred kilometres in width, was a sort of legal no-man's-land between the Maltese and the Libyan shelves. In the latter case, the two shelves would not touch one another and there would be no need for a demarcation line. But the former interpretation, given the indeterminate nature of such a large area, lending itself to dozens of possible demarcation lines, would exacerbate the difficulty still further.[23] And there would be another difficulty. Would the natural boundary the Court was called on to decide divide the continental shelves, the continental margins or the tectonic plates? This brought into the full light of day the ambivalence in the concepts of a *natural* prolongation and a *natural* boundary. Nature is indeed a kaleidoscope.

---

[21] See *Tunisia/Libya*, paras. 38 and 52-60, on these various approaches. The Court's choice—the configuration of the seabed and its present geological structure (see para. 61)—is now only of historic interest, given the abandonment in 1985 of all physical considerations whatsoever.

[22] *Ibid.*, para. 44.

[23] For the Libyan argument, see *Libya/Malta*, para. 38. The Court was able to avoid answering the difficult questions thus put to it because it rejected *en bloc* natural physical prolongation and its corollary, natural submarine boundaries.

There is another difficulty: it goes without saying that the slightest geological irregularity or the smallest wrinkle on the seabed could not be regarded as interrupting the continuity of a shelf to the point of constituting a natural boundary between two clearly separate prolongations. Hence the legal distinction between simple discontinuities and true breaks or fundamental interruptions on the seabed. The declaratory doctrine could cope with the latter, but not with the former. Where is this quantitative threshhold? How many grains of sand does it take to make a pile?

There has never been an answer to this question. The courts have contented themselves with comparisons with precedents drawn from previous decisions and State practice and limited themselves to deciding, in each of the cases brought before them, that on this particular occasion the discontinuity was not such as to constitute a fundamental interruption between two separate shelves. After all, in each case there were a number of irregularities of structure or relief, some of which were cited by one party in support of a natural boundary, others by the opposing party. On what basis, by what criteria were the courts to attribute decisive effects to some of these features and not to others?

Nature can do things badly

But there is worse: to want to place maritime boundaries where nature has put physical separations—supposing these are identifiable —amounts to trusting in the vagaries of nature, the very antithesis of an equitable maritime delimitation, since, even when it is not silent, nature is not necessarily equitable. Nature and equity are not synonymous. There is no logical reason why a maritime delimitation based on physical factors of geology or geomorphology should be equitable except by the happy accident of coincidence or chance. If the "physical feature"[24] lies very close to the coasts of one State and very far from those of the other, a natural boundary which followed this natural separation would not satisfy the demands of equity since it would cut off the first of these States from its right to maritime areas adjacent to its coasts. The principles of equity, of equality of States and of non-encroachment would be compromised if the whims of nature were allowed to dictate maritime boundaries to governments and international tribunals.

The potential for unfairness hidden in the concept of natural maritime frontiers explains why States have almost never resorted to this type of delimitation. Thus, as already pointed out, even before

[24] *Anglo-French* award, para. 107.

1969 the agreement between the United Kingdom and Norway adopted the median line, taking no account of the Norwegian Trough, which meant giving to Norway large stretches of continental shelf which "cannot in any physical sense be said to be adjacent to it, nor to be its natural prolongation".[25] Since then, there have been innumerable delimitation agreements drawing demarcation lines which ignore even very significant accidents of geology and geomorphology.[26]

The exclusive economic zone has no natural boundaries

The theory of natural boundaries raised problems enough in the context of continental shelf delimitation, but at least it was not beyond the bounds of possibility sometimes to identify peculiarities of structure or relief on the seabed. The moment one left the delimitation of the seabed behind and embarked on fishery and exclusive economic zones the difficulties became impossibilities. A flat, continuous ocean, offering an unimpeded means of communication, cannot admit of natural interruption. The exclusive economic zone concept does not rest in any way on a fact of nature. It is a legal institution, deriving entirely from the political will.

In *Gulf of Maine* the United States maintained that the North East Channel marked not only the physical boundary between its own natural prolongation and that of Canada in respect of the seabed, but also constituted a natural boundary between distinct oceanic and ecological regimes (fishery resources, currents, temperature,

---

[25] *North Sea*, para. 45.

[26] For example, the Franco-Spanish agreement on the delimitation of the continental shelf in the Bay of Gascony (1974) ignores the Cape Breton trough (*RGDIP*, vol. 80, p. 369; *Annuaire français de droit international*, 1974, p. 831; *Limits in the Seas*, No. 83; Conforti and Francalanci, p. 69; Azcarraga). The Cuba/Haiti agreement (1977) established a line of equidistance independent of the Cayman trough (*New Directions*, vol. VIII, p. 69). The Mexico/USA agreement (1978) took no account of Sigsbee Deep (*ILM*, vol. 17, 1978, p. 1073; Conforti and Francalanci, p. 172). The India/Thailand delimitation (1978) ignored the Andaman Basin (*Limits in the Seas*, No. 93). The France (Martinique and Guadeloupe)/Venezuela (Aves) delimitation (1980) followed a line of longitude unrelated to the geomorphology of the region (*RGDIP*, vol. 87, 1983, p. 724). The Norway/Iceland agreement on the Jan Mayen Continental Shelf (1981), in accordance with the recommendations of the Conciliation Commission (*ILM*, vol. 20, 1981, p. 797), took no account of the physical facts (*ILM*, vol. 21, 1982, p. 1222). (For the *Jan Mayen* case, see Churchill, Evensen, Gounaris[2] and Richardson.) There is one (probably the only) exception to this considerable practice in which the natural maritime boundary is ignored: the Australia/Indonesia treaty (1972), which takes account of the Timor trough for the delimitation of the continental shelf between the two countries (*Limits in the Seas*, No. 87). On this subject, cf. Lumb, Usman. See also Sette-Camara, *Libya/Malta*, Separate Opinion, p. 61.

salinity, vertical stratification, tidal movements). The United States represented the North East Channel as a buffer zone forming a natural boundary between two physical and ecological worlds and the Court was asked not to undo what nature had done.[27] This attempt to extend the declaratory concept, already in jeopardy in the context of the continental shelf, to the exclusive economic zone, was forcefully rejected:

> The Chamber is not . . . convinced of the possibility of discerning any genuine, sure and stable 'natural boundaries' in so fluctuating an environment as the waters of the ocean, their flora and fauna.[28]

If the courts had persisted with the declaratory concept formulated in 1969 they would have made impossible any maritime delimitation law since although, if really necessary, the idea could be applied to the delimitation of the continental shelf, it could certainly not have governed exclusive economic zone delimitation. The coming together of the continental shelf and exclusive economic zone concepts, added to the intrinsic difficulties of the natural boundary theory, happily averted this danger and ensured the unity of maritime delimitation law.[29]

All boundaries are political

But there was an even more telling objection to the declaratory concept: there are no natural boundaries. ''There is no boundary which is not political.''[30] This is true of land boundaries which, even if they follow the accidents of geography, do so only by virtue of law, in other words, they are a political phenomenon. As Judge Jiménez de Aréchaga pointed out in *Tunisia/Libya*, it was inconceivable that one would return in the maritime delimitation context to that ''dangerous doctrine of 'natural frontiers', which Rousseau demolished when he observed '*qu'elles aboutissaient à faire de l'ordre politique l'ouvrage de la nature*' ''. In the same way that ''natural land features, such as valleys, mountain crests, river thalwegs, etc., cannot by themselves determine boundaries between States'', so ''physical features such as depressions, channels, sea-bed contours,

---

[27] For a summary of the US argument, see *Gulf of Maine*, paras. 51-3.

[28] *Gulf of Maine*, para. 54.

[29] A similar observation could be made about the delimitation of the territorial sea, where the idea of a natural boundary is also inconceivable.

[30] Lapradelle, P. de, ''La frontière. Etude de droit international'', Paris, Les Editions internationales, 1928, p. 11.

geological structure, etc., cannot by themselves govern the determination of continental shelf boundaries''.[31]

Maritime boundaries, like land boundaries, are the fruit of the will of States or the decision of the international judge, and neither governments nor judges limit themselves simply to scientific fact. *Res judicata pro veritate habetur*. It is legal truth to which this maxim refers, not scientific. The judges' task is that of a judicial organ, charged to state the law, and to state the law is not the same as to give in to nature's demands. Their role must not be reduced to that of a scientific committee conferring, like an expert or super-expert, the force of law on a scientific discovery.

The slow march of case-law

It is hardly necessary to recall what a large part disputes over the so-called natural boundaries of the seas have played in cases subsequent to *North Sea*, with voluminous technical annexes, invasive scientific debate, memorable expert jousting, only to end each time with an ambiguous solution, reflecting the courts' discomfort. In *this* case, the discontinuity referred to was not of the kind or size to be regarded as giving rise to two physically distinct shelves, so it was necessary to resort to legal criteria to resolve the dispute. It was as if the courts, although aware of the inadequacies and difficulties of the declaratory concept, were reluctant openly to defy the famous, venerable and almost untouchable *North Sea* precedent, to commit parricide, as it were.

But by 1977, in the *Anglo-French* case, the essential had been pronounced: a physical characteristic

> . . . is placed where it is simply as a fact of nature, and there is no intrinsic reason why a boundary along that axis should be the boundary.[32]

But instead of sticking to that, the Tribunal chose to put itself on declaratory theory territory, pointing out that, in the present case, there were merely ''discontinuities in the seabed and subsoil which do not disrupt the essential unity of the continental shelf'',[33] and so implying that, had there been a clear break in the shelf and not just a discontinuity, the declaratory concept would have regained the upper hand.

---

[31] *Tunisia/Libya*, Separate Opinion, p. 117, para. 61. Quotation in French in original English text.

[32] *Anglo-French* award, para. 107.

[33] *Ibid.*

With *Tunisia/Libya*, the slide increased pace, reflecting, no doubt, a certain irritation on the part of the Court at the deluge of technicality which threatened to obscure the legal argument. The two parties were arguing for natural prolongation, vying with one another in scientific demonstration. Overwhelmed by the avalanche of technical problems and anxious to allow the law its say, the Court decided in favour of neither side. But, although it took the view that, in this case, the physical features were not such as indisputably to mark the limit of two distinct natural prolongations, the Court again kept open (as had the Court of Arbitration) the possibility that there might in some other case be such a natural dividing line between continental shelves. Moreover, the Court decided that it was only ''in the particular geographical circumstances of the present case'' that ''the physical structure of the continental shelf areas is not such as to determine an equitable line of delimitation''.[34] However, even if they cannot be used to identify two distinct shelves, according to the Court, mere geomorphological discontinuities can always be taken into account ''as one of several circumstances considered to be the elements of an equitable solution''.[35] This introduced a distinction between a genuine break in the shelf, determining delimitation on the basis of the separation of natural prolongations, and a mere discontinuity, as one factor to be taken into consideration alongside others. This subtle distinction betrayed the embarrassment of the Court, wanting, as it did, to escape from the natural prolongation theory, but judging that the moment had not yet come to abandon it openly.

The *Gulf of Maine* judgment took the same attitude. On the one hand, it stressed the legal, as opposed to physical, nature of delimitation:

> . . . a delimitation, whether of a maritime boundary or of a land boundary, is a legal-political operation, and . . . it is not the case that where a natural boundary is discernible, the political delimitation necessarily has to follow the same line.[36]

On the other hand, however, it was on the basis of an examination of the facts in the case that it refused to regard the North East Channel as other than a mere ''natural feature of the area'' unsuitable for inclusion among the ''factors to be used to determine the

---

[34] *Tunisia/Libya*, para. 133.
[35] *Ibid.*, paras. 68 and 80.
[36] *Gulf of Maine*, para. 56.

method of delimitation".[37] But, just as in earlier decisions, the po
ibility was not excluded that there might be "a natural separati‹
. . . from the factual viewpoint between the respective continentʌɪ
platforms of the Parties in dispute",[38] i.e. "distinctive geological
characteristics . . . such as might have special effect in determining
the division of that shelf and the resources of its subsoil".[39]

The same cautious approach was followed in the *Guinea/Guinea-
Bissau* case. Although finding that it was dealing in this case with a
single shelf the Tribunal once again reserved the position where

> [t]he characteristics of a continental shelf may serve to demonstrate the
> existence of a break in the continuity of the shelf or in the prolongation of
> territories of the States which are parties to a delimitation.[40]

From one case to the next, the conditions for recognizing the
existence of two physically distinct natural prolongations seemed
more and more difficult to meet and the scope for practical
implementation of the declaratory theory of delimitation seemed
increasingly doomed to become no more than a matter of form,
preserved for the sake of it, *pour mémoire*, one might say. In fact, in
case after case, the delimitation was attributive, and on the basis of
rules of law made by man.[41] There was a major obstacle to the
complete abandonment of the declaratory concept: as long as the
institution of the continental shelf continued to rest on the theory of
the natural prolongation of the land territory under the sea, it was
difficult for the courts to cut the umbilical cord binding delimitation
to the physical facts of the seabed. There could be no breakthrough
in respect of *delimitation* without progress over *title*. But such
progress once achieved, the way would be clear for movement on
delimitation.

B. *The Evolution of Legal Title to the Continental Shelf: From Natural Prolongation to Distance*

Over the years, from one judgment to the next, title to the
continental shelf was to detach itself increasingly from its physical
roots. The idea of natural prolongation would survive, but its content
would become less and less physical, more and more legal.

---

[37] *Ibid.*, para. 46.
[38] *Ibid.*, para. 47.
[39] *Ibid.*, para. 193.
[40] *Guinea/Guinea-Bissau*, para. 117.
[41] Cf. Sette-Camara, *Libya/Malta*, Separate Opinion, p. 60.

The warning signs

This development, recounted by the Court in *Tunisia/Libya*,[42] was foreshadowed even before the *North Sea* judgment. As early as 1953, the International Law Commission's attention had been drawn by some of its members to the case of States which had little or no continental shelf in the physical sense and which might be disadvantaged by a purely physical concept of the shelf. It was then that it was suggested that the continental shelf should be defined in terms of distance.[43] It was then also that the Commission expressed the opinion that the seabed separated from the coast by a trough close to the shore should be part of the continental shelf of the coastal State.[44] And it was at this time, too, that the physical criterion of depth was reinforced by the non-physical one of exploitability, thus permitting the continental shelf to be extended further and further into the open sea, *pari passu* with technological progress. By introducing the criterion of exploitability the Commission, in its own words, was deciding "not to adhere strictly to the geological concept of the continental shelf".[45] The endorsement of this criterion in the 1958 Geneva Convention shows that even before 1969 there was a "lack of identity between the legal concept of the continental shelf and the physical phenomenon known to geographers by that name".[46] It also shows that the distance criterion has ancient roots. As Judge Mbaye would later remark, distance "has never been truly absent from the concept of natural prolongation", and "accompanied that concept from the outset", hidden behind the notions of exploitation and bathymetry, but "when these concepts proved far too relative, resort to an exact distance became necessary in order to define the factors which determine rights to areas in or under the sea".[47]

Thus, "[t]his widening of the concept for legal purposes", which was to dominate the eventual development of the law of the continental shelf, started "very early".[48]

[42] *Tunisia/Libya*, paras. 41-50.

[43] *ILCYB*, 1953, vol. II, p. 9. In 1955, Scelle spoke of "the total inequality in the territorial extent of continental shelves which varies from zero to the infinite" (Scelle, p. 10).

[44] *ILCYB*, 1953, vol. II, p. 214, para. 66.

[45] *ILCYB*, 1956, vol. II, p. 297, para. 6.

[46] *Tunisia/Libya*, para. 42.

[47] *Libya/Malta*, Separate Opinion, p. 95. Cf. the *Anglo-French* award, para. 191: "[A]nd the very fact that in international law the continental shelf is a juridical concept means that its scope and the conditions for its application are not determined exclusively by the physical facts of geography but also by legal rules".

[48] *Tunisia/Libya*, para. 41.

The work of the Third Conference on the Law of the Sea (UNCLOS III)

The evolution thus embarked on was speeded up by the work of UNCLOS III. The inequality suffered, as a result of the natural physical prolongation concept, by those States which nature had endowed with only a narrow continental shelf was acknowledged, and consideration given to the possibility of granting every coastal State rights over the soil and subsoil of maritime areas adjacent to its coasts up to a distance of 200 miles, regardless of the physical make-up of the seabed. The distance criterion would thus have replaced the depth and exploitability criteria of the 1958 Convention, and the distance of 200 miles would have been both a minimum and a maximum. It would have secured the equality of coastal States regardless of the physical features of the seabed, and would also have put a brake on those far-reaching claims which were liable to reduce the marine areas it was hoped to preserve for the international community. The continental shelf concept would be fused with that of the exclusive economic zone. Up to 200 miles, the seabed would have formed part of the exclusive economic zone: beyond 200 miles, it would have been part of the international zone, the common heritage of mankind.

However, fixing a 200 mile limit for the rights of all coastal States over the seabed would have been to the disadvantage of those few States whose continental shelf, in the physical sense of the word, stretches more than 200 miles into the open sea. In the name of rights allegedly acquired under the regime of the old theory and basing themselves on supposedly scientific criteria, a small group of influential States sought to preserve the advantages of the natural prolongation and even took the opportunity of securing an enlarged definition to replace the classical concept of "continental shelf" with that of "continental margin" which includes, in addition to the shelf in the strict sense, the "continental slope" and the "continental rise". To make the package deal acceptable to those few States with a broad continental margin, a complicated compromise was worked out, limiting the indefinite extension of their rights. It is set out in the various provisions of Article 76 of the Montego Bay Convention:[49]

[49] 1982 Law of the Sea Convention, Art. 76 (extracts):

1. The continental shelf of a coastal State comprises the sea-bed and subsoil of the submarine areas that extend beyond its territorial sea throughout the natural prolongation of its land territory to the outer edge of the continental margin, or to a distance of 200 nautical miles from the baselines from which the breadth of the territorial sea is measured where the outer edge of the continental margin does not extend up to that distance.

(Footnote continued on p. 36)

continental shelf rights ''throughout the natural prolongation of its land territory to the outer edge of the continental margin'' when this edge lies beyond 200 miles; continental shelf rights up to at least 200 miles even when the outer edge of the continental margin lies within 200 miles; and various limitations on the extension of continental shelf rights beyond 200 miles. In addition, there was to be a Commission on the Limits of the Continental Shelf and payments or contributions for the exploitation of the continental shelf beyond 200 miles. Retained as a minimum, the continental shelf now ceased to be a maximum. The concept of the continental shelf as distinct from that of the exclusive economic zone, at least beyond 200 miles, was now entrenched. And, since it was difficult to have a different basis for rights within and beyond 200 miles, justification for this whole collection of rights, within and beyond 200 miles, came to be found in ''natural prolongation''.

As we have seen, the equality of States was the driving force which, by bringing together the continental shelf and exclusive economic zone concepts, led to the substitution of legal criteria for the previously dominant notion of the configuration of the seabed.[50] At the same time, from its original quasi-territorial status, the continental shelf became a purely maritime concept, after the fashion of other forms of jurisdiction granted to States over the sea adjacent to their coasts.

The beginnings of an about-turn in the courts

It was in 1982 that the Court took on board these facts of international law. In *Tunisia/Libya*, delivered a few months before the signing of the Montego Bay Convention, it noted the growing divergence between the natural physical prolongation concept and that of the continental shelf. ''The legal concept, while it derived

---

(Footnote continued from p. 35)

3. The continental margin comprises the submerged prolongation of the land mass of the coastal State, and consists of the sea-bed and subsoil of the shelf, the slope and the rise. It does not include the deep ocean floor with its oceanic ridges or the subsoil thereof.

10. The provisions of this article are without prejudice to the question of delimitation of the continental shelf between States with opposite or adjacent coasts.

For a history of Article 76, see, *inter alia*, Oda (Separate Opinions, *Tunisia/Libya*, pp. 211ff, and *Libya/Malta*, pp. 151ff), Caflisch [1] pp. 81ff, Hutchinson, pp. 162ff. On the problems raised by Article 76, see also pp. 129-30 below.

[50] Cf. Mbaye, *Libya/Malta*, Separate Opinion, p. 94: ''[T]he indisputable connection between the continental shelf and the exclusive economic zone argues in favour of a purely legal approach to the former, which is henceforward to be primarily defined in terms of a certain distance rather than by the physiography of the sea-bed and its subsoil''.

from the natural phenomenon, pursued its own development."[51] Although not dismissing the concept or the term "natural prolongation", it gave it evolutionary content:

> The concept of natural prolongation . . . was and remains a concept to be examined within the context of customary law and State practice.[52]

As a result, the Court took the view that international law, as formulated at UNCLOS III and as it seemed already to have been hallowed by custom, was ready to accord coastal States rights over "any seabed area possessing a particular relationship with the coastline of a neighbouring State"[53] and defined these rights by reference to a particular distance from the coast. It was in this context that the judgment referred to Article 76(1) of what was then the draft Convention, with its definition of the continental shelf "in two parts, employing different criteria":

> In so far . . . as the paragraph provides that in certain circumstances the distance from the baseline, measured on the surface of the sea, is the basis for the title of the coastal State, it departs from the principle that natural prolongation is the sole basis of the title.[54]

This new definition, it added, "cannot be ignored".[55]

So it was with clear-headedness but also a degree of caution that, in 1982, the Court broached the development of the legal title to the continental shelf. No doubt, since the Convention had not yet been signed, it did not want to take a position on the legal force of the new concept and still less on the links which were being formed between the already well-established continental shelf concept and the more recent one of the exclusive economic zone, which it regarded as "part of modern international law".[56] Several opinions appended to the judgment expressed regret that the Court had not been bolder in abandoning natural physical prolongation in favour of what it called, significantly, "the distance principle".[57]

---

[51] *Tunisia/Libya*, para. 42.

[52] *Ibid.*, para. 43.

[53] *Ibid.*, para. 41.

[54] *Ibid.*, para. 48.

[55] *Ibid.*, para. 47.

[56] *Ibid.*, para. 100.

[57] *Ibid.*, para. 48. Jiménez de Aréchaga, Separate Opinion, pp. 113-16, paras. 50-6; p. 121, para. 73; Oda, Dissenting Opinion, p. 222, para. 107; pp. 233-4, paras. 129-30; p. 257, para. 160; Evensen, Dissenting Opinion, pp. 284ff.

Even if the way was now clear for the "distance principle", courts only embarked on it with great caution. Although Canada relied on it very heavily in the *Gulf of Maine* case, the Chamber saw the principle as no more than "one more ... endeavour ... another attempt to turn equidistance into a genuine rule of law".[58] Nonetheless, the *Gulf of Maine* judgment is an important landmark in the development of a *legal* concept of title:

> '[L]egal title' to certain maritime or submarine areas is always and exclusively the effect of a legal operation. The same is true of the boundary of the extent of the title. That boundary results from a rule of law and not from any intrinsic merit in the purely physical fact.[59]

A few months later, the Arbitral Tribunal in the *Guinea/Guinea-Bissau* case[60] limited itself to endorsing the cautious position in *Tunisia/Libya,* and it was only with *Libya/Malta* that the Court decided to make the break.

3. THE ABANDONMENT OF THE DECLARATORY CONCEPT: THE ABOUT TURN IN THE 1985 *LIBYA/MALTA* CASE

In *Libya/Malta* the Court was seised with the full ramifications of the survival of the declaratory concept. Was delimitation of the continental shelf, in the light of these developments, still a matter of discovering, with the help of the physical sciences, the divisions set by nature between the continental shelves of the interested parties, or was it now a question of applying the rule of law independent of any diktat of nature? As we have seen, Libya maintained that the delimitation line should follow the rift zone which, it claimed, physically separated the shelves of the two countries. Even supposing, it added, that the rift zone did not constitute a fundamental separation between the two shelves, it was nonetheless a discontinuity of a kind, according to the 1982 *Tunisia/Libya* formula, to be regarded as a relevant circumstance which the delimitation had

---

[58] *Gulf of Maine*, para. 106.

[59] *Ibid.*, para. 103.

[60] "There are therefore two rules [for determining the continental shelf] between which there is neither priority nor precedence." The "second rule ... by reference to distance, without derogating from the rule of natural prolongation, reduces its scope by substituting it in certain circumstances specified in ... Article 76 of the 1982 Convention ...". *Guinea/Guinea-Bissau*, paras. 115-16.

to take into account. Malta, for its part, did not limit itself to denying the existence or importance of the rift zone; it argued that legal title to the continental shelf was no longer based on physical facts, but rested on the legal criterion of distance which nowadays brought together the continental shelf and exclusive economic zone concepts. This means, according to Malta, that not only can delimitation no longer be dictated by a natural separation, however important and indisputable, but that the geological and geomorphological facts relating to the seabed no longer have any role to play in delimitation and do not even constitute a relevant circumstance to be taken into account.[61]

The Court was thus required to take a position on three essential problems: the legal basis of title to the continental shelf; the incidence of title on delimitation; and the role of physical facts.

The legal basis of title to the continental shelf

According to Libya, developments in the law of the sea had not affected the principle that natural prolongation in the physical sense is the basis of legal title to the continental shelf. It argued that Article 76 of the Montego Bay Convention had acquired the force of customary international law only in respect of its reference to natural prolongation. Far from sanctioning the obliteration of this idea, UNCLOS III had given it new importance. As for the other provisions of Article 76, especially those according every coastal State rights over the seabed up to at least 200 miles from its coast, these had not acquired the force of customary international law. In any case, Libya added, the distance criterion is secondary to the critical criterion of natural prolongation; the Conference intended the latter to have pride of place, and only introduced the idea of distance into Article 76 as a peripheral and exceptional consideration. Dominated today even more than in the past by the concept of natural prolongation, Libya concluded, the continental shelf notion remains distinct from that of the exclusive economic zone, and the distance principle has no part to play.

For Malta, it was quite the opposite. The provision of Article 76 which conferred on coastal States rights over the seabed up to 200 miles regardless of its physical configuration has acquired the force of customary law. If there is any doubt about the customary force of Article 76, it is only on the subject of the rights of States with a broad continental margin "throughout the natural prolongation . . . to the

---

[61] For a summary of the parties' positions, see *Libya/Malta*, paras. 30-2, 34, 36 and 38.

outer edge of the continental margin''. Even for States with a wide continental margin, Malta added, Article 76 does not provide for the natural prolongation to flourish in all its magnificence since it terminates rights over the seabed in all cases at 350 miles from the baselines or 100 miles from the 2,500 metre isobath. So, according to Malta, it is distance which both forms the basis of the rights of States over the seabed up to 200 miles and imposes a limit to the exceptional extension of these rights beyond 200 miles. Distance, Malta concluded, pervades this article and there is now such a correlation between the notion of the shelf and that of the exclusive economic zone that it is impossible, without losing sight of the development of the customary law of the sea, to embark on a delimitation of the continental shelf without keeping in mind the concept of the exclusive economic zone.

The Court took no position on the legal force of the various elements in Article 76 or the new definition of the continental shelf but started from the idea, which it had already expressed in 1982, that:

> The institution of the exclusive economic zone, with its rule on entitlement by reason of distance, is shown by the practice of States to have become a part of customary law.[62]

It then stated that the rights in the exclusive economic zone embrace those over the seabed, so much so that

> [a]lthough there can be a continental shelf where there is no exclusive economic zone, there cannot be an exclusive economic zone without a corresponding continental shelf.[63]

In other words, even if they do not entirely coincide,

> . . . the two institutions—continental shelf and exclusive economic zone— are linked together in modern law.[64]

As a result, even in a case dealing only with continental shelf delimitation and not that of the exclusive economic zone, "the principles and rules underlying the latter concept cannot be left out of consideration".[65] This means, in practice, that from now on,

---

[62] *Libya/Malta*, para. 34.
[63] *Ibid.*
[64] *Ibid.*, para. 33.
[65] *Ibid.*

some importance must be attached "to elements, such as distance from the coast, which are common to both concepts",[66] especially where

> ... verification of the validity of title is concerned, since, at least in so far as those areas are situated at a distance of under 200 miles from the coasts in question, title depends solely on the distance from the coasts of the claimant States of any areas of seabed claimed by way of continental shelf, and the geological or geomorphological characteristics of those areas are completely immaterial.[67]

The break between the concept of the continental shelf and that of the natural physical prolongation may now be complete, but, for all that, the term "natural prolongation" has not been banished from the law of maritime delimitation. It has merely changed its meaning and now has a legal connotation, separate from physical considerations, except in the case where the continental shelf passes beyond the 200 mile mark.[68] When the continental margin does not reach 200 miles,

> ... natural prolongation, which in spite of its physical origins has throughout its history become more and more a complex and juridical concept, is in part defined by distance from the shore, irrespective of the physical nature of the intervening seabed and subsoil. The concepts of natural prolongation and distance are therefore not opposed but complementary; and both remain essential elements in the juridical concept of the continental shelf.[69]

Title and delimitation

Would the upheaval in the legal basis to title to the continental shelf have repercussions at the level of delimitation? Here also, the Court was faced, in *Libya/Malta*, with diametrically opposed views.[70]

---

[66] *Ibid.*

[67] *Ibid.*, para. 39.

[68] Cf. Mbaye, *Libya/Malta*, Separate Opinion, p. 94: "in contemporary customary law, natural prolongation is no longer what Truman referred to as such in his 1945 Proclamation".

[69] *Libya/Malta*, para. 34.

[70] The question of the relationship between title and delimitation had been raised previously by Canada in *Gulf of Maine*, but, since it rejected the Canadian thesis on the distance principle, the Chamber was able to avoid pronouncing on the issue (see p. 38 above).

According to Libya, regardless of whatever other developments there may have been in the continental shelf concept, the question of delimitation is separate from that of title. Even supposing that the continental shelf concept had undergone a fundamental transform- ation, reflected in the provisions of Article 76 of the 1982 Con- vention, this transformation, Libya argued, could have that much less an effect on delimitation in view of paragraph 10 of this Article: "The provisions of this Article are without prejudice to the question of the delimitation of the continental shelf." Libya concluded that delimitation has nothing to do with the arguments about natural prolongation and distance but is still governed solely by the rule of equitable result.

While accepting that the concepts of title and delimitation are distinct, Malta maintained that there is a certain link between them. To conclude that because the two are not synonymous there is no correlation between them would be to fall prey to a non-sequitur. The continental shelf cannot be delimited in the same way, Malta explained, according to whether the legal title to the shelf is based on natural prolongation in the physical sense, on effective occupation, or on some other legal concept. There can be no water-tight barrier between title and delimitation, sealing off one from developments in the other.

The Court had not previously had occasion to pronounce on this problem other than incidentally. It had, of course, already pointed out that the concepts of title and delimitation are not synonymous,[71] but it is clear that the reason it gave so much importance in its *North Sea* judgment to natural prolongation in the delimitation process was that it made the legal basis for the rights of the coastal State the natural prolongation of its territory under the sea. Had natural prolongation not been at the heart of title, it would not have occupied this central place in delimitation. In the *Anglo-French* case, the Court of Arbitration had rejected a method of delimitation advocated by France because it did not see it as "compatible with the legal regime of the continental shelf".[72] In *Tunisia/Libya* the link was similarly pointed out:

> . . . 'principles and rules of international law which may be applied' for the delimitation of continental shelf areas must be derived from the concept of the continental shelf itself, as understood in international law . . . .[73]

[71] *North Sea*, paras. 18 and 20; *Tunisia/Libya*, paras. 44 and 73.
[72] *Anglo-French* award, para. 246.
[73] *Tunisia/Libya*, para. 36.

The Court explained in this same judgment that it was the coast of the parties which constituted the point of departure ''in order to ascertain how far the submarine areas appertaining to each of them extend *in a seaward direction*, as well as *in relation to neighbouring States situated either in an adjacent or opposite position*''.[74] It had also noted that, insofar as the distance principle ''is the basis for the title of the coastal State'', ''[i]t is only the legal basis of the title to continental shelf rights—the mere distance from the coast—which can be taken into account as possibly having consequences for the claims of the Parties''.[75]

In *Libya/Malta*, the Court disposed of the problem in concise and definitive fashion:

> That the questions of entitlement and of definition of continental shelf on the one hand, and of delimitation of continental shelf on the other, are not only distinct but are also complementary is self-evident. The *legal basis* of that which is to be delimited, and of entitlement to it, *cannot be other than pertinent* to that delimitation . . . The criterion [of delimitation] is linked with the law relating to a State's legal title to the continental shelf.[76]

The end of declaratory delimitation

In *Libya/Malta*, the Court drew the logical conclusions from its innovatory analysis of the legal title to the continental shelf and the correlation between title and delimitation, and served the death warrant on the declaratory concept of delimitation:

> . . . since the development of the law enables a State to claim that the continental shelf appertaining to it extends up to as far as 200 miles from its coast, whatever the geological characteristics of the corresponding seabed and subsoil, there is no reason to ascribe any role to geological or geophysical factors within that distance either in verifying the legal title of the States concerned or in proceeding to a delimitation as between their claims.[77]

Whereas in previous cases the arguments for treating a physical characteristic as determining the delimitation had been rejected on the basis of the specific facts of the case, this time the Libyan

[74] *Ibid.*, para. 74.

[75] *Ibid.*, para. 48. The reason the Court, despite this acceptance of it in principle, did not take the distance concept into account in *Tunisia/Libya* was, it would seem, because the two parties had based themselves on natural prolongation and not argued the distance principle at all (*ibid.*). As already noted, some judges regretted this attitude of the Court (p. 37 above).

[76] *Libya/Malta*, paras. 27 and 61; cf. para. 34.

[77] *Ibid.*, para. 39.

argument that the rift zone should be treated "as if it were some natural boundary"[78] was thrown out because the "juridical difficulties of the rift-zone argument are conclusive against it".[79] The scientific argument is completely rejected as being irrelevant. A geological or geomorphological feature, even if it were sufficiently significant to separate physically two distinct continental shelves, would have no relevance to delimitation, governed by the rules of law and henceforth detached from any physical considerations:

> The Court is unable to accept the position that in order to decide this case, it must first make a determination upon a disagreement between scientists of distinction as to the more plausibly correct interpretation of apparently incomplete scientific data; for a criterion that depends upon such a judgment or estimate . . . is clearly inapt to a general legal rule of delimitation.[80]

Indeed, the decision sounds like a death knell:

> [T]he area of continental shelf to be found to appertain to either Party not extending more than 200 miles from the coast of the Party concerned, no criterion for delimitation of shelf areas can be derived from the principle of natural prolongation in the physical sense.[81]

There was still more: as if to strangle at birth any future attempt by parties (relying on the distinction drawn in the *Tunisia/Libya* case between physical features as direct and decisive criteria for delimitation and physical features as one among several relevant circumstances) to plead anew the physical attributes of the seabed, the Court pushed its reasoning to its logical conclusion:

> Neither is there any reason why a factor which has no part to play in the establishment of title should be taken into account as a relevant circumstance for the purposes of delimitation.[82]

Not only do courts no longer have to yield to the demands of nature; they do not even need to respond to its suggestions. Expelled from the law as a decisive element in the delimitation process, the facts of nature are not likely to make their reappearance through the back door of "relevant circumstances". The bridges are down, and retreat to any natural boundary whatsoever cut off once and for all.

[78] *Ibid.*
[79] *Ibid.*, para. 41.
[80] *Ibid.*
[81] *Ibid.*, para. 79A.
[82] *Ibid.*, para. 40.

It is remarkable that the Court should have resisted the temptation to present its new doctrine as having been foreshadowed in its previous judgments. With clarity and courage, it recalled the contrary positions it had taken previously and observed that it had found warrant for giving physical factors a possible role in delimitation "in a regime of the title itself which used to allot those factors a place which now belongs to the past, in so far as seabed areas less than 200 miles from the coast are concerned".[83] Far from resorting to the convenient fiction of a legal continuum the Court has made a clean break with the past. From now on, even in respect of the continental shelf, it is no longer a question of seeing the delimitation process as amounting to no more than a discovery of maritime areas which belong "already" and *ab initio* to one or other of the States concerned. Whatever the jurisdiction under consideration, it is never nature which fixes, or even suggests, the maritime boundary, and it is never a natural boundary the courts are called on to draw.

[83] *Ibid.*

II

THE LEGAL CONCEPT OF MARITIME
DELIMITATION

The components of the new concept

NOWADAYS, instead of discovering divisions allegedly indicated by nature in order to record them and attribute to each State what nature has "already" given it, delimitation takes the opposite course of assuming that there is an *area of overlap*, i.e., an area over which both States have legal title. Unless there are overlapping titles, there is nothing to delimit. As already noted, both the concept and term "area of overlap" appeared in the case law in 1969.[84] Over time, however, there have been two developments which have radically altered the meaning of this. On the one hand, overlap, originally thought of as exceptional, has shown itself to be the more common phenomenon. In fact, no court has ever been called on to decide a case where there was anything but an overlap of jurisdictions. On the other hand, and most importantly, "overlapping", regarded in the *North Sea* case as an overlapping of natural prolongations in the physical meaning of the term, has, in the course of a series of judgments, become an overlapping of legal titles.

There is a second aspect of the new concept of delimitation: the moment it is seen as "the means of resolving situations of overlap or interference arising from the titles of the Parties"[85] to the same maritime space, it cannot be anything other than a *division* of a space previously undivided. The language of 1969 can then be reversed. Delimitation now aspires to be a definition *de novo* of the area which is henceforth to belong to each of the States and not the determination of what "already" belongs to them.

And this leads inevitably to a third characteristic: the division of areas where two titles meet and intertwine cannot be undertaken

---

[84] See pp. 21ff above. Cf. *Tunisia/Libya*, para. 75; *Gulf of Maine*, paras. 115, 195 and 209. Some judgments also speak of the "marginal area" (*North Sea*, para. 20) or "marginal areas" (*Anglo-French* award, para. 78).

[85] Mbaye, *Libya/Malta*, Separate Opinion, p. 96.

without reducing both of them. Delimitation means *amputation*. While the declaratory concept sought to "leave as much as possible to each Party all those parts of the continental shelf that constitute a natural prolongation of its land territory into and under the sea",[86] the constitutive concept implies that each of the parties is to be deprived of part of the area to which it has legal title. Instead of trying to give effect to both titles, delimitation consists in reducing the extent of each. Delimitation is no longer *suum cuique tribuere* but to decide what each must agree to be deprived of for the other's benefit. In the declaratory concept, it is a matter of *recognizing* what is; in the constitutive, it is a case of *granting by taking away*. Encroachment and amputation are an inherent part of delimitation.[87]

This division/amputation (and here there is a fourth distinction from the former recognition theory), is carried out by *legal decision*, i.e., applying rules of law and legal criteria. While the previous concept was limited, at least for the continental shelf, to an insistence on respect for physical facts, the attributive approach always requires a division "on the basis of law", as it was forcibly put in *Gulf of Maine*.[88] It is also important to keep the "objective legal reasoning"[89] rigorous so that the delimitation process does not float in a void but is firmly anchored to legal considerations. And here is a key aspect of the concept of the delimitation process as it emerges from the case-law: the delimitation process cannot avoid including the legal basis of title as an essential element.

Title governs delimitation . . .

There has already been occasion to mention the relationship between title and delimitation. The two concepts are clearly not identical. Title is to do with defining the criteria on the basis of which a State is legally empowered to exercise rights and jurisdiction over the maritime areas adjacent to its coasts. It is especially concerned with fixing the outer seaward limits. Delimitation, for its part, consists in drawing a demarcation line, a boundary, between two neighbouring States when the geographical situation does not allow both the parties concerned to enjoy their title to its full extent. But it must be remembered that delimitation is nonetheless closely linked

---

[86] *North Sea*, para. 101C1.

[87] Cf. Evensen, *Tunisia/Libya*, Dissenting Opinion, p. 317: "the drawing of frontiers both on land and at sea must always entail restrictions on the extensions of a country's territorial expanse". On the non-encroachment principle, see pp. 60-63 below.

[88] *Gulf of Maine*, para. 59.

[89] *Guinea/Guinea-Bissau*, para. 102.

with the legal basis of title. Delimitation cannot be understood without title, which lies at its very heart. To answer the question, "by what criterion are overlapping areas to be divided?", international law has turned to considerations relating to the legal basis of title, and has decided the criteria and methods for delimitation by reference to the legal concepts governing maritime jurisdictions. Thus, delimitation law has not been cut off from its legal environment and does not find itself condemned to a stagnation incompatible with the development of the law of the sea. As we have seen, this is the approach the Court adopted in *Libya/Malta,* in both a negative and a positive sense: negatively, in rejecting all criteria for division of the continental shelf deriving from physical considerations which had lost all connection with title; positively, when it undertook an "assessment of the impact of distance considerations on the actual delimiting".[90] The actual process of delimitation is determined by the legal title to the area under consideration. This is the "logical" result—the Court's word[91]—of this "self-evident" truth:[92] the link between title and delimitation.

. . . but not by itself: the role of equity

Considerations relating to the basis of title may be the decisive factor in the delimitation process but not to the total exclusion of all else. Another element comes in: the necessity for an equitable solution. Here we touch upon one of the most important aspects of the law of maritime delimitation. As international law currently sees it, delimitation must *at one and the same time* be rooted in legal considerations of title *and* arrive at an equitable solution. Both conditions must be fulfilled; neither of them is sufficient on its own. An equitable division of the area of overlap would not meet the requirements of international law if it were not at the same time rooted in legal title; and a division rooted in legal title would not do so if it did not also produce an equitable solution.

Logically, it is the need for legal title which comes first. Equity comes in only at a second stage in order to correct, if necessary, the possibly inequitable results of applying considerations relating to title to a given situation. As will be seen later, this is the approach which governs the relations between equity and the law and determines the structure of the delimitation process.[93] But history

---

[90] *Libya/Malta,* paras. 61-2.
[91] *Ibid.*, para. 61.
[92] *Ibid.*, para. 27.
[93] On this problem, see Part IV, especially pp. 201ff below.

makes a fool of logic. Chronologically, it was the need for an equitable result which was put first and which even at times so hogged the stage that it almost obscured the need for delimitation to be grounded on the ideas underlying the legal title to the area in question. But fortunately logic has regained the upper hand. It became clear that the criteria and methods for delimitation cannot be justified solely *ex post facto* by the equitable nature of the result. *Ex ante* objective legal considerations must also be taken into account. The logical sequence cannot begin with an equitable line; it must achieve such a line having started from the legal title. The criteria and methods of delimitation provide a bridge between legal considerations relating to title and the equitable line which completes the delimitation process. It is worth quoting at this point what the Court has said in another context:

> It is not a matter of finding simply an equitable solution, but an equitable solution derived from the applicable law.[94]

Setting aside for the moment this second element (which must, however, always be kept in mind), it will be useful next to examine the part played in delimitation first by the *basis* of title, second by its *operation*.

1. DELIMITATION AND THE BASIS OF TITLE

First, a comment on terminology. It is usual to say that title to the continental shelf, which once rested on natural prolongation, is now based on distance and that the principle of distance is also the basis for title to the territorial sea and the exclusive economic zone. These were the terms in which *Gulf of Maine* and *Libya/Malta* were argued before the Court and which have been used here. It must be pointed out that they are shorthand expressions, and conceptually inaccurate.[95] Strictly speaking, neither distance nor natural prolongation forms the basis of a coastal State's legal title. It will be seen in a moment that the basis is to be found in the principle that the land dominates the sea through the intermediary of the coasts, in other words, in the principle of adjacency. Distance, as "natural

---

[94] *Fisheries Jurisdiction*, ICJ *Reports*, 1974, p. 33, para. 78.

[95] Strict logic would also require a distinction to be made between the basis of title to certain maritime areas, and the seaward limit of this title (cf. *Gulf of Maine*, para. 103). But the link between these two is so close that, in practice, no such distinction is called for.

prolongation'' used to be in the case of the continental shelf, is only
a means of expressing this basis, a way of measuring and putting it
into practical effect. Until recently, adjacency was expressed by the
concept of natural prolongation for the continental shelf and distance
for the territorial sea. Nowadays, the concept of distance is the
translation of adjacency not only for the territorial sea and the
exclusive economic zone but also for the continental shelf.[96]

In fact, as far as legal title in the strict sense is concerned, there has
never been any doubt. From the moment States were recognized as
having rights over areas of the sea—that is to say, for as long as there
has been such a thing as the territorial sea—these rights have been
based on two principles which have acquired an almost axiomatic
force, the justification for which it would now be impossible to
challenge: *the land dominates the sea* and it dominates it *by the intermediary
of the coastal front*; these two ideas fuse in the concept of adjacency.

State sovereignty and maritime jurisdiction: maritime rights as derived rights

> The land is the legal source of the power which a State may exercise over
> territorial extensions to seaward.[97]

It is this principle which, encapsulated in the phrase ''the land
dominates the sea'',[98] constitutes the ultimate source, the *Urnorm*,
so to speak, of all legal title over the sea. The principle is not about
territory as such but about the rights a State exercises over it;
maritime rights and jurisdictions do not derive ''from the landmass,
but from sovereignty over the landmass''.[99] This philosophy was
highlighted by the Court in a well-known passage from the *Aegean Sea
Continental Shelf* case:

> . . . it is solely *by virtue of the coastal State's sovereignty over the land* that rights of
> exploration and exploitation in the continental shelf can attach to it, *ipso jure*,
> under international law. In short, continental shelf rights are legally both *an
> emanation from and an automatic adjunct of the territorial sovereignty of the coastal
> State*.[100]

Maritime rights derive from statehood. They are its ''prolongation'',
''extension'', ''emanation'', ''automatic adjunct''. They adhere to

[96] On this problem, see also p. 57 below.

[97] *North Sea*, para. 96. The Court used a similar form of words in the *Fisheries* case in connection with the territorial sea: ''It is the land which confers upon the coastal State a right to the waters off its coasts'' (ICJ *Reports*, 1951, p. 133).

[98] *North Sea*, para. 96.

[99] *Libya/Malta*, para. 49.

[100] *Aegean Sea Continental Shelf*, ICJ *Reports*, 1978, p. 36, para. 86.

statehood as his shadow does to man. Although they are an "automatic adjunct" of territorial sovereignty, they are not *just* an adjunct. They are not primary, autonomous rights. They have no independent existence. They are subsidiary, *derived*, rights.

This has an important implication. Since "all States are equal before the law and are entitled to equal treatment"[101] they are all in the same position as far as the theory of coastal projections is concerned. Two hundred years ago Vattel wrote:

> A dwarf is no less of a man than a giant. A small Republic is no less of a State than the most powerful Kingdom.[102]

Whether it is large or small, whether it is endowed with a long coast and a small hinterland or an extensive territory with a short coast-line, whether it is a large continental State or a small island State, in every case its statehood gives it the same potential for generating maritime projections under the conditions laid down by international law.

This is why, in particular, the generally accepted distinctions as to the effect to be given to islands in delimitations, their size, population, economic importance, etc.,[103] apply only to dependent islands. In contrast, however small it may be, an island which is an independent State enjoys, vis-à-vis its neighbours and in the determination of its seaward maritime rights, the full panoply of its rights as a State. Accepted in theory[104] and endorsed in practice, this principle has also been recognized by the courts. The first opportunity for this was the *Anglo-French* case. In order to determine the effect of the Channel Islands on the Anglo-French delimitation, the Court of Arbitration looked at their political status. Only after determining that they were "islands of the United Kingdom" and "not separate States"[105] did it adopt the enclave formula. In *Libya/Malta*, where Libya relied on the insular nature of Malta in order to claim treatment minimizing the latter's rights, the Court, after recalling that "the entitlement to continental shelf is the same for an island as for mainland", went on to explain that

---

[101] *Libya/Malta*, para. 46.

[102] Quoted in the *Dictionnaire de la terminologie du droit international*, Paris, Sirey, 1960, under "Egalité", p. 248.

[103] On this problem, see pp. 229-35 below.

[104] See, for example, Apollis [2], p. 75 n. 176; Delin, p. 205; Ely, pp. 219, 223, 231, 234, 236; Goldie [4], p. 247; Hodgson [1], p. 186; Karl, pp. 642 n. 3, 667 n. 99, 668 n. 108; Padwa, p. 650.

[105] *Anglo-French* award, paras. 186 and 190.

... Malta being independent, the relationship of its coasts with the coasts of its neighbours is different from what it would be if it were a part of the territory of one of them.[106]

An island State is an island, but, above all, it is a State, and as such it enjoys all the power of generating maritime jurisdictions which international law accords to the coastal State, as regards both title and delimitation.[107]

Although maritime jurisdiction is an attribute of State sovereignty and although, as a result, States must be treated equally in regard to delimitation just as in the determination of their seaward jurisdiction, this does not mean that all States actually have maritime rights or that the extent of these rights is the same for all. The derivative character of maritime rights stems from the fact of the coast and this introduces discrimination between States.[108] And thence springs the second volet of the diptych.

The coastal front: maritime rights as mediated rights

In order to benefit from maritime rights it is not enough to be a State. One must also be a coastal State since it is to States with access to the sea and to them alone that international law has accorded sovereign rights over areas of the sea. A coastline is an essential element in every State projection seawards. This is illuminated by the well-known words of the Court:

> ... exclusive rights over submarine areas belong to the coastal State. The geographic correlation between coast and submerged areas off the coast is the basis of the coastal State's legal title ... *the coast of the territory of the State is the decisive factor* for title to submarine areas adjacent to it.[109]

> ... it is by means of the maritime front of this landmass, in other words *by its coastal opening*, that this territorial sovereignty brings its continental shelf rights into effect ... The juridical link between the State's territorial sovereignty and its rights to certain adjacent maritime expanses is established *by means of its coast*.[110]

---

[106] *Libya/Malta*, para. 53; cf. para. 72.

[107] In *Libya/Malta*, however, the Court modified the result produced by Malta's statehood at the stage when it checked the equity of the equidistance line against the ''general geographic context''. As we shall see, although based on the legally distinct theory of relevant circumstances, this modification nonetheless affects the role of State sovereignty in the delimitation (see pp. 249-52 below).

[108] On the role of the equality of States in the delimitation process, see p. 256 below.

[109] *Tunisia/Libya*, para. 73.

[110] *Libya/Malta*, para. 49.

A State with much land territory but no coast will not have any maritime jurisdiction. A State with little territory but with a long coastal opening will have maritime jurisdiction. This might, of course, be a matter for criticism, but that is the way the international law of the sea has wanted and decreed it.

On the other hand, even though only coastal States are entitled to maritime jurisdiction, it has not been shared equally between them. Some other scheme could have been devised but this is the one international law has chosen. As a result, the coastline determines not only the existence of maritime rights but also their extent and outer shape. As three judges in *Libya/Malta* put it, "[g]iven that sovereignty creates the legal entitlement but can only give it effect by way of the coast as 'medium', it is this medium which becomes decisive for the concretization of the area of shelf attributed".[111] This explains why the size of the hinterland is irrelevant to the determination of the extent and shape of maritime jurisdiction. The landmass stretching behind the coast does not project into the sea by leaping, so to speak, over the coastline. It is a theory of coastal projection which international law has endorsed, not territorial projection. A coastal State does not obtain a more significant maritime projection by virtue of the size of its hinterland any more than a coastal State suffers *capitis deminutio* because its hinterland is smaller. The judges are consistently firm on this point:

> The rights which a State may claim to have over the sea are not related to the extent of the territory behind its coasts, but to the coasts themselves and to the manner in which they border this territory. A State with a fairly small land area may well be justified in claiming a much more extensive maritime territory than a larger country. Everything depends on their respective maritime facades and their formations.[112]
>
> Landmass has never been regarded as a basis of entitlement to continental shelf rights . . . the concept of adjacency measured by distance is based entirely on that of the coastline, and not on that of the landmass.[113]

This is obvious when it is a question of determining the outer seaward limits.[114] But it is equally true for delimitation. State practice shows that the rules are not bent according to the respective

---

[111] Ruda, Bedjaoui and Jiménez de Aréchaga, *Libya/Malta*, Joint Separate Opinion, p. 83, para. 21.

[112] *Guinea/Guinea-Bissau*, para. 119.

[113] *Libya/Malta*, para. 49.

[114] It has been calculated, for example, that the island of Nauru, with 21 square kilometres of territory, could generate an exclusive economic zone 10,000 times the size (Lucchini and Voelckel, p. 71). Cf. p. 65 below.

size of the parties. Neither the Soviet Union in its agreements with Finland, Poland and Norway, nor the United States in its agreements with Mexico and Cuba secured an adjustment of the delimitation line because of its size. In *Libya/Malta*, Libya stressed the enormous disparity of landmass between itself and Malta, claiming that this gave it a more "intense" power to generate maritime projections. The Court reacted sharply. Since landmass does not enter into the basis of title it cannot enter into delimitation.[115]

When the maritime jurisdictions of all States have been determined and all outstanding delimitations completed, then it will be possible to draw a map of the maritime frontiers of the world, and this map will reflect the political carve-up between States, itself the fruit of history. Thus, the attribution of maritime jurisdiction reflects and sometimes even magnifies the inequalities between States. One understands why judges have declined to see their mission as one of distributive justice or international social justice, the object of which would have been to rectify the inequalities between States, or even to reduce the multiplier effect of these inequalities stemming from the derivative character of maritime jurisdiction.

Adjacency

Derived rights, mediated rights: this dual character of maritime jurisdiction expresses itself in the concept of adjacency. In adjacency is found both the historical origin of and the political justification for all coastal State appropriation of the sea: the security of close-at-hand protection gave birth to the territorial sea; exploration and exploitation of the resources of the sea near the coast and the desire of every State not to allow third States to explore and exploit resources too near to its shore are at the origin of the emergence of the continental shelf theory as well as that of the exclusive economic zone. At the legal level also "[a]djacency of the seabed to the territory of the coastal State has been the paramount criterion for determining the legal status of the submerged areas".[116] As the Court observed as early as 1969, the concept of adjacency perfectly translates the dependence of maritime rights on territorial sovereignty through the medium of the coastline.

It is hardly necessary to point out that it is not the physical fact of adjacency of the sea areas to the shore which creates title or constitutes the legal basis for it. It is by virtue of the law that one of

[115] *Libya/Malta*, para. 49.
[116] *Tunisia/Libya*, para. 73.

the attributes of a State is the power to generate, through the medium of its coastline, title to maritime areas adjacent to its coasts, and it is only "legally" that maritime rights have been defined by the Court as an emanation and adjunct of State sovereignty. As the *Gulf of Maine* judgment puts it:

> [I]t is . . . correct to say that international law confers on the coastal State a legal title to an *adjacent* continental shelf or to a maritime zone *adjacent* to its coasts; it would not be correct to say that international law recognizes the title *conferred on the State by the adjacency* of that shelf or that zone, as if the mere natural fact of adjacency produced legal consequences.[117]

2. THE EXERCISE OF TITLE AND DELIMITATION

Once the legal basis of a State's title to areas of the sea has been defined by the all-embracing concept of adjacency, it remains to specify how and how far this title is exercised.

At one point in its development, international law gave different answers to this question depending on whether it was the continental shelf or the territorial sea at issue. As far as the continental shelf was concerned, title was exercised in the direction and over an area determined by the physical configuration of the seabed. In contrast, title to the territorial sea was exercised in all directions up to a certain distance from the shore. As for the exclusive economic zone, it had not yet emerged from the embryonic stage.

This era is now over and all maritime jurisdictions are today exercised in all directions over a distance determined by the law. However, distance is not measured in the abstract but by reference to something, here by reference to the coast. In the same way, a projection does not exist in a void but again by reference to something, here too by reference to the coast. Each of the elements in this trilogy of distance/radial projection/coast merits attention.

A. Distance

The function of the idea of distance in the theory of coastal projections has been defined above.[118] Adjacency, which is the basis of the coastal State's title, is, as we have just seen, liable to differences of substance and interpretation. To define this "particular relationship with the coastline of a neighbouring State"[119] in practical terms

[117] *Gulf of Maine*, para. 103 (italics in original).
[118] See p. 50 above.
[119] *Tunisia/Libya*, para. 41.

a conversion kit is required; international law has chosen distance for this purpose. In *Tunisia/Libya*, the Court spoke of the "distance principle",[120] as we know, a successful phrase. It spoke, more accurately, in *Libya/Malta*, of the "distance criterion"[121] and referred, very accurately indeed, to the "concept of adjacency measured by distance" and the "principle of adjacency as measured by distance".[122]

The distance criterion is now the common denominator of all the rights and jurisdictions of coastal States over maritime areas. With the *Libya/Malta* decision the continental shelf ceased to go its own way and rejoined the family of other maritime regimes. Thus (a point to which we shall return) the unity of the law of maritime delimitation, despite its diversity, was guaranteed.

It is hardly necessary to point out that the concept of distance is a quantitative one. The figure varies from one maritime jurisdiction to another, although nowadays the picture is dominated by the 12 miles of the territorial sea and the 200 miles of the exclusive economic zone and the continental shelf. These figures certainly have a different impact from one area to another: the 12 miles of the territorial sea, the 24 miles of the contiguous zone and the 200 miles of the exclusive economic zone are the maximum which a coastal State may, but need not, claim, while the 200 miles of the continental shelf must be seen as an inherent right, independent of any occupation, proclamation or other constitutive act.[123]

In essence quantitative, the criterion of distance is spatial in its application; although expressed by a figure, it is measured in space. "The distance ... measured on the surface of the sea":[124] this phrase of the Court's is not a literary image; it merely puts into words the fact that all considerations other than the purely spatial are entirely excluded.

The spatial character of delimitation

If there were just one coast, its projection would extend as far as permitted by international law: 12 miles for the territorial sea, 24 miles for the contiguous zone, 200 miles for the exclusive economic zone and the continental shelf. But when the space is too small and the projections of the two coasts cross and overlap, an appropriate

---

[120] *Ibid.*, para. 48.

[121] *Libya/Malta*, paras. 34 and 77.

[122] *Ibid.*, paras. 49 and 61.

[123] Cf. the 1982 Law of the Sea Convention, Articles 3, 4, 56 and 77.

[124] *Tunisia/Libya*, para. 48.

criterion is needed, and a suitable method must be applied in order to avoid the cut-off operating to the benefit of one at the expense of the other.

At first sight, the best way of dividing overlapping areas of maritime projections of the coasts of two neighbouring countries is to do so equally. As the *Gulf of Maine* Chamber said, this is a criterion "which need only be stated to be seen as intrinsically equitable"[125] and the Court advocated it from the start.[126] In the words of the *Frontier Dispute (Burkina Faso/Mali)* case, "although equity does not necessarily imply equality . . . where there are no special circumstances the latter is generally the best expression of the former".[127] It must be emphasized that the equality sought is an equality of *spatial amputation*. It is not an equality of the extent of maritime areas which will accrue, after the delimitation, to each of the States outside as well as within the area of overlap. It is the sectors of overlap, over which the two States have concurrent title, which have to be divided equally, and not all the areas appurtenant to them. Nor is it a question of dividing equally the areas *claimed* by the two sides, i.e., of splitting the difference. Such an approach would risk provoking the systematic maximization of the parties' claims and lead to a shift from the judicial task towards conciliation and compromise. These different concepts must never be confused.[128]

As for what method would be suitable to achieve a balanced spatial reduction of the two overlapping areas, it is in the nature of things that it should have the same character as the legal title on which the projections are based. In other words, like the latter, it will be spatial. For this purpose, the most appropriate method is that of equidistance, the spatial nature of which is indisputable, since it is by

---

[125] *Gulf of Maine*, para. 197. The theme reappears several times, for example, in paras. 115, 195, 209, 217 and 228.

[126] *North Sea*, paras. 57, 99 and 101C2.

[127] ICJ *Reports*, 1986, p. 633, para. 150.

[128] In his Dissenting Opinion in *Gulf of Maine*, Judge Gros criticized the slide from the concept of a division of the "marginal areas" when the titles of the two parties converge, to the concept of a division of the totality of the parties' maritime areas. He writes:

> In a territorial dispute, it is only the land actually disputed that is measured up, and everything recognized as incontestably belonging to one party is left out of the operation; nobody thinks to object against one party that it already has more land than the other. (*Gulf of Maine,* p. 381, para. 34).

As for dividing equally the areas claimed by the two parties, this was expressly recommended by three judges in the *Libya/Malta* case, on the grounds that such a division is sometimes "a means of fully satisfying the requirements of equity" (Ruda, Bedjaoui and Jiménez de Aréchaga, *Libya/Malta*, Joint Separate Opinion, p. 91, para. 38).

reference to the distance between the two coasts that it determines what reduction has to be made to each of the two competing titles. Although it may affect the quantum, the equidistance method leaves the principle of distance intact. Moreover, of all methods, equidistance would seem to come closest to achieving the objective of an equal division of the overlapping area. Technical studies would be helpful here in order to establish more precisely the effect of this method. This is a case where the scientists could give the lawyers useful assistance.

It should not, however, be overlooked that a more or less equal division of the overlapping area can be obtained by other methods, "differing from it in varying degree even while prompted by similar considerations",[129] for example, the perpendicular,[130] or the bisector of the angle formed by the two coastlines.[131] In some respects, these are just variations on the equidistance theme. This is particularly the case with the perpendicular to the general line of the coast, a method recommended in the past for delimiting the territorial seas because, when used between adjacent straight coasts, it achieves the same equal division of the overlapping area as does the median line between opposite coasts. Gidel, for example, saw the perpendicular as a "special variant of the median line understood in its broad sense".[132]

It is clear, however, that none of these various methods, even if justifiable in certain geographical situations, would be appropriate for the general application of the spatial criterion. The bisector method is possible only where two clearly distinguished coastlines form a sharply defined angle; otherwise it rests on artificially reconstructed coastal directions. And the perpendicular method is too unsophisticated to achieve the desired goal of an equal division of overlapping areas when the coastline is not straight and it is difficult to identify its general direction. The development, thanks in particular to the work of Boggs,[133] of the more sophisticated scientific technique of equidistance, made it possible to substitute this for the perpendicular in the delimitation of the territorial sea, and it

---

[129] *Gulf of Maine*, para. 200.

[130] The perpendicular to the coast was chosen for the segment of the boundary in *Tunisia/Libya* (para. 120). The perpendicular to the imaginary closing line of a gulf was used for the last segment of the boundary in *Gulf of Maine* (para. 220).

[131] This was the method used by the Chamber for the sector within the Gulf of Maine in order to produce a result "as close as possible to an equal division of the first area to be delimited" (*Gulf of Maine*, para. 213).

[132] Gidel, vol. III, pp. 759, 768, 769. Cf. Münch [1], p. 156.

[133] See especially Boggs [2], pp. 447ff; Boggs [3], pp. 178ff; Boggs [4], pp. 256ff.

is against this background that the Committee of Experts consulted by the International Law Commission in 1953 rejected the perpendicular as such in favour of the median line "drawn according to the distance principle".[134] The Commission and the 1958 Law of the Sea Conference followed suit; UNCLOS III and the 1982 Convention would do the same.[135] It was, indeed, in the end, a "line drawn in strict compliance with the canons of geometry", in other words, according to the "technical method of equidistance",[136] which became the starting-point for the legal basis of title.

The principle of non-encroachment

The idea of distance would thus seem to be, to borrow a term from theology, consubstantial with the equidistance method. In the words of the Court, the distance from the coast is a "relevant element" in delimitation, and equidistance is "the result to which the distance criterion leads".[137] When maritime areas to which two States have title overlap, the equidistance method allows each of them to exercise sovereign rights up to a certain distance from its coasts wherever these rights come up against the equivalent rights of the other State. At the same time the principle of non-encroachment is safeguarded since, except for a few special situations which then require correction, equidistance allows the boundary to be fixed at the maximum distance from both States and so avoids any excessive amputation of their maritime projections. This point calls for some explanation.

The non-encroachment principle was conceived originally as a principle according to which an equitable delimitation line was not to cut off one of the States from part of its maritime projection. More precisely, this principle was used by the Court in the *North Sea* case for the rejection of the equidistance line in situations where the configuration of the coasts—concavities, salients or islets—causes the equidistance line to deviate and bite into areas forming the natural prolongation of one of the parties. This is the result it condemned, saying:

> . . . the use of the *equidistance method would frequently cause areas which are the natural prolongation or extension of the territory of one State to be attributed to another* when the configuration of the latter's coast makes the equidistance line

[134] *ILCYB*, 1953, vol. II, p. 79.
[135] On the perpendicular method, see also p. 274 below.
[136] *Gulf of Maine*, paras. 201 and 212.
[137] *Libya/Malta*, paras. 34 and 63.

swing out laterally across the former's coastal front, *cutting it off from areas situated directly before that front.*[138]

Already in this negative form, the non-encroachment principle has a spatial character. What equity requires to be rejected is essentially a delimitation line passing too close to one of the coasts. But the non-encroachment principle also has a positive aspect: it envisages that the line will be sufficiently far from the coasts. Here, too, the chief concern is spatial.

Historically and politically, these two aspects have always been linked. The institution of the continental shelf and later of the exclusive economic zone was due, as previously pointed out, to the desire of coastal States both to secure for themselves exclusive rights to natural resources over a sufficiently large area in front of their coasts and to prevent third States coming to explore or exploit natural resources too near to their coasts. Gradually, as we shall see, political concerns, connected with the protection of security and defence interests, became linked to economic considerations.[139] Nowhere was this double basis of the non-encroachment principle more strongly expressed than in the *Guinea/Guinea-Bissau*[140] award and in the speech made by Judge Lachs, President of the Arbitral Tribunal, before delivering the award:

> As stated in the award, our principle concern has been to avoid, by one means or another, one of the parties finding itself faced with the exercise of rights, opposite to and in the immediate vicinity of its coast, which might interfere with its right to development or put its security at risk.

But the link between the negative and positive aspects of the non-encroachment principle is also logical. A State which fears lest a delimitation line based on equidistance will pass, in a sense, beneath its windows, will invoke the inequity of such a line: it will emphasize the negative aspect of the non-encroachment principle. But this same State could equally well rely on the idea that it has the right, like any other coastal State, to the maximum maritime projection compatible with international law. It is to be noted that the Tribunal is very strict when it describes the principle of non-encroachment as:

---

[138] *North Sea*, para. 44.

[139] Cf. Jiménez de Aréchaga, *Tunisia/Libya*, Separate Opinion, p. 119, para. 70 and p. 121, para. 72. The former President of the Court criticizes the lines claimed by Libya and Tunisia for coming "too close" on the one hand to the Tunisian port of Sfax, on the other to the Libyan port of Tripoli (*Tunisia/Libya*, p. 122, para. 75).

[140] *Guinea/Guinea-Bissau*, paras. 92, 98, 103 and 124.

> ... *the negative expression of the positive rule* that the coastal State enjoys sovereign rights over the continental shelf off its coasts to the full extent authorized by international law in the relevant circumstances.[141]

In fact, the non-encroachment principle lies at the very heart of the delimitation process. One cannot repeat too often that delimitation is a matter of amputating the projections of the two States by comparison with what each of them would be legally entitled to if the other did not exist. In this sense, as pointed out previously, encroachment and cut-off are inherent in the whole idea of delimitation. In the final analysis, the choice of criteria and methods for delimitation is none other than the choice of criteria and methods suitable for the drawing of what one might call the line of amputation, the line of sacrifice, i.e., to determine the distance at which each State must agree to halt projections which otherwise it would have been able to extend to the full distance and in all the directions permitted by international law. But, at the same time, a balance must be struck between the right and the sacrifice of the one and the sacrifice and right of the other. A's projection must not unreasonably encroach on that of B since B is entitled to the enjoyment, if not total at least reasonable, of its own projection; but, conversely, no more may B's projection encroach unreasonably on that of A, since A also has the right to the enjoyment, if not total at least reasonable, of its own projection. The non-encroachment principle must not be approached from the point of view of just one of the States concerned; it must be understood in its entirety as dominating the whole concept of delimitation.

It has often been observed that every freedom must stop at the point where its exercise begins to intrude on someone else's. The same is true of maritime delimitation: one party's projection must stop when it would run the risk of impinging on that of the other. To put it precisely, it is a question of deciding how far it is possible to go without going too far. At one and the same time, a delimitation must be a line of amputation and encroachment and a line of non-amputation and non-encroachment. All the evidence suggests that, to tackle this balancing trick, the purpose of which is to reconcile the conflicting and contradictory demands of the two parties, only a spatial criterion will do. The line of division must be kept at more or less the same distance from the two coasts in such a way as to ensure each gets the same measure of positive projection and the same measure of negative cut-off. In order to meet this criterion, the

---

[141] *Libya/Malta*, para. 46.

appropriate method is that of equidistance which, according to the Court's definition in the *North Sea* case,

> ... leaves to each of the parties concerned all those portions [of the continental shelf] that are nearer to a point on its own coast than they are to any point on the coast of the other party.[142]

If it should turn out, however, that, as the result of a particular geographical feature, the equidistance line threatens to come too close to the coast of one of the parties, a correction would be necessary. But this is a point which arises at another level and will be dealt with later.

B. Radial Projection

Territorial sovereignty across the coastal span projects in all directions. The land dominates the sea and does so in all directions. By definition, the projection of the coast is omni-directional, that is to say, radial. These propositions might seem too obvious even to discuss, and there would indeed be no need to linger over them were it not for the controversies to which they have given rise in two cases. Set out for the first time by Canada in *Gulf of Maine* and then taken up again by Malta in *Libya/Malta*, the radial projection theory was contested by the other side, not so much the idea itself, at the level of legal title, as its application to delimitation. As for the Court, it remained silent.

Omni-directional title

In truth, the phrase "radial projection" hides an idea of great simplicity. When one uses a fixed distance in order to define a coastal State's projection into the sea, the maritime area which accrues to it extends in all directions over the prescribed distance. No direction is more important than another. One may not be favoured over another. The term may be new but the idea stretches back into the beginnings of the law of the sea. By definition, the range of gun-fire—the famous cannon-shot rule—which inspired and for so long dominated the theory of the territorial sea, had a radial character. A cannon shoots in all directions, whence the idea that, to draw the outer, seaward limit of the territorial sea, it was enough to draw arcs of a circle, starting from points on the coast, in other words, the envelope of arcs of circles technique (also known as the "tangential

---

[142] *North Sea*, para. 6.

curve" technique) which became the preferred method. This method, described and illustrated in graph form by Boggs in 1930 and Münch and Gidel in 1934,[143] consists in defining the outer limit of the territorial sea as the curve tangential to the arcs of circles of a radius equal to the width of the territorial sea, drawn from every point on the coast. Given, however, that only the outer envelope of these arcs of circles is retained, the arcs inside the envelope in the last resort are not decisive nor, indeed, even useful, in constructing the outer limit. They are, in a sense, lost, just as are their coastal starting points. This means, as Gidel and Boggs pointed out, that only a limited number of coastal points have any effect on the construction of the outer limit and these are the points, in the language of today, which control the drawing of the line.

The envelope of arcs of circles idea was thought up by technicians and proposed to the 1930 Hague Codification Conference by the United States delegation. The International Court of Justice described it in 1951, in the *Fisheries* case, saying that it was "not obligatory by law".[144] During the 1950s the Committee of Experts and the International Law Commission recommended its use.[145] It ended up becoming the legally required method for fixing the outer limit of the territorial sea, under Article 6 of the 1958 Convention on the Territorial Sea and Contiguous Zone, and Article 4 of the 1982 Law of the Sea Convention. Directly echoing Boggs, these provisions describe this method as producing "a line every point of which is at a distance from the nearest point of the baseline equal to the breadth of the territorial sea".

The link between the envelope of arcs of circles method and radial projection is obvious. The arcs of circles method simply translates the principle of omni-directional projection into technical terms. As Judge Read wrote in his opinion in the 1951 *Fisheries* case:

> In the earliest days, the cannon on the coast, when traversed, traced arcs by the splash of their shots. Later, the imaginary cannon traced imaginary arcs which intersected and marked out the limit based on cannon shot.[146]

The arcs of circles method, conceived and legally sanctioned for purposes of establishing the outer limit of the territorial sea, is appropriate whenever the outer limit of a maritime jurisdiction is defined in terms of distance from the coast. Although the 1982

[143] Boggs [1], pp. 545ff; Münch [1], pp. 75ff; Gidel, vol. III, pp. 510ff.
[144] ICJ *Reports*, 1951, p. 129.
[145] *ILCYB*, 1953, vol. II, p. 76; 1954, vol. I, pp. 85 ff; 1956, vol. II, p. 268.
[146] ICJ *Reports*, 1951, p. 192.

Convention did not refer to it for fixing the outer limit of the exclusive economic zone, it is appropriate in this case also: many States have in fact used it. As to the continental shelf, the arcs of circles method was out of the question so long as the width of the shelf was defined according to the criteria of depth, exploitability and natural prolongation; but it reasserts itself with the new idea according to which the shelf is defined primarily according to a spatial criterion, as was always the case for the territorial sea and as it is for the exclusive economic zone. The radial effect makes it possible to create that "belt" of which the Court spoke in reference to the territorial sea,[147] that envelope of ocean space adjacent to the coastal front which is intrinsic to the criterion of distance.

One consequence of radial projection is that there is no fixed relationship between the extent of the maritime rights generated by a coast and its length, any more than there is a fixed relationship between the extent of the maritime rights generated by a coast and the size of its hinterland.[148] This explains the intense interest all States now have in the least stretch of maritime front, the smallest island, over which they can claim sovereignty. By creating an economic zone of 200 miles, France has managed to become the third world power in terms of the size of the maritime areas under its jurisdiction despite the fact that it does not occupy third place according to the length of its coastline and even less so in respect of the size of its land territory.[149] The size of the exclusive economic zone proclaimed by the United States in 1983 is equally eloquent.[150] These facts, which no-one disputes, are none other than the application of the theory of coastal projections and an illustration of the principle that the land projects legally towards the sea in all directions, assuming, of course, that this projection does not run into

[147] *Ibid.*, p. 129.

[148] Cf. p. 54 above. With a 12 mile territorial sea, for example, a tiny island 1 mile across (and so with an area of 0.78 square miles) would generate, thanks to its coastal opening of 3.14 miles, a territorial sea of 490 square miles. To generate the same area of territorial sea, a mainland territory would need a coastline 41 miles in length, in other words, thirteen times the length of the small island. Another example: a circular island with a coastal length of 1 mile (which means a diameter of 0.32 miles) generates a territorial sea of 464 square miles, while a mainland territory with the same length of coast generates only 12 square miles of territorial sea, almost 40 times less.

[149] Lacharrière G., de, "La zone économique française de 200 milles", *Annuaire français de droit international,* 1976, p. 647.

[150] See the map published at the time of this proclamation (*ILM*, vol. 22, 1983, p. 463). Cf. Alexander, L.M., "The Extended Economic Zone and US Ocean Interests", *Columbia Journal of World Business*, 1975, p. 36; Quéneudec, J.P., "La proclamation Reagan sur la zone économique exclusive des Etats-Unis", *Annuaire français du droit international*, 1975, p. 710.

a projection coming from a neighbouring territory, in which case the problem of delimitation will arise.

Omni-directional delimitation

If a coast radiates in all directions when it is on its own, why should it cease to do so when its projection enters into competition with that of the coast of another State? The reduction of the distance to which it can project is the result of the cut-off effect inherent in delimitation, but there is no reason why the directions in which it projects should themselves be restricted. If there is radial projection seaward, then there must be radial projection in delimitation.

However, what seems to be self-evident has twice been challenged. It is not without interest to recall the particular context in which the debate took place.

In *Gulf of Maine*, the United States maintained that its coastal front at the far end of the Gulf and the coastal front of Canada which borders the Gulf to the east both project into the sea in a direction at right angles to the coast; but, added the United States, the American coastal front at the far end of the Gulf, for reasons it is not necessary to dwell on here, must be regarded as the "primary" and as such be given more weight than the Canadian coastal front, considered to be "secondary".[151] In countering this argument, Canada did not limit itself to rejecting any coastal hierarchy but also put forward the radial projection theory. It argued that the American coast does not, any more than the Canadian, project into the sea at right angles to the general direction of the coast:

> The maritime zone of a coastal State . . . is not to be thought of as a platform in front of its coast, but as a broad belt of sea surrounding its territory in every direction.[152]

This is the context in which the concept and term "radial projection" were used for the first time. In its judgment, the Chamber rejected the American argument as implying a hierarchy between natural phenomena which did not admit of value judgments. It did not refer to the radial projection theory.[153]

---

[151] United States Memorial, paras. 287 and 309.

[152] Canadian Counter-Memorial, paras. 151 and 564-8; Canadian Reply, para. 73.

[153] *Gulf of Maine*, paras. 36-7. It must, however, be noted that, by making the delimitation of the inner sector of the Gulf of Maine on the basis of a "division of the area of overlapping created by the lateral superimposition of the maritime projections of the coasts of the two States" (*Gulf of Maine*, para. 209), the Chamber implicitly rejected the theory of the frontal projection and perpendicular in favour of the radial projection and omni-directional theory.

Sketched out in *Gulf of Maine*, the controversy surrounding radial projection was to reach new dimensions in *Libya/Malta*. Libya did not deny that an isolated island in the ocean could ''radiate'' 360 degrees around its coasts, but it contested the use of radial projection for delimitation purposes. In the latter case, it argued, the only relevant segments are those which face one another, and all that matters is the projection of each of these segments in the direction of the one facing it. In the case at issue, therefore, all that needed to be taken into account was the segments of the Maltese coast and of the Libyan coast which directly face one another (i.e., facing respectively due south and due north), the Maltese segment projecting only in a southerly direction and the Libyan only in a northern. The practical purpose of this thesis was to deny to Malta all rights over the seabed to the east and south-east of the Maltese islands. Malta protested against this resurgence of the frontal projection theory, arguing that its coasts give rise to rights in all directions.[154]

As we see, in this case discussion of radial projection came, once again, as a reaction to frontal projection arguments. As in *Gulf of Maine*, the Court in *Libya/Malta* was again able to decide the point at issue without entering into the substance of the argument. In its judgment, even though the Court limited the eastward delimitation to a meridian passing approximately at right angles to the two coastal segments facing one another, it did so, as we shall see, in order to protect the interests of Italy, in other words, for reasons which had nothing to do with the Libyan arguments about the relevant coasts and without reference to the problem of the direction of maritime projections.[155] It should be noted, however, that far from rejecting the Maltese argument according to which the coast of Malta is capable of projecting to the east and south-east just as in any other direction, the Court was at pains to point out:

A decision limited in this way does not signify . . . that the claims of either Party to expanses of continental shelf outside that area have been found to be unjustified[156]

thus leaving untouched the question of the legal possibility of the Maltese coasts projecting to the east and south-east as well as to the

---

[154] Libyan Memorial, pp. 156-7; Libyan Counter-Memorial, pp. 34-5, 39; Libyan Reply, p. 78. Maltese Reply, para. 97; Maltese Oral Pleadings, CR 84/26, pp. 41ff and 85/7, pp. 22ff.

[155] *Libya/Malta*, paras. 20-3. See also pp. 254ff below.

[156] *Ibid.*, para. 21.

south. The radial projection theory may not have been endorsed by the Court, but neither was it rejected by it.[157]

In truth, there is no reason why a coast should project in all directions if it faces the ocean on its own, but only frontally when faced with a parallel coast so that its projection intersects that of another coast. This is fully borne out by the practice in delimitation agreements. There are many examples where sometimes very short coasts have radiated in all directions and created for one or other (or perhaps both) of the parties maritime jurisdictions stretching in all directions and overflowing, on both sides, a so-called face to face relationship.[158] In the same way, the delimitation line drawn by the Court of Arbitration between France and the United Kingdom in the Atlantic region would make no sense if the Court had thought that the Scilly Isles and Ushant projected only frontally towards one another and had not taken the normal view that they project in all directions.

Inherent in the theory of maritime projections, radial projection governs delimitation as it does title. The arcs of circles which translate it into practice at the level of title do likewise at the delimitation level. These arcs will be drawn, starting from the two coasts, in all directions, and delimitation will take place wherever the arcs emanating from one coast cross with those emanating from the other. In this respect, there is an obvious relationship between equidistance as a method of delimiting overlapping maritime areas and the arcs of circles technique as a means of establishing the outer limit of a maritime jurisdiction defined by distance. The basic elements of the arcs of circles method, in fact, provided the inspiration for Boggs' suggestion, in his classic studies of 1937 and 1951,[159] that the boundary of the territorial sea between neighbouring States be fixed according to a line each point of which would be at an equal distance from the nearest point on each of the coasts. In both cases, it was, at the beginning at least, by means of arcs of circles that the method was to be applied. (Since then, more elaborate

---

[157] The authors of the Joint Separate Opinion regretted that the judgment might be interpreted, not as a rejection of the radial projection theory, but "as encouraging the insistence upon this claim" (Ruda, Bedjaoui and Jiménez de Aréchaga, *Libya/Malta*, Joint Separate Opinion, pp. 76-7, para. 2. Cf. Schwebel, *ibid.*, Dissenting Opinion, p. 179).

[158] See, for example, agreements between France and Mauritius (1980), *Limits in the Seas*, No. 95; France/St. Lucia (1981), *RGDIP*, vol. 85, 1981, p. 651; France/Australia (1982), *RGDIP*, vol. 87, 1983, p. 726; Italy/Spain (1974), *Limits in the Seas*, No. 96—in this agreement the short Minorca coastline facing the long Sardinian coast benefited from a coastal projection in all directions.

[159] Boggs [2] and [4].

procedures have been developed.)[160] Just as with the arcs of circles method, the equidistance method meant giving effect, in constructing the line, only to certain points on the coast, others having no influence. In both cases, the coastal re-entrants, the concavities, benefit from the seaward projection generated by the salients, the convexities. The equidistance method is to delimitation what the arcs of circles method is to the determination of the outer limits: the most developed technical expression of the distance criterion and of multidirectional projection. They are like twins: there cannot be one without the other.

C. Coasts

Distance and multidirectional projection both require for their implementation a starting point: it is from the coasts that State sovereignty extends itself legally seawards. The concepts of distance and radial projection are bound up with that of coasts and it is only for the convenience of analysis that they are dealt with separately here.

Coasts and title

The extent and shape of a State's maritime projection defined in terms of distance and governed by the radial projection concept will be determined by the pattern of its coastal opening; hence the crucial importance of the geographical configuration of the coastline. With the method known as the *tracé parallèle* (which, according to the Court in the description it gives for the territorial sea, "consists of drawing the outer limit of the belt of territorial waters by following the coast in all its sinuosities")[161] the line of the outer limit faithfully reflects the shape of the maritime front in its every detail, whether it is a matter of the territorial sea or of any other jurisdiction measured by distance. With this method, coastal geography exercises the maximum influence. But, as the Court pointed out, although this method "may be applied without difficulty to an ordinary coast, which is not too broken", it cannot be applied to a coast "deeply indented and cut into" or "rugged". In these cases, it is necessary to turn to the arcs of circles method mentioned above or the straight baselines method which "consists of selecting appropriate points on the low-water mark and drawing straight lines between them".[162]

[160] On modern techniques of constructing lines of equidistance, see, *inter alia*, Beazley [2] and [4]; Hodgson and Cooper; Shalowitz, vol. I, pp. 230ff; Voelckel [2].

[161] *Fisheries*, ICJ *Reports*, 1951, p. 128.

[162] *Ibid.*, pp. 129-30.

Like the arcs of circles method, the straight baselines method has become customary international law and found expression in the 1982 Convention.[163]

The combination of these two methods leads to an important conclusion. It may be true that State sovereignty projects itself seawards by means of the maritime front. However, what the law looks to is not the actual coastline in all its minutest detail and every irregularity, but a stylized coast determined by baselines and points deemed to be representative. This has not stopped the Court taking the view that the arcs of circles method, as well as the straight baselines method, correctly secures the application of the principle that the belt of territorial waters must follow the general direction of the coast.[164] Nowadays, international law considers baselines and basepoints a valid legal expression of the coastline for all maritime jurisdictions, not just the territorial sea. It is no accident that one normally uses the shorthand expression, ''200 nautical miles from the coast'', rather than the more accurate ''200 nautical miles from the baselines from which the breadth of the territorial sea is measured''. This assimilation of baselines and coasts is revealing.

It goes without saying that the choice of basepoints and the drawing of straight baselines are not left to the discretion of the coastal State. Simplified representation does not mean arbitrary representation. The choice of basepoints for drawing the envelope of arcs of circles is usually dictated by geography, the most prominent points determining the outer envelope. In the case of rocks or islets lying off the coast, however, there will be an element of legal decision-making. But even if the jurist has to ask himself which island or rock should legally serve as the basepoint, once he has made his decision, the cartographer and the computer lose all freedom.

These observations corroborate the statement made earlier, in the context of radial projection, that the extent of a maritime jurisdiction, although determined by the shape of the coastline, is not in a constant relationship to it throughout the length of the coastal front. The length of the coastline is an element in the shape of the coast, but it is not the only one. Of course, a long coast has more chance of generating a large expanse of maritime space than a short one, but this common-sense observation cannot be expressed mathematically. Maritime jurisdictions are not measured by the

---

[163] Article 7. The ''baselines from which the breadth of the territorial sea is measured'' were also used for measuring the contiguous zone, the exclusive economic zone and the continental shelf (1982 Convention on the Law of the Sea, Articles 33, 57, 76).

[164] *Fisheries*, ICJ *Reports*, 1951, pp. 129-30.

length of the coast, and two coasts similar in length may, because of other coastal characteristics, generate maritime areas very different in size. It is the coastal opening which radiates seaward, not just the length of the coastline as measured by the surveyor. As the examples previously mentioned demonstrate,[165] if a mile of coast of one State gives rise to a certain area of territorial sea, continental shelf or exclusive economic zone, this does not mean that a mile of another State's coast must produce the same area of territorial sea, continental shelf or exclusive economic zone. In addition, the number of basepoints determining the outer limit varies according to the configuration of the coast. The further from the coast the arcs of circles method is applied, the fewer the basepoints, and the greater the length of the outer limit determined by each.[166]

Coasts and delimitation

As in the case of title, distance and radial projection take the coastal front as the starting point for delimitation purposes, but with one important difference: the starting point here is the geography of two maritime fronts, not just one, and these have to be considered together.

Rarely has case-law been so consistent and unanimous as on the primacy of the coastal geography in matters of delimitation. This doctrine has been the subject of many pronouncements of principle:

It is ... necessary to examine closely the geographical configuration of the coastlines of the countries whose continental shelves are to be delimited.[167]

[T]he method of delimitation which it adopts ... must be one that has relation to the coasts of the Parties actually abutting on the continental shelf ... [168]

The coast of each of the Parties ... constitutes the starting line from which one has to set out in order to ascertain how far the submarine areas appertaining to each of them extend in a seaward direction, as well as in relation to neighbouring States situated either in an adjacent or opposite position.[169]

The delimitation line to be drawn in a given area will depend upon the coastal configuration.[170]

[165] See p. 65 n. 148 above.

[166] The *Gulf of Maine* case showed that Canada and the United States both constructed the outer limits of their exclusive fisheries zones on the basis of only a few points (Cf. C1/CR 84/6, p. 68).

[167] *North Sea*, para. 96.

[168] *Anglo-French* award, para. 248.

[169] *Tunisia/Libya*, para. 74.

[170] *Gulf of Maine*, para. 205.

It must be pointed out that the relationship between the two coasts plays as important a role in delimitation as the configuration of each of them independently. This explains, as will be seen, the care often taken over the distinction between a geographical relationship of adjacency and one of opposition, as well as over the comparison of the length of coastal fronts.[171]

There has been some discussion as to which coastal segments are to have their configuration taken into account for delimitation purposes. This problem can probably be resolved quite simply. Since delimitation presupposes an overlapping of projections, the relevant segments for delimitation purposes are those whose projections intersect projections from the other coast. Coastal segments whose projections do not overlap have no effect upon delimitation. Thus, in the *Anglo-French* case, the Court of Arbitration rejected the French argument that delimitation in the Atlantic region should be governed by the general direction of the coasts within the Channel: ''It is not . . . obvious'', said the Court,

> how or why the coasts within the Channel should . . . acquire an absolute relevance in determining the course of the boundary itself in the Atlantic region . . .

> [T]he method of delimitation which it adopts for the Atlantic region must be one that has relation to the coasts of the Parties actually abutting on the continental shelf of the region.[172]

The Court put it particularly clearly in *Tunisia/Libya*:

> . . . for the purpose of shelf delimitation between the Parties, it is not the whole of the coast of each party which can be taken into account; the submarine extension of any part of the coast of one Party which, because of its geographic situation, cannot overlap with the extension of the coast of the other, is to be excluded from . . . consideration by the Court.[173]

In *Gulf of Maine*, the Chamber similarly rejected the American argument that the maritime boundary in the outer section of the Gulf, in open seas, should be governed by the coastal configuration at the far end of the Gulf.[174]

---

[171] See pp. 235ff below.

[172] *Anglo-French* award, paras. 246-7.

[173] *Tunisia/Libya*, para. 75.

[174] *Gulf of Maine*, para. 224. Although these principles, a logical consequence of the coastal projections theory, are endorsed by most of the cases, there is a discordant note in *Guinea/Guinea-Bissau*, resulting from a macro-geographic view of the coast in question.

There is no doubt that of all the methods available, equidistance is the best way of ensuring that the coastal configuration is reflected in the delimitation. It is, the Court has said, "a geometrical delimitation method . . . whereby the delimitation line is directly governed by points on the coasts concerned", and which has "the virtue—though it may also be the weakness— . . . to take full account of almost all variations in the relevant coastline".[175] An equidistance line is not constructed on the basis of a general direction established in a debatable manner. It takes account of the successive changes in the direction of each of the coasts concerned and thus is an objective reflection of the complexity of the coastal configurations.[176]

This aspect has, however, sometimes been questioned on the ground that only salient points on the coastline have any repercussion on the delimitation line, and that a single basepoint can control the line over quite a distance. This cannot be disputed, but it is not really a matter for criticism. It is a logical consequence of the theory of coastal projections that the maximum extent of the maritime space of each, in practice as in theory, is to be determined by the most prominent points on the shoreline. It is the contrary solution which would be unacceptable. Treaty practice and case-law both support this view. For example, the agreement between Argentina and Uruguay over the River Plate results in the whole line, up to 200 nautical miles seaward, being controlled by the two salient points marking the ends of the imaginary line closing the River Plate.[177] In the delimitation between India and Sri Lanka, almost 50 miles of the delimitation line are controlled by a single basepoint on the coast of Sri Lanka, and the last 58 miles depend on a single point on the coast of Sri Lanka and a single point on the coast of India.[178] The line decided on by the Chamber in *Gulf of Maine* for the outer sector (which is not, however, strictly speaking, an

---

The Arbitration Tribunal in this case referred to the "continuous coastline" (i.e. the whole coastline) of the two countries. It even added the coast of a third State, Sierra Leone, leading it to make the delimitation on the basis of a "long coastline" by relation to the "whole of West Africa", and a line in the general direction of the coast starting from a third country (paras. 92, 103-4 and 108-10). Cf. p. 238 below.

[175] *Tunisia/Libya*, paras. 76 and 126.

[176] Cf. Oda, *Libya/Malta*, Dissenting Opinion, p. 140, para. 30: "If geography is respected, the ascertainment of objective 'equidistance' by means of the geographical or geometrical method of plotting equidistance will be quite independent of the subjectively defined 'relevant coasts' ". Equidistance is particularly suitable in the case of irregular indentations because of the use of basepoints. Each basepoint represents a certain stretch of coast, at the mid-point between the preceding and following basepoints.

[177] 1973, *Limits in the Seas*, No. 64.

[178] 1977, *Limits in the Seas*, No. 77.

equidistance line) rests throughout its whole length on just two coastal points.[179] The median line between Malta and Libya, which the Court took as the line of departure in *Libya/Malta*, is controlled by just two points on the coast of Malta and by almost as few on that of Libya.[180]

All these characteristics the equidistance method shares with the arcs of circles and straight baselines methods, both of which are now accepted unreservedly for fixing the outer limits. One should not complain, any more than with the arcs of circles method, that equidistance reflects points on the coast rather than the coasts themselves. It is hard to see why the "loss" of a certain number of coastal points or segments, and the control of sometimes long segments of the line by only a few points, should escape criticism when it is a case of fixing the outer limits, but become reprehensible the moment it moves from title to delimitation.

It goes without saying that, just as is the case in implementing the arcs of circles method in such a way as to reflect the coastline for purposes of title, the implementation of the equidistance method so as to reflect the coastline for purposes of delimitation presupposes that the baselines and basepoints fulfil certain conditions. In the majority of cases, it is again geography which decides the basepoints. They are "*geometrically determined*, not artificially picked up, as the drawing of the delimitation line progresses".[181] In this sense, it is clear that "any cartographer can *de facto* trace such a boundary on the appropriate maps and charts, and those traced by competent cartographers will for all practical purposes agree".[182] In some cases, a choice will still have to be made, for example between a line drawn on the basis of salient points on the continental coast and one drawn on the basis of salient points on the islands, islets or rocks lying off the coast. The real problem of equidistance will then be not so much its intrinsic value as the question: "equidistance between what and what?". In *Gulf of Maine*, for example, the Chamber pointed out the possible inconvenience of taking as basepoints "tiny islands, uninhabited rocks or low-tide elevations, sometimes lying at a considerable distance from terra firma",[183] and it objected to the equidistance method proposed by Canada in that it would mean, in the inner section of the Gulf, "the adoption of a line all of whose basepoints would be located on a handful of isolated rocks, some very

---

[179] *Gulf of Maine*, para. 224.
[180] *Libya/Malta*, para. 70.
[181] Oda, *Libya/Malta*, Dissenting Opinion, p. 140, para. 30. Emphasis in original.
[182] *North Sea*, para. 22.
[183] *Gulf of Maine*, para. 201.

distant from the coast, or on a few low-tide elevations''.[184] Likewise, in *Libya/Malta*, the Court said:

> ... the equitableness of an equidistance line depends on whether the precaution is taken of eliminating the disproportionate effect of certain islets, rocks and minor coastal projections.[185]

In a word, the choice of basepoints must be reasonable and equitable. The rectification of the basepoints is, moreover, one of the most suitable and most commonly used methods of correcting inequity in an equidistance line, permitting the effects of certain islands, salients or other minor accidents to be ironed out or eliminated. This does not put in question the validity of the equidistance method, but becomes relevant at the second stage of delimitation, when the equidistance line is put to the test of equity. This is the context in which the problem will be considered in Part IV of this book.

Coastal length and delimitation: the so-called principle of proportionality

In almost every case brought before the judges the party with the longest coastal front argues that this gives it the right to a greater area of maritime jurisdiction. This theory is sometimes pushed further, and it is argued that the extent of maritime rights accruing to each State should be more or less in the same ratio as the length of the maritime fronts. The proportionality argument is usually linked with others which it is intended to reinforce. In *Libya/Malta*, however, once the rift zone theory was put aside, the argument of proportionality appeared in all its purity. As the Court put it, ''[n]othing else remains in the Libyan submissions that can afford an independent principle and method for drawing the boundary, unless the reference to the lengths of coastlines is taken as such''.[186] The enormous difference in length between the coast of Malta and that of Libya made the proportionality argument particularly tempting in that case.

The theory of the comparison of coastal lengths was considered in greatest depth in the joint opinion of Judges Bedjaoui, Ruda and Jiménez de Aréchaga in *Libya/Malta*. It may be true, the three judges noted, that maritime rights are ''an emanation of statehood'', but nonetheless the ''extent and limits'' of those rights ''are given

---

[184] *Ibid.*, para. 210.
[185] *Libya/Malta*, para. 64.
[186] *Ibid.*, para. 58.

concrete form by the coastal front, and as a function of its geography, which comprises all its physical characteristics, length included". The shore, they observe, "is a more or less important, more or less extensive, means of access to the sea", a "parameter . . . expressed in units of measurement". Since a great variety of elements in the coastal configuration are taken into account—orientation, curvature, opposite or adjacent relationship, general direction—"it would appear striking and unusual, unjustifiable and unwarranted, not to deal likewise with the length of the coasts". In short, because it is access to the sea which gives title to maritime jurisdiction, the "breadth of contact with the sea" cannot but govern the delimitation.[187]

If it had to be seen as an inherent part of the delimitation process, this theory would run into all sorts of obstacles, practical and circumstantial as well as juridical and fundamental. It is as well, therefore, that the judges have been rather cautious towards it.

First, the idea of coastal length is a deceptively simple one. There are many ways of measuring the length of a coast. One can follow its every turn, but one can also follow its general direction. An indented coastline will seem longer or shorter depending on whether or not the indentations are included. In the *North Sea* case, the Court suggested measuring the length of the coasts "according to their general direction in order to establish the necessary balance between States with straight, and those with markedly concave or convex coasts, or to reduce very irregular coastlines to their truer proportions".[188] This is the method the Court was to apply in *Tunisia/Libya*.[189] In *Gulf of Maine*, the parties discussed whether the shores of the Bay of Fundy should be taken into account for the purpose of determining proportionality. The Chamber deemed it possible at one and the same time to draw a straight closing line across the Bay, thus making the Canadian coast one side of a rectangle, and to take account of part of the shores of the Bay for proportionality purposes.[190] In *Guinea/Guinea-Bissau*, calculation of the length of coastline included

[187] Ruda, Bedjaoui and Jiménez de Aréchaga, *Libya/Malta,* Joint Separate Opinion, pp. 82ff, paras. 20ff.

[188] *North Sea*, para. 98.

[189] *Tunisia/Libya*, para. 131. The Court states, however, in another passage in the same judgment, that "the element of proportionality is related to lengths of the coasts of the States concerned, not to straight baselines drawn round those coasts" (*ibid.*, para. 104).

[190] But only that part of the Bay which was more than 12 miles wide (*Gulf of Maine*, paras. 31 and 221). The Chamber's solution was criticized by Judge Schwebel (*Gulf of Maine*, Separate Opinion, p. 354). The US coasts were measured according to the coastal front method.

some island formations.[191] This is a situation where maps can be made to say more or less what one wants, and it is not unusual to find parties, on the basis of identical cartographic data, producing quite different figures for the length of their coasts.

This first practical difficulty is compounded by the no less hazardous need to decide which segments of coast to include in the reckoning. A litigant always hopes to improve his case by lengthening his own relevant coasts and shortening those of the other party. This thorny problem has been mentioned above.[192]

It seems even more difficult to decide which maritime areas ought, according to the proportionality theory, to be in the same ratio to one another as the coastlines. Is only the area of overlap to be taken into account? Or should it be the ratio between the totality of the maritime areas attributable to the interested parties throughout the area in dispute? If so, how is one to define the limits of the latter?[193] In these circumstances, it is understandable why the scholarly models of proportionality which the parties have submitted to the courts seem never to have convinced them. In *Libya/Malta*, for example, the Court observes:

> ... the geographical context is such that the identification of the relevant coasts and the relevant areas is so much at large that virtually any variant could be chosen, leading to widely different results.[194]

There is sometimes another, completely insurmountable, obstacle: the parties may ask the judge or arbitrator for only a partial delimitation of a given area. This was the case in *Gulf of Maine* where the Chamber was called on to draw the maritime boundary only between an agreed point to the north and an agreed area to the south. Further north and further south, the delimitation was left for subsequent negotiation.[195] It may also happen that the court itself decides to limit the delimitation to a restricted sector in order to preserve the rights of third States. In *Tunisia/Libya*, the Court refrained from fixing the terminal point of the delimitation line so as not to prejudge "the delimitations [which may] ultimately [be] agreed with third States on the other side of the Pelagian Sea".[196] In

---

[191] *Guinea/Guinea-Bissau*, para. 97.

[192] See p. 72 above.

[193] The question is by no means theoretical, as is shown by the difficulties the Court ran into in *Tunisia/Libya* regarding the inclusion of areas of territorial and internal waters in the maritime areas to be compared (*Tunisia/Libya*, paras. 103-5 and 131).

[194] *Libya/Malta*, para. 74.

[195] See *Gulf of Maine*, para. 23.

[196] *Tunisia/Libya*, para. 130; cf. para. 33 and 133C3.

Libya/Malta, it gave its decision "limited . . . geographical scope", delimiting only "the area in which, as the Court has been informed by Italy, that State has no claims".[197] It is obvious that in this sort of situation, where each of the parties may at some time be allocated additional stretches of sea, any calculation of the ratio between maritime areas is extremely precarious. As the Court puts it, "to apply the proportionality test simply to the areas within these limits would be unrealistic" because of "the probability that future delimitations with third States would overthrow not only the figures for . . . areas used as the basis for calculations but also the ratios arrived at".[198]

But even more damning than these difficulties of applying the proportionality theory to particular situations are the fundamental objections of principle. We have seen previously[199] that, as far as title is concerned, the length of the coastline (one among several elements determining its configuration) does not have any direct and independent effect. There is no constant and automatic relationship between the length of a coast and the maritime area it generates seaward. If this is true of title, why should it not be true of delimitation? Since international law has not accepted the principle of dividing maritime areas according to the length of the coastline,[200] it cannot accept that delimitation between neighbouring States must necessarily reflect the relationship between their coastlines measured with a length of string.

It is understandable why, with increasing firmness from one judgment to the next, the courts have resisted the temptation of a delimitation formula whose deceptive simplicity would have been incompatible with the theory of coastal projections. In 1977 the *Anglo-French* award denied that proportionality could be "an independent source of rights to areas of continental shelf". Proportionality, it said, "is not in itself a source of title" and "an equitable delimitation . . . is not . . . assigning to them . . . areas . . . in proportion to the length of their coastlines".[201] In *Gulf of Maine*, the Chamber, in its turn, refused to regard proportionality as "an autonomous criterion or method of delimitation":[202]

    . . . to take into account the extent of the respective coasts of the Parties

---

[197] *Libya/Malta*, para. 21.
[198] *Ibid.*, para. 74.
[199] See pp. 70-71 above.
[200] The Court has pointed this out: *Libya/Malta*, para. 54.
[201] *Anglo-French* award, paras. 101 and 246.
[202] *Gulf of Maine*, para. 218.

concerned does not in itself constitute either a criterion serving as a direct basis for a delimitation, or a method that can be used to implement such delimitation . . . a maritime delimitation can certainly not be established by a direct division of the area in dispute proportional to the respective lengths of the coasts belonging to the parties in the relevant area. . . .[203]

In *Libya/Malta* the Court again formally refused to take coastal length into account as a "principle of entitlement . . . and . . . method of putting that principle into operation":

> . . . the use of proportionality as a method in its own right is wanting of support in the practice of States, in the public expression of their views at (in particular) the Third United Nations Conference on the Law of the Sea, or in the jurisprudence. It is not possible for the Court to endorse a proposal at once so far-reaching and so novel.[204]

The refusal of the courts to recognize coastal length as such as one of the elements of legal title and a direct basis for delimitation does not mean, however, that coastal length has no role at all to play. Even though there may not be, in the matter of delimitation, any "proportionality principle" legally requiring that each State be allocated maritime areas proportionate to the length of its coastal front, there is, nonetheless, a "factor of proportionality", the function of which is to check *a posteriori* that a delimitation based on legal elements does not produce an unreasonable disproportion between the areas. Although it is not one of the "principles and rules of international law applicable to the delimitation", proportionality is "one possibly relevant factor, among several other factors, to be taken into account . . . at a certain stage in the delimitation process".[205] It is thus only at the second stage of the delimitation process that proportionality is introduced "as an aspect of equity".[206]

Equidistance, a method inherent in the concept of delimitation

Whether one starts from the basis of title or its exercise, from the principle of adjacency or the criterion of distance, from the idea of coasts or of radial projection, all roads eventually lead to equidistance. It is not a question at this point of drawing attention to the practical advantages of this method, its convenience, its

---

[203] *Ibid.*, para. 185.

[204] *Libya/Malta*, para. 58.

[205] *Ibid.*, paras. 57-8.

[206] *Tunisia/Libya*, para. 131 and *Libya/Malta*, para. 77; and see pp. 235ff below.

simplicity, its *prima facie* equitable character. We shall come back to these later.[207] At this stage the virtues to be emphasized are the legal ones. It is these which require the use of equidistance, as a matter of law, for a delimitation conceived as the division, according to spatial criteria, of areas of overlapping coastal projections, which are themselves spatial in character.

This way of looking at things may seem to run counter to the well-established case-law which insists again and again that equidistance is not "a method having some privileged status in relation to other methods";[208] that it has no "intrinsic merits" which could make it the preferred method;[209] that ". . . the equidistance method is just one among many and there is no obligation to use it or give it priority";[210] that it is not "the only appropriate method of delimitation . . . nor even the only permissible point of departure", and that it cannot be regarded as "a general rule, or an obligatory method of delimitation, or . . . a priority method, to be tested in every case".[211]

Closer inspection may show this insistence that equidistance has no intrinsic merit to be less of an impregnable judicial constant than might seem at first sight. The refusal in the earlier judgments to accord equidistance any special legal function was part and parcel of the ideas then prevailing in respect of the continental shelf. At a time when the continental shelf was linked to natural prolongation and when there was no "principle of proximity inherent in the whole concept of continental shelf appurtenance", it was obviously impossible to see equidistance as part of "the natural law of the continental shelf", i.e., to treat it as "logically necessary, in the sense of being an inescapable *a priori* accompaniment of basic continental shelf doctrine".[212] But the theory of the continental shelf today is no longer that of 1969, and the refusal to allow that equidistance has any "fundamentalist" character or "juristic inevitability"[213] has lost its *raison d'être*. The language of 1969 has lapsed from grace. Reversing the order of the words, proximity (which is but another way of saying distance) is nowadays a fundamental part of the concept of the continental shelf, as well as the territorial sea, the contiguous zone and the exclusive economic zone. Equidistance flows from the

---

[207] See p. 205 below.
[208] *Tunisia/Libya*, para. 110.
[209] *Gulf of Maine*, para. 162.
[210] *Guinea/Guinea-Bissau*, para. 102.
[211] *Libya/Malta*, paras. 43 and 77.
[212] *North Sea*, paras. 46 and 56.
[213] *Ibid.*, para. 37.

"natural law" of each of these jurisdictions. It is "logically necessary" and has a "character of so to speak juristic inevitability". True enough, the courts continue to repeat the traditional formulae about the absence of any intrinsic merit in equidistance, or any quality of privilege or precedence, but this is a hangover from the past, a survival of ideas no longer valid. Just as the light of a dead star still reaches us years later, out of date juridical ideas take time to die out. So it was with the theory of natural physical prolongation and the declaratory concept of the delimitation of the continental shelf, the death of which, though it took place several years earlier, was pronounced only in 1985. So it is with the anti-fundamentalist statements about equidistance, still with us even though they are no more than the echo of doctrines belonging to history.

Libya/Malta, *a transitional judgment*

The 1985 judgment in *Libya/Malta* is a particularly significant example of the way courts, while looking to the present and future, still think it necessary to keep one foot in the past. In this judgment, after so many years—and judgments—of hesitation, the Court at last recognizes the primacy of distance in respect of title and, simultaneously, in the delimitation of maritime areas, including the continental shelf. From this primacy it draws the inevitable *negative* conclusion, that the physical facts of natural prolongation are irrelevant. However, it shrinks from following its logic through, and rejects the equally inevitable, *positive* result of the concept it has just adopted, equidistance "as a provisional point of departure" in the delimitation process.[214]

> The Court is unable to accept that, even as a preliminary and provisional step towards the drawing of a delimitation line, the equidistance method is one which *must* be used ... The application of equitable principles in the particular relevant circumstances may still require the adoption of another method, or combination of methods, of delimitation, even from the outset.[215]

But when it comes to the delimitation in practice, the Court adopts a noticeably different approach. It states that it

> intends to proceed by stages; thus, it will first make a provisional delimitation ... it will then examine this provisional solution in the light of the

[214] *Libya/Malta*, para. 42.
[215] *Ibid.*, para. 43.

requirements derived from other criteria, which may call for a correction of this initial result.[216]

In view of the link between title and delimitation, it seems logical to the Court

> that the choice of the criterion and the method which it is to employ in the first place to arrive at a provisional result should be made in a manner consistent with the concepts underlying the attribution of legal title.[217]

The Court concludes that it has "little doubt"[218] that, in the case of a delimitation exclusively between coasts facing one another, it should proceed by drawing a median line "by way of a provisional step in a process to be continued by other operations".[219] Is this in the hope of reconciling what it has said it does not want to do with what it has nonetheless done? Or fright at its daring? Whatever the explanation, the Court judged it necessary to tone down the striking effect of the way it had proceeded, returning a few pages later to the traditional line:

> The introduction of this criterion of distance has not . . . had the effect of . . . conferring upon the equidistance method of delimitation the status of . . . a priority method, to be tested in every case. The fact that the Court has found that, in the circumstances of the present case, the drawing of a median line constitutes an appropriate first step in the delimitation process, should not be understood as implying that an equidistance line will be an appropriate beginning in all cases, or even in all cases of delimitation between opposite States.[220]

Just as in 1982 the Court half-opened the door on the "distance principle", so in 1985 it half-opened the door on equidistance as a first step, but without immediately opening it wide. It is to be hoped that the Court will take the next opportunity to do so. The position it has taken on the distance criterion makes a similar development on equidistance logically inevitable. The completion of the process initiated by *Libya/Malta* is in sight.

Equidistance not an obligatory method

Let there be no misunderstanding. This plea for the recognition of the fundamental and inherent character of equidistance does not

---

[216] *Ibid.*, para. 60.
[217] *Ibid.*, para. 61.
[218] *Ibid.*
[219] *Ibid.*, para. 62.
[220] *Ibid.*, para. 77.

mean that every maritime delimitation should legally be equidistant. It is no more true today than in 1969 that there is a rule of law requiring every maritime boundary to be drawn according to the equidistance method and proscribing every other method. Otherwise, the decision would be legally predetermined and there would be no point in going to law. The rejection of the Danish and Dutch contentions on this point is decisive, and the main conclusion of the 1969 decision—"the use of the equidistance method of delimitation [is] not . . . obligatory"[221]—remains as true as ever.

But, if this main conclusion of the *North Sea* judgment remains valid, it is for a reason other than that which motivated the Court in 1969. The real reason for the non-obligatory nature of equidistance is no longer to be found in the non-fundamental character of this method but in the fact, mentioned already, that although international law requires delimitation to be rooted in title, it also insists on an equitable outcome. Both conditions must be fulfilled. One alone is not sufficient. That is why "under existing law" the equidistance line "is . . . only provisional".[222] This result of the distance criterion, the equidistance line, must at a second stage be tested, as a matter of equity, against the relevant circumstances. This dual nature of delimitation is a translation of the principle, stated in the *North Sea* case and repeated in all the judgments since, including *Libya/Malta*, that equidistance is not a legally obligatory method. Anchoring delimitation in title turns equidistance into the method legally required *as the point of departure*. The need for an equitable solution leads to the rejection of the idea of an equidistance line as the legally required *point of arrival*. We shall return to this aspect in detail in Part IV.

[221] *North Sea*, para. 101.
[222] *Libya/Malta*, para. 63.

III

NATURE AND LAW IN MARITIME DELIMITATION

T HE preceding discussion makes it easier to grasp the subtle relationships which both unite and disunite nature and law in the matter of maritime delimitation. It goes without saying that the two belong to different categories. On the one hand, facts, circumstances, situations independent of human will, predetermined, permanent and intangible; on the other, directives and norms at one and the same time emanating from the human will and intended to determine it, contingent and always subject to change. But, although separate, the two are always intertwined since the norm can depend for its content on the realities of nature. However, even if it takes account of facts and nature, the law inevitably transcends them. In the words of François Gény, the ''made'' always triumphs over the ''given''. In essence, law is always a phenomenon of culture; it is never a fact of nature.

Obvious though it may be, this observation is as true of maritime delimitation as of anything else. For several decades now, States have been claiming maritime rights over distances further and further from their coasts, not in order to conform to a requirement of nature, but to give expression to a will that is purely political. Even in the heyday of natural prolongation, the continental shelf was a legal institution: it was the human will which chose to take the physical fact of the continental shelf as the basis for defining the rights of the coastal State to certain submarine areas. What was true of the continental shelf in its origins is even more true of the continental shelf as it is conceived today. It is equally true of the territorial sea and the exclusive economic zone. Adjacency, as already noted, is a legal phenomenon, as is coastal projection. Coasts project into the sea only because States have wanted them to; and they project in the way States want.

Law, man-made as it is, can, as just noted, take account of the facts of nature, attributing certain effects to them, but these effects will vays be determined by the law, never imposed on it. Thus, in espect of title, the maritime projection rests on the combination of a legal fact—State sovereignty—with a fact of nature—the maritime front. The coastal opening is itself a hybrid concept: a cultural phenomenon in so far as it is political history which determines whether or not a State has access to the sea and political history which fixes the extent of this access; a fact of nature insofar as the geographical configuration of this access is a predetermined fact. As far as delimitation is concerned, it is the law which decides the criterion to govern the division of overlapping areas, but this criterion is itself also a compound: distance, radial projection, equidistance and equity are entirely ''made''; the coasts on which distance, radial projection, equidistance and equity depend are entirely ''given''.

''There is no question of refashioning nature''

If there is any one dominant principle in the ideology of maritime delimitation, it is the one laid down by the Court in the *North Sea* case:

> Equity does not necessarily imply equality. *There can never be any question of completely refashioning nature*, and equity does not require that a State without access to the sea should be allotted an area of continental shelf, any more than there could be a question of rendering the situation of a State with an extensive coastline similar to that of a State with a restricted coastline ... *It is therefore not a question of totally refashioning geography* whatever the facts of the situation ...''.[223]

Since then, this principle has never been questioned. The *Anglo-French* award rejected any ''refashioning of geography'' in the name of equity,[224] and the *Libya/Malta* judgment cites among the principles applicable to any maritime delimitation,

> the principle that there is to be no question of refashioning geography, or compensating for the inequalities of nature; ... the principle that although all States are equal before the law and are entitled to equal treatment, 'equity does not necessarily imply equality' ... nor does it seek to make equal what nature has made unequal.[225]

In a word, delimitation must take the coasts as they are, in their likeness if their configuration is similar, with their differences if

[223] *North Sea*, para. 91.
[224] *Anglo-French* award, para. 195. See also paras. 101, 244, 248 and 249.
[225] *Libya/Malta*, para. 46.

nature has made them dissimilar. Just as a State without access to the
sea will be disadvantaged by comparison with a State which has a
coast, so, in relations between two neighbouring coastal States, one
may be better off than the other because of the configuration of their
respective coastlines. Delimitation does not seek to "make equal
what nature has made unequal". From this point of view, the Court
was right when it said that "[t]he principle of equality of States has
. . . no particular role to play in the applicable law".[226]

It should be remembered that the nature to be respected, and the
geography to be followed, are not pure nature and pure geography.
Even if it is "natural" and "geographic", the coastal opening is
nonetheless the fruit of political history. It is, after all, the latter
which has given maritime access to one and denied it to another, or
which has caused one to benefit from a "good" coastal configuration
and given another a "bad" one. Delimitation depends on a nature
already formed by law, on a geography as much political as natural.

The significance of the principle that nature and geography are not
to be refashioned should not be exaggerated. It is simply a matter of
not refashioning nature "entirely", remaking geography "totally".
Sometimes overlooked, these adverbs in fact make all the difference.

"There is no question of completely *refashioning nature"*

If international law had stuck strictly to the principle that
delimitation must not reshape geography, this would have meant
taking nature as it is, with all its quirks, however inequitable the
result might seem. After all, neither physical geography nor the land
boundaries as carved out by political history can be judged according
to reason or justice. Maritime boundaries would then have been a
faithful reflection of the political and physical course of the shoreline.
Whether they were reasonable or fair would not have been the
question. On the other hand, however, it would not have been
inconceivable to use maritime delimitations to make maritime
boundaries more just and reasonable than are land frontiers, and to
apply to the sea the international social justice which is so conspic-
uously lacking in the distribution of *territorial* sovereignty. It would
not, *a priori,* be more, or less, justifiable to seek to put right the
inequalities of nature than not to do so.

The logic of coastal projection might have dictated the former
approach. Since it is the coasts which serve as intermediary between
State sovereignty and maritime jurisdictions, why not, for

[226] *Ibid.*, para. 54.

delimitation purposes, take the coasts as they are? The courts do, indeed, at times seem to have been attracted by this idea. The *North Sea* judgment, for example, after noting that, since the land dominates the sea, "it is ... necessary to examine closely the geographical configuration of the coastlines of the countries" concerned, added:

> This is one of the reasons why the Court does not consider that markedly pronounced configurations can be ignored....[227]

Later, in *Gulf of Maine*, the Chamber was to reject "the idea ... that certain geographical features are to be deemed aberrant by reference to the presumed dominant characteristics of an area, coast or even continent":

> ... the facts of geography are not the product of human action amenable to positive or negative judgment, but the result of natural phenomena, so that they can only be taken as they are.[228]

But this insistence on pursuing nature and geography to the very limit has remained a minority view, and the judgments which contain these pronouncements have themselves not applied them. The rule of customary international law which has prevailed is that, although delimitation ought not to involve a refashioning of nature "entirely", "totally", "completely", it may quite properly make some correction.

This touches on one of the most troubling aspects of maritime delimitation. Given the two possible approaches, the law has tried to steer a middle course, to respect nature while changing it, to correct geography while still conforming to it. This is precisely the reason for introducing equity into the delimitation process. Maritime boundaries could have been the product exclusively of the political and natural reality of the coastal contours, but, for the sake of equity, international law wanted to improve on this. As Judge Lachs, President of the Guinea/Guinea-Bissau Arbitration Tribunal, put it, equity thus serves to "make a bridge between nature and the law". This has not been a soft option for the courts since, in each and every case, they have to strike the difficult balance between the safety of respect for nature and the temptation to rewrite geography so as to impose their own idea of justice. The path between blind pursuit of the given and the total freedom of *ex aequo et bono* is not an easy one.

---

[227] *North Sea*, para. 96.
[228] *Gulf of Maine*, paras. 36-7.

To effect what might seem a squaring of the circle, the law has adopted a bold approach. The delimitation line is first drawn in faithful reflection of the coasts exactly as they are, fashioned by history and geography. The court then checks whether a small geographical feature on one of the coasts leads to a displacement of the line, or a major deviation, causing a disproportionate, and therefore inequitable, amputation or encroachment. "We seek to ensure", said Judge Lachs, "that neither of the two [States] is subjected to any significant cut-off to the advantage of the other, and that its coastline, or rather, the effect of its coastline, cannot be unduly reduced owing to a whim of nature".

This approach, which will be examined in more detail when we look at the delimitation process itself,[229] may seem a happy reconciliation of the contradictory aims of respect for geography and the pursuit of equity. We should not delude ourselves. What this approach does is none other than to move away from nature and take liberties with geography, to impose human judgment at the very moment of proclaiming that the facts of nature take priority.

When the International Court of Justice recommends, in the *North Sea* case, that no account be taken of islets, rocks or minor coastal projections, "the disproportionally distorting effect of which can be eliminated"[230] or considers that "so great an exaggeration of the consequences of a natural geographical feature" (a concave coastline) "must be remedied or compensated for as far as possible, being of itself creative of inequity",[231] is it doing anything other than suggesting a correction to nature in the name of equity? When it suggests "abating the effects of an incidental special feature" which, by disturbing a general configuration characterized by the resemblance of the two coasts, would risk causing "an unjustifiable difference of treatment",[232] is it not making a judgment about the hierarchy of elements none of which is more or less natural than the others? And when it contemplates measuring the coasts according to their general direction, ignoring indentations and salients, in other words, attributing to them a length other than their real one, what is it doing if not correcting nature?

Some years later, the Anglo-French Court of Arbitration, while also insisting on the need to refer to "the actual geographical conditions",[233] in its turn was to suggest, in the name of equity,

[229] See pp. 225ff below.
[230] *North Sea*, para. 57.
[231] *Ibid.*, para. 89.
[232] *Ibid.*, para. 91.
[233] *Anglo-French* award, para. 240.

"an ... abatement of the inequitable effects of the distorting geographical feature",[234] explaining that it was necessary to avoid "particular configurations of the coast", "individual geographical features" or "particular geographical features"[235] producing an "inequitable" delimitation.[236] When the Court says that the coasts of France and the United Kingdom would be comparable "in the absence of" or "leaving out of account" such and such an all too real geographical feature—the Channel Islands, for example, or the projection westwards of the Scillies—and decides to base itself on the situation as it would "otherwise" have been, is it not rewriting nature? To draw an initial line in the Channel without taking account of the Channel Islands, to say that the Scillies, like Ushant, "both constitute natural geographical facts ... which cannot be disregarded ... without refashioning geography",[237] and then to give half-effect to the Scillies but full effect to Ushant is surely, however described, a touching up of nature. To which may be added, in passing, the oddity of a logic which says that two coasts are comparable once their differences are set aside. It is like saying that if men did not have so many distinguishing features they would all be the same.

More generally, are the courts not making geography to measure each time they decide to ignore an island or to give it only partial effect, each time they undertake the delimitation as if the island did not exist or was closer to the shore than it really is?[238]

This game of words in which a very real geographical feature may be erased or mutilated under the pretence that it is "particular", "unusual", "incidental", and where the effect, however real, which this feature exercises over a delimitation line may be reduced or eliminated simply because it is deemed "exaggerated", sometimes encourages States to make surprising demands. Under cover of "abating the effects of an incidental special feature", sizeable areas of the parties' territory may fall victim to strange attempts at conjuring. In *Gulf of Maine*, for example, Canada tried, in effect, to secure the disappearance of Cape Cod and Nantucket Island, and the United States that of the whole Canadian province of Nova Scotia.[239]

---

[234] *Ibid.*, para. 251.
[235] *Ibid.*, paras. 100, 101 and 251.
[236] *Ibid.*, para. 240.
[237] *Ibid.*, paras. 248 and 254.
[238] For the problems of islands, see pp. 225ff below.
[239] Cf. p. 228 below.

IV

MARITIME DELIMITATION AND LAND DELIMITATION

O NE can better understand the peculiar nature of maritime delimitation, a newcomer to the international law scene, by comparing it with the long-established and well-developed institution of delimitation on land.

Delimitation on land is a legal and political process for deciding the spatial extent of the sovereignty of two neighbouring States. It determines the spatial boundaries of those juxtaposed and contiguous sovereignties which go to make up the society of nations. It rests basically on the principle that sovereignties may not overlap and that a given area must therefore inevitably belong by law to one or other of the States in question. In the event of a dispute, the right course, in the words of the Court in the *Minquiers and Ecréhos* case, is "to determine which of the parties has produced the more convincing proof of title" to the disputed area.[240] If both parties can lay claim to a title, it is the one who can establish the more convincing, the weightier, title, who will be regarded as having sole title in law to the coveted area, which will thus be deemed to be part of its sovereign territory.

The declaratory theory of the continental shelf, set out by the Court in 1969, to some extent derives from the same philosophy. As in the case of land delimitation, continental shelf delimitation was not intended to divide an undivided space but to determine the area to which each of the parties had, and had uniquely, legal title. Nowadays maritime delimitation is quite different. Far from assuming that there can be only one legal title to a given area, it postulates the existence of two equally valid titles in competition with one another over the same area. It is not a question of which proof is the more or less convincing, which title the weightier, but of requiring from each of the parties with these equally well-founded

---

[240] ICJ *Reports*, 1953, p. 52.

titles a reasonable sacrifice such as would make possible a division of
the area of overlap.

This explains the different role played by effectiveness in land and
maritime delimitations. Occupation, the effective exercise of State
sovereignty, acts of sovereignty: all are factors which help to
determine which title is the better and hence legally the only one in
the context of land delimitation, but they are of no relevance in
maritime delimitation. The Court has said so clearly from the very
beginning as far as the continental shelf is concerned. The right over
the continental shelf, it has stated, "does not depend on its being
exercised".[241] In *Tunisia/Libya*, the Court was concerned with the
conduct of the parties and the presence of oil wells in the area of
delimitation, but this was not so much from the point of view of
effectiveness as to "take into account whatever indicia are available
of the line or lines which the Parties themselves may have considered
equitable or acted upon as such".[242] There was, nonetheless, still
the risk of the law of delimitation moving towards a situation of
weighing up titles on the basis, *inter alia,* of effectiveness. This would
not only have encouraged States to acts of occupation such as
untimely drilling, but also have meant big changes in the law of the
sea. This explains the reservations expressed by some of the
judges.[243] The fact remains that, in *Gulf of Maine*, where the
behaviour of the parties was again invoked by the States in dispute,
the Chamber did not find it a convincing argument in the circumstances, although it did not reject it as irrelevant in itself.[244]

It is not surprising, against this background, that the process of
maritime delimitation is noticeably different from that of land
delimitation. The constituent elements are not the same, the ideas
and the ways of expressing them are different, there are not the same
controversies. There is one point in common, however: equity, as
distinct from *ex aequo et bono*, enters into both types of delimitation,
and is seen in both as an integral part of the law.[245] It is clear,
however, that the role it enjoys and the place it occupies in maritime

---

[241] *North Sea*, para. 19.

[242] *Tunisia/Libya*, para. 118.

[243] Cf. Gros, *Tunisia/Libya*, Dissenting Opinion, p. 155, para. 22 ("The
transformation of the unilateral into the equitable remains unexplained"); and
Evensen, *ibid.*, Dissenting Opinion, p. 318.

[244] *Gulf of Maine*, paras. 126-54. The *Guinea/Guinea-Bissau* award shows the same
hesitation (paras. 62 and 105).

[245] *Frontier Dispute (Burkina Faso/Mali)*, ICJ *Reports*, 1986, pp. 567-8, para. 28. Cf.
Bardonnet, D., "Equité et frontières terrestres", *Mélanges offerts à Paul Reuter*, Paris,
Pedone, 1981, p. 35.

delimitation cannot be compared with the far more modest position it holds in land delimitation. In short

> ... the process by which a court determines the line of a land boundary between two States can be clearly distinguished from the process by which it identifies the principles and rules applicable to the delimitation of the continental shelf.[246]

Maritime boundaries and land boundaries

Although the process of maritime delimitation differs fundamentally from that of land delimitation, the result tends to be much the same.

At first sight the two types of boundary seem to have nothing in common except the name. The "continuity" of the sea militates against both the "strict compartmentalization of State jurisdictions"[247] and any precise demarcation. On the other hand, in contrast to land boundaries which separate sovereignties in their totality, maritime boundaries (with the exception of those of the territorial sea) separate only sovereign rights with a functional, and hence limited, character.

On reflection, however, these differences seem to be more a matter of nuance than real conflict. Even if it is impossible to envisage any demarcation of territory on the sea, technology does now make it possible to define a maritime boundary with great accuracy, and experience shows that States do not overlook a few minutes or seconds more or less of latitude or longitude. Nor should one exaggerate the differences between maritime jurisdictions and true "zones of sovereignty".[248] First, the entry of security considerations into the relatively select club of relevant circumstances, at first hesitant, then increasingly sure, has turned maritime boundaries more and more into political frontiers on the sea.[249] Then, it would be unrealistic to ignore certain tendencies to the "territorialization" of the 200 mile zone: nobody knows what the future may hold. In his final statement in *Gulf of Maine*, the United States agent made an important reference to the "political" risk to his country of a line which would place part of the American coast face to face, not with Europe or the high seas, but with "Canadian waters". "The issue of cut-off", he added, "raises the most fundamental questions of

---

[246] *Frontier Dispute (Burkina Faso/Mali)*, ICJ *Reports*, 1986, p. 578, para. 47.

[247] De Visscher, p. 42.

[248] *Guinea/Guinea-Bissau*, para. 124.

[249] See pp. 264-6 below.

sovereignty'' for "no State knows with any certainty what the future of the economic zone regime will hold''.[250]

In these circumstances, it is not surprising that the legal regime of maritime boundaries should have been assimilated by the courts, in certain respects, to that of land boundaries.

As early as 1969, the Court drew a first analogy, observing that, as with land boundaries, maritime boundaries may remain undefined over quite long periods without this uncertainty affecting the rights of the States concerned.[251]

On the other hand, in the *Aegean Sea Continental Shelf* case, the Court said:

> Whether it is a land frontier or a boundary line in the continental shelf that is in question, the process is essentially the same, and inevitably involves *the same element of stability and permanence*, and is subject to the rule excluding boundary agreements from fundamental change of circumstances.[252]

As a direct consequence of this analysis, the Court took the view that the delimitation between the continental shelves of Greece and Turkey "relat[es] to the territorial status of Greece''.[253]

Finally, in ruling on the *Application by Italy for Permission to Intervene* in *Libya/Malta*, the Court referred to a dictum of the Permanent Court according to which, in a dispute relating to sovereignty over a piece of land territory, account must always be taken of claims to sovereignty from a third State, and declared that "this observation . . . is no less true when what is in question is the extent of the respective areas of continental shelf over which different States enjoy 'sovereign rights' ''.[254]

The term "boundary'', used more and more frequently today in place of "delimitation line'', is not, as one can see, a usurpation. The process of maritime delimitation is and remains an exercise *sui generis*; the dividing line to which it leads is undoubtedly very like a land boundary. It is not simply a linguistic convenience that the *Guinea/Guinea-Bissau* judgment transferred to maritime areas the distinction between *limit* and *boundary*, borrowed from land territory:

---

[250] CR 84/26, pp. 49-50.

[251] *North Sea*, para. 46.

[252] ICJ *Reports*, 1978, p. 35, para. 85.

[253] *Ibid.*, p. 37, para. 90.

[254] ICJ *Reports*, 1984, p. 26, para. 43. This position was, however, rejected, or at least given a different shade of meaning, in somewhat delphic terms, in the *Frontier Dispute (Burkina Faso/Mali)* case (as cited at p. 93 n. 246 above).

... a limit indicates the extent of a domain, whereas the role of a boundary is to separate two States.[255]

It is indeed a boundary separating States which is produced by the division of overlapping areas, the very essence of maritime delimitation. Sooner or later, the theory of maritime delimitation will complete the theory of the State in international law.

---

[255] *Guinea/Guinea-Bissau*, para. 49.

PART II

THE LAW OF
MARITIME DELIMITATION:
UNITY OR DIVERSITY

PART II

THE LAW OF MARITIME DELIMITATION:
UNITY OR DIVERSITY

THE *law* or *laws* of maritime delimitation? So far we have proceeded as if the existence of a single law applicable to all maritime delimitations presented no problem. It is obvious that there are powerful unifying influences at work here. The practical importance of the delimitation of the continental shelf, and the bitterness of the legal controversies to which it has given rise, have led to the extrapolation, not always conscious, of the continental shelf rules to other situations. In a way, the law of continental shelf delimitation has been regarded as the prototype of all maritime delimitation law. The role of equity, its links with the law, the dialectic of equitable principles, relevant circumstances and an equitable outcome, the controversy over equidistance, all these are considerations which, starting with the law of the delimitation of the continental shelf, have invaded the law of maritime delimitation *tout court*.

On closer inspection, however, there is no shortage of distinguishing features, and centrifugal tendencies stand out behind all the talk of unity. Maritime delimitations are too diverse in their modalities, their purpose and their legal regime for unity to be taken as self-evident: in their modalities, since some are the result of an agreement between the States concerned, and others are decided by an international judge or arbitrator; in their purpose, since they relate to jurisdictions differing in scope and nature (it is not obvious *a priori* that the delimitation of the territorial sea, the continental shelf and the exclusive economic zone should observe the same legal rules and principles); and finally, in the legal regime governing them, since some delimitations are determined by the provisions of multilateral treaties binding on the parties while others are regulated by customary international law.

The courts' stance has not been uniform in the face of this coexistence of unifying factors and the seeds of divergence. In some respects, the unifying tendency has prevailed, while in others the centrifugal force has had the upper hand. There would be nothing more to say about this were it not that in each case the solution adopted seemed to give rise to reservations.

Delimitation may be carried out in two different ways: by negotiated agreement between the States concerned or, in the case of disagreement, by the decision of a third, judicial or arbitral, party. This is of little importance, say the courts, since the applicable rules of law are the same. On this point, it is the unifying forces which have predominated, but wrongly, for the differences between the two ways of delimitation cannot be eradicated; they will persist whatever the assertions of unity. The identity the courts say exists between the rules governing all maritime delimitations however carried out has more to do with rhetoric than legal analysis.

Delimitation may affect maritime areas as diverse as the territorial sea, the continental shelf and the exclusive economic zone. On this point, the language of unification is less certain. As a result of the demise of the theory of natural physical prolongation and the victory of the distance criterion, there has been a considerable rapprochement between the delimitation of the continental shelf and the exclusive economic zone. Although cracks still appear, unity between the two has almost been achieved. Delimitation of the territorial sea has lagged behind somewhat, not keeping up with the developments which have characterized the delimitation of other maritime jurisdictions. In this respect, the development has been one of diversification though here, too, there is a unifying tendency. The unity of the theory of coastal projections and the unity of the concept of maritime delimitation have been important forces in the replacement of the diversity of maritime jurisdictions by a common law which is now taking place.

Finally, the formal sources of the applicable law remain twofold, treaty and customary international law. Here the breach might have been irremediable, for why should the courts have developed a body of customary rules were it not to differentiate them from treaty rules? Paradoxically, this gap was scarcely opened up when the courts themselves filled it by interpreting the treaty regime in such a way as to make it coincide, in substance, with customary international law. And so unity prevailed. But, dare one say it, this unity has taken the wrong direction. Instead of gravitating towards treaty provisions, which are full of law-making potential, the courts have concentrated on customary international law, which is far poorer in this respect. Fortunately, this trend is now going into reverse. It is to be hoped that the elements of the law of maritime delimitation will regroup around rules of law, and that these will regain, within the framework of customary international law, the richness and precision which the treaty norms had until the courts altered their meaning.

And so the answer to the question posed at the beginning of this chapter, ''Unity or diversity in the law of maritime delimitation?'', must for the moment be hedged. Sometimes it is unity which prevails, sometimes diversity. But current solutions are always open to revision; indeed, they are already being questioned. As far as modalities are concerned, there is bound to be a split between negotiated and third-party delimitations since, on this point, diversity is in the nature of things. And if one looks at it in terms of the kind of maritime jurisdiction being delimited, unity is still a potential rather than an established reality. However, things are moving in the right direction and there is no doubt that normative unity will soon prevail. What about the problem as regards the applicable principles and rules of international law? The unity between the treaty regime and the rules of customary international law achieved somewhat artificially by the courts is no doubt definitive, but its content and direction are changing. Behind the accommodating language of the law of maritime delimitation what, in fact, strikes the observer is a picture of basic unity covering a certain degree of diversity.

I

NEGOTIATED AND THIRD-PARTY DELIMITATIONS

A MARITIME delimitation is normally achieved by means of a negotiated agreement. If the parties do not reach agreement, the delimitation is decided by a judicial or arbitral body, which takes its decision in the light of the applicable rules and principles of international law,[1] at least, of course, if the parties have not left the court the problem of deciding *ex aequo et bono* or chosen some other method of settling their dispute. These remarks

[1] The extent of the task entrusted to the judge or arbitrator varies. At one end of the scale is a simple indication of the principles and rules of international law according to which the parties will negotiate their delimitation following the judicial or arbitral decision (*North Sea*); at the other is a precise determination of the boundary, which is sometimes drawn on a map (*Beagle Channel*; *Dubai/Sharjah*; *Gulf of Maine*; *Guinea/Guinea-Bissau*). Between these two extremes, there can be various intermediary formulae, not always easy to interpret. In *Tunisia/Libya*, the Court was asked to define the applicable principles and rules of international law, and to "clarify the practical method for the application of these principles and rules in this specific situation, so as to enable the experts of the two countries to delimit these areas without any difficulty". The parties undertook to meet to put these principles and rules into effect with a view to concluding a treaty. In the absence of agreement they were to return to the Court to ask it for such "explanations or clarifications as may facilitate the task of the two delegations, to arrive at the line separating the two areas of the continental shelf". The Court saw its task as "to be precise as to what it decides", so as to leave the experts only a "technical task" (*Tunisia/Libya*, paras. 29-30). It attached a map to the judgment "for illustrative purposes only, and without prejudice to the role of the experts in determining the line with exactness" (para. 129). As difficulties arose in implementing the judgment, the Court, at Tunisia's request, provided an interpretation of certain passages in its *Application for Revision and Interpretation of the Judgment of 24 February 1982*, (ICJ *Reports*, 1985, p. 192). In *Libya/Malta*, the Special Agreement asked the Court to define the applicable principles and rules of international law and to indicate "how in practice such principles and rules can be applied by the two Parties in this particular case in order that they may without difficulty delimit such areas by an agreement . . . in accordance with the decision of the Court". The Court took the view that, to fulfil its task, it had to take a position on the methods of delimitation, and to translate them into "at least an approximate line which could be illustrated on a map" (*Libya/Malta*, para. 19). The parties can, if they wish, ask the judge or arbitrator for only a partial delimitation of their maritime boundary, leaving the rest for negotiated settlement (see p. 109 below).

are obvious to the point of banality. But looked at more closely, things are less simple. Having two modes of delimitation has always caused problems and it is not certain that a point of equilibrium has yet been reached.

Are there norms binding on the courts?

Rules of law which the judge or arbitrator might apply to a dispute did not emerge all at once. Obviously, neighbouring States were entitled to agree, by means of a treaty, on the line delimiting their maritime jurisdictions, and this called for no special comment. States had long been in the habit of delimiting their territorial sea in this way and, following the 1945 Truman Proclamation, they turned naturally to the negotiated solution to delimit this newcomer to maritime jurisdictions, which the continental shelf then was. The problem was how to proceed in cases where States failed to reach agreement. Recourse to judicial or arbitral settlement presupposed that there existed principles and rules of law which the judge or arbitrator could apply, but in fact the position was far from clear.

When the International Law Commission first tackled the problem in the course of its work on the law of the sea after 1950, it had something to go on as far as territorial sea delimitation was concerned, but it was confronted with a total legal vacuum in respect of the continental shelf. In respect of the territorial sea, State practice, the work of the 1930 codification conference and legal doctrine allowed the view that some rules had been formed, though opinion differed as to what those rules were.[2] In respect of the continental shelf, in contrast, the subject was so new that several members of the Commission thought it premature to pronounce any rule whatsoever. In the face of this lacuna in international law, recourse to the International Court of Justice or arbitration seemed difficult, and it was suggested that the way out was simply to provide that, in case of disagreement, the dispute should be resolved by one of the appropriate procedures for pacific settlement.[3] There was even a proposal for submission to arbitration *ex aequo et bono* or conciliation.[4] It was not without difficulty that, after consulting a Committee of Experts whose technical report[5] served as a legal guide, the Commission arrived at the well-known formulae which were to be written into Article 12 of the 1958 Geneva Convention on

---

[2] Cf. p. 135 n. 98, below.
[3] *ILCYB*, 1953, vol. II, p. 216, para. 84.
[4] *Ibid.*, pp. 48-9.
[5] *Ibid.*, pp. 77-9.

the Territorial Sea and Contiguous Zone and Article 6 of the 1958 Geneva Convention on the Continental Shelf.[6] At first sight these provisions seem to be addressed not to the judge or arbitrator but to States: it is States, according to the letter of the Convention, who are required to determine the boundary between them according to the principle of equidistance, unless another boundary line is justified by special circumstances. In reality, it is the judge or arbitrator who will have to implement the equidistance/special circumstances rule since, in practice, the difference of views between States will turn on whether or not there are special circumstances and, if there are, on the impact of these circumstances on the equidistance line.

But what was to happen when delimitation was not governed by the 1958 provisions, in other words, when it was between States not party to the Geneva Conventions? Would there, even in this case, be principles and rules of international law which the courts could apply? Governments have never seemed to have any doubts on this score, since it is on the basis of principles and rules of law that they have all, without exception, asked the courts to decide every time they have sought to resolve a dispute of maritime delimitation by judicial or arbitral settlement. As early as 1969, the Court took the view that the non-applicability of the 1958 provisions did not mean that "rules are lacking"[7] and since then awards and judgments have insisted on the duty of the judge and arbitrator to decide on the basis of law and not *ex aequo et bono*.[8] It will always be to the International Court of Justice's credit that it formulated the norms to be followed in cases where there was no applicable treaty provision, thus permitting every maritime delimitation to be determined by law.

Although doubts about the existence of legal norms binding on the courts are now a thing of the past, this prehistoric period of the law of maritime delimitation has left its traces and the normative density of the law remains to this day a matter of controversy.

Are there norms binding on States?

Under the 1958 system there was no rule of law restricting the contractual freedom of States since governments had the right to accept or reject equidistance whether or not there were special

---

[6] Rather curiously, Article 24(3) of the Convention on the Territorial Sea and Contiguous Zone did not adopt the same formula for the delimitation of the contiguous zone, to which it applied equidistance without the special circumstances restriction. On the genesis of the 1958 provisions see p. 170 below.

[7] *North Sea*, para. 83.

[8] We will come back to this in detail in Part III, especially pp. 163ff.

circumstances. In *Gulf of Maine*, however, the Chamber was to describe the 1958 provisions as having a certain normative element in respect of negotiated delimitations: by "going a little far in interpreting the text . . . a rule . . . may be regarded as logically underlying the principle just stated", that is "that any agreement . . . should involve the application of equitable criteria".⁹

It was, in fact, only with the 1969 judgment in the *North Sea* case that the idea of restricting the contractual freedom of States took shape, subjecting negotiated delimitations themselves to rules of law. Two legal obligations were spelt out by the Court and carefully distinguished. The first, of a procedural character, is the "primary obligation to effect delimitation by agreement".¹⁰ The second is substantive: the obligation in delimitation agreements to respect certain fundamental rules, or, more precisely, the obligation in the course of negotiations to follow equitable principles and to reach an equitable result. The Court traced this two-pronged rule for negotiated delimitation back to the 1945 Truman Proclamation, which "must be considered as having propounded the rules of law in this field". The Court added: "These two concepts, of delimitation by mutual agreement and delimitation in accordance with equitable principles, have underlain all the subsequent history of the subject", explaining that it is a question of "actual rules of law . . . which govern delimitation . . . that is to say, rules binding upon States for all delimitations".¹¹ This double obligation, procedural and substantive, is also incorporated in the "fundamental norm" which the *Gulf of Maine* judgment would later describe as governing "every maritime delimitation between neighbouring States", whether it is a case of a delimitation decided by the courts or a delimitation negotiated by the States concerned.¹² And, finally, it was echoed in Articles 74 and 83 of the 1982 Montego Bay Convention, which provide that "[t]he delimitation . . . shall be effected by agreement on the basis of international law . . . in order to achieve an equitable solution".

At the procedural level, what was simply encouragement to agree has become a legal obligation to seek an agreement. But although the theme has been a constant ever since 1969, it is not easy to see exactly what it implies. Is it not obvious that the States concerned are not

---

⁹ *Gulf of Maine*, para. 89.

¹⁰ *North Sea*, para. 72.

¹¹ *Ibid.*, paras. 47, 85 and 86. Apart from the passages quoted from the *North Sea* case, see, for example, *Gulf of Maine*, paras. 22, 87, 89-90, 92, 95, 112 and 113; *Libya/Malta*, para. 46.

¹² *Gulf of Maine*, para. 112.

going to pass the task of effecting a delimitation between them to a judicial or arbitral body without first trying to reach an agreement? Is it not also obvious that "the duty of Parties to seek first a delimitation by agreement"[13] does not rule out the possibility of a disagreement and so does not exhaust the matter? The courts have certainly been aware of the risk of seeing the rule of the "priority" of the search for an agreement as a "self-evident truth",[14] which is why they have tried to give it real meaning, first, by explaining that governments have an obligation to negotiate in the sense understood by international law, i.e., that States are bound to conduct "meaningful" negotiations,[15] to negotiate "in good faith and with the genuine intention of achieving a positive result",[16] and secondly by stating that a delimitation may not be made unilaterally and that a unilateral delimitation will not be opposable to the other States concerned.[17]

The submission of negotiated settlement to substantive rules originated in the particular circumstances of the *North Sea* case. The facts are well known. The parties disagreed as to whether Denmark and the Netherlands were entitled to claim an equidistant delimitation or whether the Federal Republic of Germany could claim a different one. But the problem was presented differently before the Court, which was asked, in a more general and abstract manner, to define the principles and rules of international law applicable to delimitation, the parties undertaking to effect the delimitation at a later stage "by agreement in pursuance of the decision requested from the International Court of Justice". It was in response to this invitation that the Court undertook "to indicate . . . the principles and rules of law in the light of which the methods for eventually effecting the delimitation will have to be chosen",[18] thus sowing the seed of the principle that negotiated delimitations are subject to fundamental legal norms.

This idea, which emerged in the specific context of the 1969 case, was to make progress over the years.

At UNCLOS III, the successive negotiating texts bearing on the

---

[13] *Libya/Malta*, para. 46.

[14] *Gulf of Maine*, paras. 22 and 87.

[15] *North Sea*, para. 85.

[16] *Gulf of Maine*, para. 112; cf. para. 87.

[17] "[A]n attempt by a unilateral act to establish international maritime boundary lines regardless of the legal position of other States is contrary to recognized principles of international law" (*Tunisia/Libya*, para. 87). In the same sense, *Gulf of Maine*, paras. 87 and 112.

[18] *North Sea*, para. 84.

delimitation of the continental shelf and the exclusive economic zone were drafted as rules incumbent on States when negotiating their delimitations. In the wake of these drafts, Articles 74 and 83 of the 1982 Convention provided that the delimitation of the exclusive economic zone and the continental shelf should be effected "by agreement *on the basis of international law* . . .". The negotiators thus appear not to be entirely free: the agreement is to be effected "on the basis of international law".[19]

The courts were to follow a similar route. After recalling that any maritime delimitation may be effected either by an agreement or, where such an agreement cannot be achieved, by resort to a third party, the *Gulf of Maine* judgment explained that, "[i]n either case, delimitation is to be effected by the application of equitable criteria and by the use of practical methods capable of ensuring, with regard to the geographic configuration of the area and other relevant circumstances, an equitable result". The Court added that "the fundamental norm of customary international law governing maritime delimitation . . . is ultimately that delimitation, *whether effected by direct agreement or by the decision of a third party*, must be based on the application of equitable criteria and the use of practical methods capable of ensuring an equitable result".[20] The same approach was adopted in *Libya/Malta*, where the Court stated that equitable principles of a normative character "govern not only delimitation by adjudication or arbitration, but also, and indeed primarily, the duty of the Parties to seek first a delimitation by agreement".[21]

The identity of the rules for negotiated and third party delimitations: the theory of the "consensual basis" of all delimitations

It would seem, therefore, that international law is not content to submit negotiated delimitations to substantive rules but requires that these rules be identical to those which the judge or arbitrator has to

---

[19] As far as the delimitation of the territorial sea is concerned, there is no such obligation in Article 15 of the Convention. It should be noted that Articles 74 and 83 are silent on the content of the law the parties are to apply. These articles add, in paragraph 2, that "[i]f no agreement can be reached within a reasonable period of time, the States concerned shall resort to the procedures provided for in Part XV" (on these procedures, see Caflisch [2], pp. 107ff), but again nothing is said about the substantive rules to be applied. The question of the actual content of the law of maritime delimitation is completely ignored, and must be decided without any reference to the 1982 Convention.

[20] *Gulf of Maine*, paras. 112-13.

[21] *Libya/Malta*, para. 46.

apply when deciding a delimitation on which the parties have failed to agree. As justification for this conception of the unity of the normative corpus, the courts have relied on the theory that all maritime delimitations are identical in character. Whether negotiated by the parties, it is said, or decided by a judge or arbitrator, delimitations all have a consensual basis. In 1969 the Court had referred to the famous dictum of the Permanent Court in the *Free Zones* case: "the judicial settlement of international disputes . . . is simply an alternative to the direct and friendly settlement of such disputes between the parties".[22] This identification between third party and agreed delimitations was to be expounded in *Gulf of Maine*, where the Chamber states that:

> any delimitation must be effected by agreement between the States concerned, either by the conclusion of a direct agreement or, if need be, by some alternative method, which must, however, be based on consent.[23]

This kinship between the two methods of delimitation, it may be noted in passing, explains their complementary nature. The same delimitation may be part negotiated, part adjudicated. Moreover, since a negotiated delimitation and a third party delimitation are both consensual in nature, they cannot, by definition, conflict with one another. In the *Anglo-French* case, the Court of Arbitration was careful to identify those segments of the delimitation line on which the parties were agreed and limited itself to filling the "gaps".[24] In *Gulf of Maine*, the Chamber considered itself bound by the indication in the special agreement of the starting point for the maritime boundary and the zone in which this line was to end. This reflected the parties' intention to determine by negotiation the boundary line above the starting point and below the terminal point. The adjudication was limited to the section in between.[25] In short, as the

---

[22] PCIJ, *Series A/B*, No. 42, p. 116; *North Sea*, para. 87. This theory was taken up and developed in the *Frontier Dispute (Burkina Faso/Mali)* case: "A judicial decision, which 'is simply an alternative to the direct and friendly settlement' of the dispute between the Parties ... merely substitutes for the solution stemming directly from their shared intention, the solution arrived at by a court under the mandate which they have given it. In both instances, the solution only has legal and binding effect as between the States which have accepted it, either directly or as a consequence of having accepted the court's jurisdiction to decide the case" (ICJ *Reports*, 1986, p. 577, para. 46).

[23] *Gulf of Maine*, para. 89.

[24] *Anglo-French* award, paras. 111, 117 and 121.

[25] *Gulf of Maine*, paras. 22-3. The Chamber's obligation to abide by the provisions of the Special Agreement relating to the zone in which the line was to terminate was the

(Footnote continued on p. 110)

Court said in its decision on the *Application for Revision and Interpretation of the Judgment of 24 February 1982*:

> It is always open to the parties to a dispute to have recourse to a conjunction of judicial determination and settlement by agreement.[26]

An artificial equation

Of the various elements making up this mosaic of ideas, the least open to question is undoubtedly the statement that judges and arbitrators are required to apply principles and rules of law. We can be grateful that the initial stage, when there was a question mark over the very existence of legal norms on the subject, is now a thing of the past.

Nor would one think of challenging the proposition that the parties may not make a unilateral delimitation and are bound, in the first instance, to seek delimitation through agreement. By its very nature, maritime delimitation has an international character and its validity must be appraised in terms of international law.[27] A delimitation cannot be effected unilaterally, without taking into account the position of other States, and it is opposable to other States only to the extent that they accept it. Bilateralism is inherent in delimitation.[28]

(Footnote continued from p. 109)
subject of a question from Judge Gros (C 1/CR 84/17, p. 64). In its reply, Canada said: "There is nothing unusual for two governments which have agreed on a segment or point of their maritime boundary, or an area within which a segment or point should be located, to so inform a court of justice or arbitration, which will continue the work the parties had only managed to begin. Far from constituting an encroachment on such a court's freedom of appraisal, I should have thought that co-existence between a partially negotiated delimitation and a delimitation partially decided by adjudication fell squarely within the proper ambit of the judicial function" (C 1/CR 84/19, p. 17-18). For the United States reply, see C 1/CR 84/17, p. 64.

[26] ICJ *Reports*, 1985, p. 218, para. 47.

[27] Cf. *Fisheries*, ICJ *Reports*, 1951, p. 132: "The delimitation of sea areas has always an international aspect; . . . the validity of the delimitation with regard to other States depends upon international law".

[28] The provisions of the 1958 and 1982 Conventions on the delimitation of the territorial sea, and those of the 1958 Convention on the delimitation of the contiguous zone, could be interpreted as an invitation to States to determine the limits of their territorial sea vis-à-vis their neighbours unilaterally, this being sanctioned in advance by international law provided they do not go beyond the equidistance line. The obligation not to make a unilateral maritime delimitation would therefore seem to have been dispensed with in the case of the territorial sea and the contiguous zone. But these slight differences do not appear to have more than a curiosity value. In substance, the territorial sea regime established by the 1958 and 1982 Conventions is identical to that established for the continental shelf by Article 6 of the 1958 Convention. If a State makes

It is with the third element in the courts' conception—the identity between negotiated delimitations and third party delimitations— that one leaves the reassuring realm of certainties for a more debatable area of judicial development.

The proposition that the parties are required, when negotiating their maritime delimitations, to apply exactly the same rules of law as would a judge or arbitrator is highly debatable. Certainly, during negotiations a government may seek to strengthen its position by relying on legal pronouncements and precedent. It is equally certain that two governments can agree to seek a delimitation in conformity with the rules of law, that is to say, in practical terms, to try to reach a solution identical to that which a court would reach.[29] And finally, the case-law is certainly always a useful point of reference and a valuable source of ideas for the negotiators. But governments can, if they want, set aside legal considerations and adopt any line which seems to them equitable in the circumstances. For that purpose, they may choose whatever method or combination of methods they wish, or they may choose not to follow any method at all but simply to draw on the map a line which seems satisfactory to them for reasons best known to themselves. It is not an accident that so many delimitation agreements are silent as to the methods they have used. By definition, the parties must consider the line adopted to be equitable, otherwise they would not have subscribed to it.[30] States can be influenced by many considerations: geographical, economic, military, political. A government may accept a less favourable delimitation on one of its coasts in exchange for a more favourable delimitation on another coast, or for economic or political advantages in other fields. It is enough to look at agreements such as those

a unilateral delimitation of its territorial sea up to the equidistance line, this delimitation will be opposable to its neighbouring State only in so far as it does not object to it. If the neighbouring State thinks that special circumstances justify a different delimitation, there will be a dispute which can be resolved by negotiation or by judicial means, just as in the case of the continental shelf. Some States have also delimited their continental shelves by domestic legislation, and the effects vis-à-vis third countries have been the same as those in a unilateral delimitation of the territorial sea.

[29] Some delimitation agreements concluded by France expressly refer to international law. For example, the France/Venezuela Agreement (p. 29 n. 26 above) includes the following in its preamble: "Basing themselves on the relevant rules and principles of international law and taking into consideration the work of the Third United Nations Conference on the Law of the Sea". Cf. the agreements between France and Mauritius; France and St. Lucia; France and Australia (p. 68 n. 158 above); France and Tonga (1980) (*RGDIP*, vol. 84, 1980, p. 968).

[30] See p. 154 below.

concluded between Argentina and Chile[31] or between France and Monaco[32] to be persuaded of the possibility of a divorce between negotiated delimitations and legal considerations. It is out of the question that in such cases a court deciding on the basis of law would have reached identical or even similar results.

If negotiated delimitations were subjected to legal norms, this would mean that there were *jus cogens* rules restricting the contractual freedom of States and, as a corollary, that a delimitation agreement disregarding such rules would arguably be invalid. This is certainly not the case. The principles and rules of international law set out by the courts in respect of maritime delimitation are purely suppletive and States are free to agree to reject them. The Court recognized this in 1969 when it said that

> [w]ithout attempting to enter into, still less pronounce upon any question of *jus cogens*, it is well understood that, in practice, rules of international law can, by agreement, be derogated from . . . .[33]

An agreement in which the parties rejected equitable principles (although these are said, in *Libya/Malta*, to be applicable to third party settlements as well as negotiated ones)[34] would certainly be valid: it is not because an agreement would correct the inequalities of nature, or cause an encroachment on the maritime projection of one of the States, or ignore a relevant circumstance, or base itself on distributive justice, that it would fail to constitute law between the parties. Even if the governments concerned undertake in advance to respect the principles and rules of law stated by a court, they remain free, in the end, to conclude an agreement on a different basis. The agreements concluded by the Federal Republic of Germany with its neighbours following the Court's 1969 judgment, even though they claim to be on the basis (*auf der Grundlage*) of the judgment, rest in fact

---

[31] Treaty of Peace and Amity (1984) (English translation, *ILM*, vol. 24, 1985, p. 11; French translation, *RGDIP*, vol. 89, 1985, p. 854).

[32] Maritime delimitation convention of 1984 (*RGDIP*, vol. 90, 1986, p. 308). According to a particularly well-placed commentator, this agreement "was inspired by considerations of courtesy and good-neighbourliness, and adopted an *ad hoc* solution which had nothing to do with law and is explained only by the special nature of the relations between the two countries" (Guillaume [2], p. 284).

[33] *North Sea*, para. 72. It is a little surprising that, in the same judgment, the Court said that it was not a matter "for the unfettered appreciation of the Parties" (para. 83). This phrase can be explained by the context, since the parties had specifically asked the Court for legal guidelines and the Court had considered it could not divest itself of this invitation.

[34] *Libya/Malta*, para. 46.

on considerations of economics and expediency unconnected with the Court's legal guidelines, in particular, those relating to natural prolongation.[35] Has it ever been suggested that they are therefore invalid? On the contrary, in its 1985 decision on the *Application for Revision and Interpretation of the Judgment of 24 February 1982*, the Court said that, even if the parties were committed in their Special Agreement to effect the delimitation in accordance with the principles and rules indicated by the Court, "they may . . . still reach mutual agreement upon a delimitation that does not correspond to the decision". In this case, "their accord will constitute an instrument superseding their Special Agreement".[36]

One can understand, in these circumstances, why the courts do not readily accept the precedents provided by State practice as a source of customary law.[37] This is as true of those agreements which adopt equidistance as of those which reject it, of those which base themselves on proportionality as of those which do not, of those which conform to physical facts as of those which ignore them.

States may enjoy complete contractual freedom. Courts and arbitrators, called on to decide on the basis of international law, do not. The judge or arbitrator, as we have seen,[38] is required to find a solution which not only seems equitable to him but is also grounded on legal considerations. And, whereas the equity applicable to governments in a negotiation has a very broad, ill-defined meaning, the equity of the judge or arbitrator is narrowly confined *infra legem*. It is the *"legal* concept of equity"[39] which the courts are required to implement. For them, justice is not "abstract justice but justice according to the rule of law".[40] The difference between these two sorts of equity—that of governments who negotiate a delimitation and that of the courts who determine it—is fundamental.

---

[35] For the agreements relating to the delimitation of the North Sea, including those concluded following the Court's *North Sea* judgment, see *Limits in the Seas*, No. 10 (Revised). Cf. Jagota [2], p. 111; Prescott, p. 285; Wenger, A., "'Pétrole et gaz naturel en mer du Nord. Droit et Economie", Paris, Technip, 1971, p. 132ff. ("An examination of the map shows . . . the extremely limited influence of the principles laid down by the International Court of Justice concerning the definitive delimitation of the German zone . . . in practice, [the agreements] have reflected only the economic interest of the coastal States . . . This compromise was made without taking account of the grand principles laid down by the Court"; p. 135).

[36] ICJ *Reports*, 1985, p. 219, para. 48.

[37] On the role of practice in the formation of customary law in maritime delimitation, see pp. 147-56 below.

[38] See pp. 48ff above.

[39] *Tunisia/Libya*, para. 71.

[40] *Libya/Malta*, para. 45.

This means that governments and courts are in completely different positions.[41] In contrast to governments, the courts cannot make their decision simply by reference to the facts, ignoring the rules of law. To reach their conclusion they must start from the facts *and* the law. This is not the case with States. As far as governments are concerned, in the end, the method is of little importance. For the courts it is the essential link between the underlying facts and the eventual delimitation. In short, as the Court put it unequivocally in *Libya/Malta*:

> ... although there may be no legal limit to the considerations which States may take account of, this can hardly be true for a court applying equitable procedures.[42]

Although it may be true that judicial or arbitral settlement is an alternative to the friendly settlement of international disputes, the theory that judicial settlement is based on consent cannot be pushed too far without the risk of turning into fiction. If two States submit their dispute to a court it is precisely because they have failed to settle it on a consensual basis. One may question the courts' motives in making this somewhat artificial assimilation. Is it not rather giving the courts, under cover of making negotiated delimitations amenable to the rules of law, the freedom of decision which belongs to States? In suggesting that the parties are bound to reach the solution which a court deciding in accordance with the rules of international law would have reached, is one not, in fact, trying to do exactly the opposite, i.e., to allow the courts to reach a decision as little predetermined by the law as that which governments are entitled to reach as a result of negotiation? If this really were the aim, the courts' insistence on the distinction between equity and *ex aequo et bono* would be of little value, and they would risk reducing to nothing the magnificent effort of nearly twenty years in constructing, almost *ex nihilo*, a coherent law of maritime delimitation. The theory that all maritime delimitations, whether negotiated or third-party, are identical, got off to a false start and has had disastrous consequences. It is one example of judicial construction it is to be hoped will disappear.

---

[41] See Jiménez de Aréchaga, *Tunisia/Libya*, Separate Opinion, p. 117, para. 61: "...there is a world of difference between the two situations". Cf. Sette-Camara, *Libya/Malta*, Separate Opinion, p. 62.

[42] *Libya/Malta*, para. 48.

II

A COMMON LAW FOR THE DELIMITATION OF ALL MARITIME AREAS?

THERE is no doubt that maritime jurisdictions have different purposes and different modalities. In essence, however, delimitation is always the same. And is it not normal for identical exercises to have identical rules? As we have seen, the concepts and controversies arising out of the problems of continental shelf delimitation have spread to the exclusive economic zone. There has been so much less interest in the delimitation of the territorial sea that when one talks of a common law of maritime delimitation, it is essentially the continental shelf and exclusive economic zone of which one is thinking. But the problem of territorial sea delimitation should not be ignored. As for the delimitation of internal waters and the contiguous zone, these are issues which remain open.[43]

1. DELIMITATION OF THE CONTINENTAL SHELF AND THE EXCLUSIVE ECONOMIC ZONE

By the time UNCLOS III became the forum for the development of the new concept of the exclusive economic zone, a concept so quickly to become a part of customary international law, the main lines of the law of continental shelf delimitation had already been drawn, in Article 6 of the 1958 Convention and in the *North Sea*

---

[43] The 1958 and 1982 Conventions are silent on the delimitation of *internal waters*. It has been suggested that it would be appropriate to apply the rules relating to the territorial sea (Caflisch [2], p. 41 and [3], p. 391). As for the delimitation of the *contiguous zone*, we have seen (p. 105 n. 6) that the 1958 Convention provides, except where the parties agree otherwise, for equidistance without mention of special circumstances. The 1982 Convention, on the other hand, contains no provision at all. There are various possible explanations for this silence, which it has been suggested should be remedied by the application of the rules relating to the delimitation either of the territorial sea or the exclusive economic zone and the continental shelf (Caflisch [2], pp. 55ff and [3], pp. 392ff). The tendency of the law of maritime delimitation towards unity means the problems of internal waters and the contiguous zone should not be insuperable.

judgment of the International Court of Justice. Were the rules governing the delimitation of the continental shelf also to apply to exclusive economic zone delimitation? The question was to be posed at the Conference immediately it came to drafting the provisions relating to the delimitation of these two jurisdictions. It would later be raised in the courts.

Logically, the solution to this problem should also have answered the question about the unity or duality of delimitation lines. An identity of the rules governing delimitation should have implied an identity of the line of delimitation. Duality in the rules of delimitation would normally have translated into a duality of delimitation lines. That is not the way things turned out, however. There has been no difficulty in accepting that the same rules govern the delimitation of the shelf and the zone but, despite the growing tendency to unification, there is still argument as to whether a single maritime boundary divides the two jurisdictions. This disassociation of the rules governing delimitation and the drawing of lines is worth pausing over.

A. Identical Rules of Delimitation

There has never been any serious difficulty in fashioning a body of norms common to the delimitation of the continental shelf and the exclusive economic zone.

At UNCLOS III, the texts governing the delimitation of these two jurisdictions were subject to exactly the same arguments and developed in exactly the same way. The drafts never differentiated between the two regimes, and successive negotiating texts used the same wording for the articles relating to delimitation of both the continental shelf and the exclusive economic zone.[44] The controversy over equidistance and equitable principles affected both texts in exactly the same way and in the same terms; the same philosophies confronted one another in both problems. One can point at most to just one occasion when the chairman of the negotiating group wondered "whether some kind of distinction in this respect, as related to the applicable criteria of delimitation, offered elements conducive to our search for a compromise".[45] But this suggestion was not followed up and, as we know, Articles 74 and 83 of the 1982 Convention govern continental shelf and exclusive economic zone delimitation in absolutely identical terms.

---

[44] On the genesis of Articles 74 and 83, see pp. 147-8 below.
[45] Quoted by Oda, *Tunisia/Libya*, Dissenting Opinion, p. 239, para. 137.

Nor do the courts seem to see any difference between the rules governing delimitation of the continental shelf and those applying to delimitation of the exclusive economic zone. As Judge Jiménez de Aréchaga wrote in 1982, ''. . . both of these delimitations are governed by the same rules''.[46] Judge Oda observed at the same time that ''the principles and rules of international law applicable to the delimitation of the continental shelf will not be different from those applicable to the delimitation of the exclusive economic zone''.[47] More recently, the *Gulf of Maine* judgment referred to the ''symmetry of the two texts relating to the delimitation of the continental shelf and of the exclusive economic zone'' and added that the fundamental norm it laid down is applicable to ''all kinds of maritime delimitation'' and to ''every maritime delimitation between neighbouring States''.[48] Finally, it may be noted that the *Guinea/Guinea-Bissau* arbitral award referred to exactly the same sources of law and applied the same principles and rules for delimiting both the continental shelf and the exclusive economic zone without even suggesting that any distinction could be made in this respect.[49]

Is there any need to ask why the unity of the legal regime for the delimitation of the shelf and the zone has been so easily accepted? It may be that the controversy over the place to accord to equidistance and equitable principles in the articles dealing with delimitation was enough to absorb the interest of delegations to UNCLOS III and that nobody had any reason to raise a new difficulty. The case-law relating to the continental shelf was, moreover, well enough developed for it to seem pointless to think up new rules for delimitation of the exclusive economic zone. This shows, once again, the extent to which continental shelf delimitation has served as the model for the delimitation of other maritime areas: it is from the rules relating to continental shelf delimitation and by reference to these rules that the common law of maritime delimitation has developed.

B. A Single Maritime Boundary

Can, or should, the delimitation of the continental shelf and the exclusive economic zone result in the same demarcation line, or is it more appropriate to have one for the shelf and another for the zone?

---

[46] *Tunisia/Libya*, Separate Opinion, p. 115, para. 56.
[47] *Ibid.*, Separate Opinion, p. 247, para. 145; cf. p. 249, para. 146.
[48] *Gulf of Maine*, paras. 90 and 112.
[49] *Guinea/Guinea-Bissau*, paras. 43 and 87ff.

This, reduced to essentials, is the problem of the single maritime boundary.

But, first, a preliminary comment. The problem does not affect the delimitation of the territorial sea. It is easy to understand why. Between coasts facing one another at a distance of less than twice the width of the territorial sea (and so, in general, less than 24 miles apart), the line delimiting the maritime jurisdictions of the two States will separate only their territorial seas since, for lack of space, neither State will have a continental shelf or exclusive economic zone. Where the two States are more than twice the width of the territorial sea apart, each will have full rights over the territorial sea. Only the continental shelf and the exclusive economic zone will have to be delimited, and it is only between these two latter jurisdictions that the question of a single boundary can arise. In the case of adjacent coasts, a line drawn seawards from the coast will usually for the first twelve miles separate only the territorial waters of the two countries. Beyond that, one can ask if it is the same line which laterally separates their continental shelves and exclusive economic zones or not. Here again, it is only for these last two that the problem of a single boundary arises.[50]

Since the problem is thus limited to the continental shelf and the exclusive economic zone, is it conceivable that different lines divide these two jurisdictions, given that their delimitation is governed by the same rules?

It is obvious what is at stake here. If one of the parties has obtained, by agreement or through judicial means, a continental shelf delimitation which seems to it to be unfavourable, it will quite naturally seek to obtain a different delimitation for the exclusive economic zone; the other party, in contrast, will want to extend to the exclusive economic zone the favourable delimitation it has obtained for the continental shelf. This explains why, for example, in the Gulf of Gascony, France supports the single boundary theory, since the 1974 agreement on the continental shelf was clearly much to its advantage.[51] Spain, on the other hand, wants a different

[50] The maritime delimitation agreement between France and Monaco (p. 112 above), which determines the lateral limits between the French and Monacan maritime areas, defined separately first ''the limits of the territorial waters of the two States'', then the ''limits of the maritime areas beyond their territorial sea''. It is only in respect of this second segment that one can speak of a single maritime boundary in the strict sense. Likewise, in *Guinea/Guinea-Bissau*, the ''line delimiting the maritime territories'' of the parties traced by the Tribunal in accordance with the Special Agreement delimits the territorial sea of the two countries before becoming a single maritime boundary separating their continental shelf and exclusive economic zone (cf. p. 125 below).

[51] See p. 29 n. 26 above.

delimitation for the exclusive economic zone.[52] The question will present itself less frequently in reverse. In the *Jan Mayen* case, the exclusive economic zone delimitation came first, with an agreement favourable to Iceland. The question at issue between Iceland and Norway was whether this same line should delimit the continental shelf.[53]

At the conceptual level, it is more difficult to understand how identity of rules and the drawing of a delimitation line can get out of phase with one another. The explanation given is essentially that, although identical in content, the rules applicable to the delimitation of the continental shelf and the exclusive economic zone can lead to different results. The relevant circumstances are not necessarily the same when it is a question of the seabed or the water column. What is equitable for the seabed may not be so for the superjacent waters.

Surprising though it may seem, scholars have scarcely touched on the problem, and their differing positions have been argued only briefly.[54] It is in the context of judicial procedures that the problem has been raised, and then usually only indirectly, rarely head-on. It is therefore necessary to look at the slow progress of judicial thinking on this difficult issue before venturing upon consideration of the subject as a whole.

a) The slow progress of judicial interest

Even before customary international law endorsed the institution of the exclusive economic zone, the problem of the single boundary had been raised in regard to fishing zones. The Anglo-French Court of Arbitration observed in 1977 that, entrusted by the Special Agreement with the delimitation of the continental shelf between France and the United Kingdom, it did not have "any competence to settle differences between the Parties regarding the boundary of their . . . respective fishery zones, and still less to pronounce upon the boundary of the Economic Zone" established by French legislation.[55] Nevertheless, the Court of Arbitration, in delimiting the continental shelf around the Channel Islands, took account of the fisheries zones established in the area. The continental shelf delimitation line, states the award, must be drawn in such a way as not to encroach on the Channel Islands' twelve mile fishing zone. In

[52] Cf. Guillaume [2], p. 287.

[53] See p. 131 below.

[54] By way of example one can quote: in favour of the unity of the lines, Guillaume [2], p. 328; in favour of their duality, Caflisch [3], pp. 422, 426. Cf. O'Connell, vol. II, pp. 727ff; Reuter, [2], pp. 260ff; Oda [2]; Orrego Vicuña, pp. 121ff.

[55] *Anglo-French* award, para. 13.

fact, the limit of the continental shelf was fixed so as to coincide with the limit of this fishing zone.[56] While proclaiming that the delimitation of the continental shelf is independent of that of fishing zones—and could therefore theoretically be different—the Court of Arbitration seems nonetheless to have preferred not to separate them.

Tunisia/Libya

In *Tunisia/Libya*, the International Court of Justice was seised only of the continental shelf delimitation and dealt exclusively with that issue. It referred to the exclusive economic zone only incidentally and it was *à propos* the continental shelf that it raised the "distance principle".[57] The problem of the relationship between the two institutions and thus of whether there were one or two lines really came to light only in the oral proceedings and in some of the separate opinions accompanying the judgment.

During the oral proceedings, precise questions were put to the parties on the subject. Judge Oda asked whether, in view of the identity between the draft provisions of the 1982 Convention (then still on the negotiating table) on the delimitation of the continental shelf and of the exclusive economic zone, the delimitation of these two areas might be or ought not to be different, and whether the circumstances to be taken into consideration in delimiting the continental shelf could or could not be different from those to be taken into consideration for the delimitation of the exclusive economic zone. Judge Schwebel asked whether, supposing that Tunisia enjoyed historic rights over sedentary fisheries, Libya could have the exclusive rights of exploitation in the sub-soil of the places where these fisheries were located.[58]

The answers given by the parties diverged dramatically. While Libya admitted that the boundaries of the continental shelf and the exclusive economic zone "ought not, in the majority of cases, to be different", it thought that "nevertheless, there may be factors relevant to fishing, such as established fishing practices, which have no relevance to shelf resources", and that, "conversely, there may be factors relevant to shelf resources—such as geological features controlling the extent of a natural prolongation—of no relevance to fishing". "The two boundaries need not necessarily coincide",

[56] *Ibid.*, paras. 187 and 202.

[57] *Tunisia/Libya*, para. 48.

[58] For the text of these questions, see ICJ *Memorials, Tunisia/Libya*, vol. V, p. 246; cf. Oda [2], p. 350.

Libya concluded, suggesting that "a vertical superimposition of rights" belonging to different States is not unknown and not in the least impractical. For Tunisia, on the other hand, "given that the coastal State . . . has sovereign rights in the exclusive economic zone for the purpose of exploring and exploiting the natural resources of the seabed and subsoil, it is difficult to see how the limits of the exclusive economic zone could differ from those of the continental shelf within the 200 miles . . . The circumstances which are relevant for the delimitation of the continental shelf are also relevant for the delimitation of the exclusive economic zone." Tunisia therefore objected to any separation between rights over the seabed and rights over the water-column: "Such a division would lead to insurmountable difficulties in practice".[59]

These questions might have led the parties to an *aggiornamento* of their positions. But they both preferred to stay within the bounds of the classic continental shelf theory, and it was on this ground that the Court answered them. Having been asked by the parties to deal simply with the continental shelf problem, the Court did not regard it as necessary to make its decision in terms of the exclusive economic zone, or even to pronounce on the relationship between the concept of the continental shelf and that of the exclusive economic zone.[60] Nonetheless, in delimiting the continental shelf, the Court referred, as had the Anglo-French Court of Arbitration, to factors relating to fisheries, in other words, to the superjacent waters.[61]

Several of the separate opinions echoed the controversy. Judges Jiménez de Aréchaga, Oda and Evensen said they were in favour of the unity of delimitation, for reasons connected as much with the increasing absorption of the continental shelf concept into that of the exclusive economic zone as for practical motives.[62] Some members of the Court went further, expressing regret that the judgment confined itself to continental shelf delimitation and did not base itself squarely on the exclusive economic zone, since, in their view, it was this latter concept which would henceforth prevail, and the two delimitations, were now, of their very nature, identical.[63]

---

[59] ICJ *Memorials, Tunisia/Libya*, vol. V, pp. 503, 507-8. Cf. Oda *Tunisia/Libya*, Dissenting Opinion, p. 232, para. 127 and Oda [2], p. 351.

[60] *Tunisia/Libya*, paras. 48 and 100.

[61] *Ibid.*, paras. 93-5.

[62] *Ibid.*, Jiménez de Aréchaga, Separate Opinion, p. 115, para. 56 and p. 130, para. 99; Oda, Dissenting Opinion, p. 232, para. 126; Evensen, Dissenting Opinion, p. 287, para. 9 and p. 288, para. 10.

[63] *Ibid.*, Oda, Dissenting Opinion, p. 234, para. 130 and p. 249, para. 146; Evensen, Dissenting Opinion, p. 287, para. 9; p. 288, para. 10 and p. 319.

Gulf of Maine

Against such a background, the submission of the delimitation of the maritime boundary between Canada and the United States in the Gulf of Maine area to a Chamber of the Court was obviously going to arouse much interest. The parties asked the Court, in their Special Agreement, to define "the course of the single maritime boundary that divides the continental shelf and fishery zones" of the two countries in this area. They added that neither State would in future be able to "claim or exercise sovereign rights or jurisdiction . . . over the waters or seabed and subsoil" beyond the single boundary thus defined. As the parties emphasized, the reference to the concept of a single maritime boundary meant that the case was to break new ground.

Although the Special Agreement spoke of the continental shelf and fishery zones, the words "exclusive economic zone" were not mentioned. This silence is explained by the fact that at the time the Special Agreement was concluded, neither party had proclaimed such a zone or even taken a position in regard to this new institution of the law of the sea. The United States was, however, to proclaim an exclusive economic zone in the course of the written proceedings.[64] Canada observed that, on its side, all the elements of an economic zone were already in place and it reserved the right to proclaim such a zone in the future. However, neither party presented the problem in terms of the relationship between continental shelf and exclusive economic zone delimitations. They contented themselves with stating that what they had in mind was a single, multipurpose boundary to delimit the totality of jurisdictions and rights which international law currently accorded to coastal States, or might in the future accord them. According to the two parties, it was not for the Court to contemplate separately a delimitation of the continental shelf on one hand, and of fishery or exclusive economic zones on the other, nor to ask itself if the delimitations could or should coincide. It was a single line they wanted, obtained by "a single, synthetic, global operation".[65]

At the end of the first phase of the oral proceedings, the President of the Chamber put the following question to the parties:

> In the event that one particular method, or set of methods, should appear appropriate for the delimitation of the continental shelf, another for that of

[64] See p. 65 n. 150 above.
[65] Canadian Pleadings, C1/CR 84/6, p. 13. The United States said it agreed with this analysis (C1/CR 84/24, p. 19).

the exclusive fishery zones, what do the Parties consider to be the legal grounds that might be invoked for preferring one or the other in seeking to determine a single line?

The wording of this question seemed to suggest that the Court was inclined to exclude from the discussion the concept of the exclusive economic zone in favour of the narrower fishery zone concept used by the Special Agreement. It also suggested that the Chamber saw the problem in terms of the relationship between a delimitation of the continental shelf and of fishery zones, and that it was preparing, as a result, to reject the global approach adopted by the parties during the proceedings.

In his reply, the Canadian agent dealt with the question in the terms in which it was put. He admitted that the circumstances relevant to the delimitation of these two areas might, in theory, differ: "the dilemma you have identified might well arise in certain cases", he said. In such a case, it would be appropriate to give preference to the method dictated by the relevant circumstances applicable to each particular section of the single line the Chamber was asked to draw. In the present case, however, no such discrepancy presented itself. The United States, for its part, insisted that it had no reason to envisage giving preference to factors connected with either the shelf or the water column. In its view, the Chamber's task was to consider the relevant circumstances as a whole, without distinguishing between the factors relating to the seabed and those relating to the water column: it was a question of an "integrated whole" calling for an "overall solution".[66]

The Chamber noted in its judgment the parties' wish for a single line "applicable to all aspects of the jurisdiction of the coastal State, not only jurisdiction as defined by international law in its present state, but also as it will be defined in future".[67] But these, however, were not the terms in which the Chamber reasoned. Instead, it saw its task as the drawing of "a single boundary for two different jurisdictions".[68] "... [T]he delimitation has a twofold object", said the Chamber.[69] Taking this as its starting point, it set off in search of criteria and methods of delimitation which were not linked

[66] Question from the President: C1/CR 84/17, p. 61; Canadian Reply: C1/CR 84/22, pp. 34ff; United States Reply: C1/CR 84/24, pp. 19ff. For a summary of the question and replies, see *Gulf of Maine*, para. 161.

[67] *Gulf of Maine*, para. 26.

[68] *Ibid.*, para. 27. This idea came up several times in the judgment. See, for example, paras. 119, 161, 168 and 194.

[69] *Ibid.*, para. 193.

exclusively to either of these objects and which did not give prefer-
ential treatment to one to the detriment of the other, but were equally
suitable for a division of either.[70]

The Chamber thus rejected the concept the parties had put to it,
of a single line, synthetic in nature. It conceived the problem,
instead, as the relationship between two delimitation lines in respect
of two different areas, and looked at it, not from the point of view of
the relationship between a continental shelf and exclusive economic
zone delimitation, but that between a continental shelf and fishery
zones delimitation. The parties' emphasis on the exclusive economic
zone and the United States' proclamation of such a zone during the
hearings clearly failed to persuade the judges. The Chamber noted
the proclamation of this zone, observing that its extent coincided
with that of the fishery zone created previously, but added[71] that
"this did not of course modify the terms of the Special Agreement".
Within the restricted territory thus chosen, the single boundary for
the continental shelf and the fishery zones, the Chamber limited itself
to stating that "there is certainly no rule of international law to the
contrary"[72] and that it did not run up against any obstacle to the
accomplishment of the operation asked of it. It took no position on
whether a court could refuse the single boundary asked for by the
parties or whether, conversely, it could regard the single boundary
as required by law even when the parties envisaged a duality of lines.
As to the general problem of the single boundary for both the
continental shelf and the exclusive economic zone, this was touched
on only incidentally:

> . . . it can be foreseen that with the gradual adoption by the majority of
> maritime States of an exclusive economic zone and, consequently, an
> increasingly general demand for single delimitation, so as to avoid as far as
> possible the disadvantages inherent in a plurality of separate delimitations,
> preference will henceforth inevitably be given to criteria that, because of
> their more neutral character, are best suited for use in a multi-purpose
> delimitation.[73]

Although it does not exclude the possibility of different lines to
delimit the continental shelf and the exclusive economic zone, the
Gulf of Maine judgment is, nonetheless, an important contribution to

---

[70] *Ibid.*, paras. 47, 119, 168, 193 and 194.
[71] *Ibid.*, para. 68.
[72] *Ibid.*, para. 27.
[73] *Ibid.*, para. 194.

the development towards a single boundary, determined by the application of the same "neutral" criteria of the coastal geography and by resort to the same "neutral" methods of a geometrical character.[74]

In his dissenting opinion, Judge Gros vigorously attacked the idea of a single maritime boundary. He said that "the Parties appeared to think that the mere fact of their having asked for a single boundary in the Special Agreement sufficed to impose it on the Chamber" and that neither the parties nor the Chamber had sought to establish "whether there existed in international law any rule prescribing or authorizing the use of a single line for the continental shelf and the fishery zone". Not only, he explains, does the parties' expression of a wish for a single line "not bind the Chamber if the law applicable to the relevant circumstances of the case does not allow the application of such procedure" but the very idea of a single maritime boundary runs into serious objections. "The two elements have always been treated separately." All in all, concludes Judge Gros, "while the crucial question in the present case has been posed, it has not been answered".[75]

It is not easy to assess the single maritime boundary approach adopted in *Gulf of Maine*. It has to be acknowledged that, by laying stress on their shared wish for a single line rather than on the development of international law towards single boundaries—in other words, by putting the subjective justification for a single boundary before its objective justification—the parties hardly helped the Chamber tackle the question head-on. It would seem from the passage quoted above that the Chamber was conscious of the problem, and that its own inclination, which for practical reasons it preferred not to express, took it in the direction of the single boundary. The trouble Judge Gros took to refute this suggests that this was indeed the unspoken tenor of the judgment.

Guinea/Guinea-Bissau

Some months after *Gulf of Maine*, an arbitration tribunal composed of three judges of the International Court of Justice had to decide a second case concerning a single maritime boundary. The Special Agreement between Guinea and Guinea-Bissau asked the Arbitration Tribunal to determine "the course of the line delimiting the

---

[74] *Ibid.*, paras. 195 and 199; cf. para. 161.
[75] *Ibid.*, Gros, Dissenting Opinion, p. 363, para. 5; p. 367, para. 12; pp. 370-1, para. 17; p. 376, para. 25.

maritime territories'' appertaining to each of the two countries. As already noted, the Tribunal not only applied the same rules of law to the delimitation of both the continental shelf and the exclusive economic zone, but, in delimiting these two areas, drew a single boundary without raising any of the problems connected with this concept.[76] The Tribunal did not ask itself whether this formula rested on the will of the parties or also, objectively, on the law of the sea. Nor did it ask whether international law proscribes such a formula, authorizes it, or makes it obligatory. In a way, the Tribunal seemed to perceive the single boundary as a fact of the current law of the sea, against which it saw no need to raise, or even examine, any objection.

Libya/Malta

Libya/Malta was to present the Court with a problem very similar to that it had faced in *Tunisia/Libya*. It was again only a matter of the delimitation of the continental shelf, and the question again arose of the relationship between the delimitation of the shelf and that of the exclusive economic zone. Neither country had claimed an economic zone. Malta had proclaimed a 25 mile exclusive fishery zone. What was directly at issue was not, therefore, the problem of a single maritime boundary, but only one of whether the distance principle which characterized the exclusive economic zone concept had permeated the theory of the continental shelf to the point where it controlled the delimitation of both areas. Malta maintained that, even if the dispute related exclusively to the delimitation of the continental shelf, so that the general question of the coincidence between continental shelf and exclusive economic zone delimitation did not need answering, it had nonetheless become ''impossible . . . without losing sight of the development of the customary international law of the sea, to attempt any delimitation of the continental shelf which simply ignores the concept of the exclusive economic zone''. As a result, it claimed, this concept could not be ''eliminated from the present debate''; and the question of the exclusive economic zone must be ''kept in mind''.[77] For Libya, however, the continental shelf and exclusive economic zone remained two fundamentally different institutions, and there was no reason, in a

---

[76] *Guinea/Guinea-Bissau*, para. 87. See p. 118 n. 50 above for the application, in this award, of the principle of the single maritime boundary to the delimitation of the territorial sea.

[77] Counter-Memorial of Malta, paras. 80-1; Reply of Malta, paras. 45-7; Pleadings, CR 84/24, pp. 57-8; 84/26, pp. 35-6; 85/7, pp. 55-6.

case dealing only with the continental shelf, to be concerned with the rules governing the delimitation of the economic zone.[78]

The Court ruled clearly in favour of a link between the two concepts:

> In the view of the Court, even though the present case relates only to the delimitation of the continental shelf and not to that of the exclusive economic zone, the principles and rules underlying the latter concept cannot be left out of consideration.[79]

As a result, "the distance criterion must now apply to the continental shelf as well as to the exclusive economic zone",[80] in respect of both title and delimitation.[81] On the other hand, the Court did not need—because the question was not asked—to take a position on the issue, properly speaking, of the single maritime boundary.

b) The present state of affairs

What is striking about the case-law reviewed above is its relative cautiousness. It is true that positions adopted by the courts are developed and refined from case to case, but it is hard, nonetheless, to avoid the impression that the courts have not really tried to tackle the question head-on. This caution can no doubt be explained by the uncertainties which, throughout UNCLOS III, surrounded the relationship between the new concept of the exclusive economic zone and that of the continental shelf, the content of which was simultaneously to be questioned. Although some of these uncertainties have been removed, others remain, so much so that the relationship between the continental shelf and the exclusive economic zone is today still a matter of controversy. So it is in terms rather of trends than of definite facts that the problem must be considered.

---

[78] Libyan Counter-Memorial, paras. 3.14 and 3.39; Pleadings, CR 84/29, p. 18; 84/30, pp. 21, 32, 41; 84/31, pp. 39, 56; 84/33, p. 37.

[79] *Libya/Malta*, para. 33.

[80] *Ibid.*, para. 34.

[81] With just one exception, none of the separate or dissenting opinions in this case challenges this position of principle. In their Joint Opinion, Judges Ruda, Bedjaoui and Jiménez de Aréchaga raise no objection (*Libya/Malta*, pp. 76ff). Judges Mosler (p. 119), Oda (p. 156, para. 60), Mbaye (pp. 94-5) and Valticos (pp. 106-7, para. 9) expressly approve it. Judge Sette-Camara, however, finds the reference to the "magic criterion of 200 miles" inappropriate in the case of the continental shelf, as also the use of the distance principle, which he considers peculiar to the exclusive economic zone: "The *excursus* of the judgment on the exclusive economic zone was unnecessary and does not contribute to the clarity of the reasoning" (pp. 69, 71).

There is no doubt that considerations of convenience and practicality play a role in the debate about the single maritime boundary. For some, the vertical superimposition of rights is a complication to be avoided at all costs; for others, it is only the lesser evil. But it is clear that, in essence, this debate is a reflection of the difference of views seen in the case-law and among scholars regarding the relationship between the concepts of the continental shelf and the exclusive economic zone in the current law of the sea. It is because, and to the extent that, the law of the sea is moving towards a common outer limit that there is an increasing tendency in the direction of a single maritime boundary. This correlation calls for some explanation.

1. Towards a common outer limit

The fragmentation phase

Over quite a long period of time, the only maritime jurisdiction of any importance was the territorial sea, which had a single outer limit covering both the water column and the seabed. It seemed hard to imagine that the outer limit of the territorial sea might apply only to the superjacent waters, while another limit, situated futher seaward, would apply to the seabed and subsoil.[82] As late as 1955, Scelle expressed hostility to the ''heretical or schismatic conception of the shelf'': ''the discontinuity between submerged territories is pure fiction'', he wrote; ''the sea is physically one'', and it is a serious error to attack the ''oneness of the maritime domain''.[83] The fragmentation of the outer limits, however, became more and more pronounced up until about 1970. The continental shelf theory, which achieved an irresistable momentum after the 1945 Truman Proclamation, endorsed the split between rights to the water column and rights to the seabed, and thus the duality of the outer limits of the coastal State's maritime jurisdictions.[84] This split was even more firmly established with the emergence of the idea of a fishery zone side by side with the continental shelf concept. From now on, the coastal State was able to draw several outer limits from its shore-line, each valid for a specific purpose and each with its own criteria. The territorial sea, the contiguous zone and the fishery zone were defined

[82] Cf. Gidel, vol. I, pp. 498ff.

[83] Scelle, pp. 15, 51, 52.

[84] The Court took note of this split in *North Sea*, para. 59. Cf. Fitzmaurice, *Fisheries (Jurisdiction)*, Separate Opinion, ICJ *Reports*, 1973, p. 27, para. 7.

in terms of distance from the baseline; the continental shelf, in terms of a combination of depth and exploitability.

The restoration phase

During the 1970s this movement went into reverse. The breaking-up and fragmentation of the seaward limit was to be replaced by restoration and reunification. There were two factors underlying this development. First, a number of coastal States wanted to reserve for themselves exclusive rights of exploration and exploitation of the fishery resources of the water column to a distance of 200 miles from their coasts. Secondly, several States wanted to put an end to the inequality created between States by the concept of the continental shelf, which had prevailed in the 1958 Convention and the *North Sea* case, according to whether nature had endowed them with a larger or smaller continental shelf. As we know, these two trends gave birth to the institution of the exclusive economic zone with a multi-purpose character, the outer limit of which, fixed at a uniform maximum distance of 200 miles from the baseline, constitutes a single spatial limit for all the rights and jurisdictions of the coastal State, in respect of both the seabed and the superjacent waters. Just as the outer limit of the territorial sea marked the end of the rights and obligations which are the attributes and constituent elements of sovereignty *stricto sensu*, so the outer limit of the exclusive economic zone henceforth marks the end of the bundle of other rights and oblig-ations of the coastal State. It is this concept which the 1982 Convention endorsed when, in Article 56, it defined "the rights, jurisdictions and obligations of the coastal State in the exclusive economic zone" as covering the resources of both "the waters superjacent to the seabed" and "the seabed and its subsoil".

The situation would have been very simple had not an influential minority of States, endowed by nature with a wide continental shelf, insisted that the minimum limit of 200 miles for the continental shelf, on which all States agreed, should not be regarded as a maximum.[85] As we know, there was a compromise solution to the problem. Article 76 of the Montego Bay Convention, while fixing the outer limit of the continental shelf at at least two hundred miles, provided that, in certain cases, the continental shelf could extend beyond this distance "to the outer edge of the continental margin". Since it was inconceivable that different legal regimes might apply to the seabed

---

[85] See pp. 35-6 above.

within and beyond 200 miles, it became necessary to preserve a single regime, distinct from that of the exclusive economic zone, for the whole of the seabed from the baseline up to the outer limit. This explains the provision in Article 56(3) of the Convention according to which "[t]he rights set out in this article with respect to the seabed and subsoil shall be exercised in accordance with Part VI".

The unification of the 200 mile outer limit is, therefore, not complete. In some cases, there remain two different outer limits, one for the water column at 200 miles from the coast, the other for the seabed at a greater distance. The single 200 mile outer limit is, however, the most frequent. Only a handful of States can lay claim, thanks to the generosity of nature, to an outer limit for their continental shelf different from that for their exclusive economic zones. Moreover, it is not certain whether continental shelf rights beyond the 200 mile limit have acquired the status of customary international law and are applicable to States not party to the Convention. In contrast, the existence of continental shelf rights up to at least the 200 mile limit of the exclusive economic zone has certainly acquired the validity of customary international law, given the consent of all States thereto and the absence of any opposition. It would today, it has been said, be "unthinkable that a State would try to exploit the submarine areas off the coasts of another State at less than 200 nautical miles from the shore".[86]

As we have seen, the Court in *Libya/Malta* took note of the customary extension of the continental shelf to a distance of at least 200 miles from the coasts and of the coincidence thenceforth, in the majority of cases, between the outer limit of the shelf and that of the economic zone. Leaving aside the exceptional, and still legally uncertain, case of States with a wide continental shelf, the single outer limit for the shelf and the zone is now an indisputable element of the law of the sea.[87]

---

[86] Jiménez de Aréchaga, *Tunisia/Libya*, Separate Opinion, p. 115, para. 53. The question of the status in customary law of the Article 76 provisions was discussed in *Libya/Malta*: Libya maintained that only the provision about the rights to the continental shelf throughout the natural prolongation of its land territory to the outer edge of the continental margin had this status (CR 84/31, pp. 51ff); Malta, on the other hand, argued that the rule according to which the continental shelf extended to a distance 'of at least 200 miles had acquired customary law status but that the customary character of the enlarged concept of the continental shelf remained under discussion (CR 85/7, pp. 39ff). The Court took no position on the customary law status of the various elements of Article 76.

[87] The unity of the limit does not imply an identity of legal regimes. There are differences between that of the continental shelf and the exclusive economic zone. While continental shelf rights "do not depend ... on any express proclamation" (1982

2. Towards a single maritime boundary

Given the link between title and delimitation, the tendency towards a common outer limit for the continental shelf and the exclusive economic zone was bound to be reflected in a parallel tendency towards a single maritime boundary.

State practice

The direction State practice has taken in this respect is most revealing. More and more often, States are no longer content to delimit their continental shelf, but agree on a maritime boundary applying also to their exclusive economic zone (or what passes for this if there has been no proclamation of an exclusive economic zone as such). Agreements defining a single maritime boundary, with various names but all covering the same reality, have for several years outnumbered those dealing simply with the delimitation of the continental shelf.[88] The *Jan Mayen* case also shows the reluctance of States to adopt different delimitations for the shelf and the zone.[89] Although Iceland and Norway had not excluded from the start a delimitation line for their continental shelf different from that for their exclusive economic zone, the Conciliation Commission recommended that they make the boundary of the shelf coincide with that of the zone, and the two States followed this recommendation. Thus, in asking the Court to draw a single maritime boundary, first, the

---

Convention, Article 77(3)), rights over the exclusive economic zone presuppose proclamation by the interested State. The breadth of the exclusive economic zone itself depends on what the latter wants, subject only to the international law limitation to a maximum breadth of 200 miles (1982 Convention, Article 57). In addition, the obligations of the coastal State are not exactly the same vis-à-vis the continental shelf and the exclusive economic zone (cf. Sette-Camara, *Libya/Malta*, Separate Opinion, p. 71).

[88] The agreements concluded by France in recent years are often called maritime delimitation conventions, and state that they are determining a line of delimitation "between the maritime areas over which the two States respectively exercise sovereign rights" or that the limit they fix "constitutes the boundary between the zones over which the contracting parties exercise or will exercise sovereign rights or jurisdiction in accordance with international law" (see, for example, the agreements with Venezuela (p. 29 n. 26 above); and with St. Lucia and Australia (p. 68 n. 158 above)). Agreements defining a "maritime boundary" often contain similar clauses (see, for example, the USA/Cuba agreement (1977), *ILM*, vol. 17, 1978, p. 110; USA/Mexico (1970 and 1978), *Limits in the Seas*, No. 45; *ILM*, vol. 17, 1978, p. 1074; USA/Venezuela (1978, *New Directions*, vol. VIII, p. 84; USA/Cook (1980) and USA/New Zealand (1980), *Limits in the Seas*, No. 100; Burma/Thailand (1980), *Limits in the Seas*, No. 102 (the agreement expressly states that the boundary separates simultaneously both the continental shelf and the exclusive economic zone of the two parties); etc.).

[89] See p. 29 n. 26 above.

United States and Canada, then Guinea and Guinea-Bissau, placed themselves in the mainstream of an existing trend and thereby reinforced it. It is not an exaggeration when *Gulf of Maine* refers to "an increasingly general demand for single delimitation".[90]

The infatuation with the single boundary revealed by State practice is not, however, universal. First, some recent agreements continue to deal only with the continental shelf or the exclusive economic zone. Secondly, there is at least one important agreement in which the States concerned, in recognition of certain exceptional features specific to the situation, have established different limits for the seabed and fishery zones.[91] Nor should one forget that governments sometimes disagree about the extension to the exclusive economic zone of limits previously agreed for the continental shelf. A case in point, for example, is the disagreement, already mentioned, between France and Spain over the Gulf of Gascony.[92]

However interesting State practice may be, it is not proper, for reasons previously indicated, to draw from it dogmatic conclusions as to the existence of a rule of customary international law which imposes a single boundary on the judge or arbitrator, as a matter of legal obligation; no more can the existence of exceptions or divergence of views alone justify by itself the opposite finding.

As a result, the question of the unity or duality of the lines delimiting the continental shelf and the exclusive economic zone has to be treated on its own merits.

Articles 74 and 83 of the 1982 Convention

One can ignore for this purpose any textual approach based on Articles 74 and 83 of the Montego Bay Convention. It would be just as misleading to conclude from the fact that there are two articles regulating the delimitation of the exclusive economic zone and the shelf that there are two lines of delimitation, as to see in the identical language of the two provisions justification for a single maritime boundary. Moreover, as we have seen, it is possible to attribute different meanings to these texts, despite their identical wording, by showing that the relevant circumstances and equitable considerations may not be the same in both cases. In the light of the compromise reached at UNCLOS III on the relationship between the shelf and the zone, one might also be tempted to see Article 74,

---

[90] *Gulf of Maine*, para. 194.

[91] Australia/Papua-New Guinea Agreement relating to the Torres Strait (1978), *ILM*, vol. 18, 1979, p. 291. See Burmester.

[92] See p. 118 above.

inserted into Part V relating to the zone as defined in Articles 56 and 57, as referring to the delimitation of a zone encompassing the rights over the seabed up to 200 miles; Article 83, inserted in Part VI, would then regulate the delimitation of the shelf distinct from the zone, in other words, beyond 200 miles, up to the outer edge of the continental margin. Would it then be necessary to accept that up to 200 miles, on the basis of Article 74, the line of delimitation would have to be the same for the zone and the shelf, for the superjacent waters and the seabed? These exercises in exegesis all seem equally pointless.

Considerations of expediency

The considerations of expediency are more interesting. It has often been pointed out that the duality of delimitation lines would mean a superimposition of rights, a situation hardly ''tolerable as a matter of international *ordre public*'', according to one member of the Court.[93] On the other hand, it should not be forgotten, as Libya pointed out in its answers to Judge Schwebel's questions in 1981, that cases of vertical superimposition of rights are not unknown. From the moment it is envisaged that a State may exercise rights over the seabed beyond 200 miles while its rights over the water column may never be exercised beyond this distance, there is automatically a situation of superimposed legal regimes. Moreover, *Gulf of Maine* has shown that a single maritime boundary itself leaves a ''grey area'' of superimposition of rights, even within 200 miles of the two States, when it is not an equidistant boundary.[94] Finally, practice suggests that although the difficulties of duality have led States to resort only exceptionally to such a solution, they have not been dissuaded from ever resorting to it. Practical considerations are, therefore, not decisive.

Legal considerations

The matter has, in the end, to be settled on the basis of legal principles. If delimitation had continued to be effected by reference to the physical characteristics of the seabed, it would have been possible to accept that the circumstances to be taken into consideration were not the same in delimiting the shelf and the zone. There would then have been nothing wrong in maintaining that, since the

---

[93] Oda, *Tunisia/Libya*, Dissenting Opinion, p. 232, para. 126.
[94] Cf. the Canadian Counter-Memorial, paras. 572ff.

equities are different, the delimitation lines might also be so.[95] But this is not the case, since "the distance criterion must now apply to the continental shelf as well as to the exclusive economic zone".[96] This means that there is no longer any legal reason to object to the existence of common norms for the delimitation of the shelf and the zone leading to a single maritime boundary common to both.

This conclusion is, of course, only valid if the continental margin does not go beyond 200 miles. Where this is not the case, and assuming that the relevant provisions of Article 76 have acquired the force of customary law, the criterion of natural physical prolongation makes its re-entry, and the duality of boundaries, outlawed by the distance criterion up to 200 miles, resumes its rights. The single boundary is thus excluded as a possibility when coasts are more than 400 miles apart and when the outer edge of the continental margin of the two States extends more than 200 miles from their coasts. In such a case, it may be necessary to delimit the continental shelf, but the economic zones of the two countries do not have to be delimited since they do not touch one another. The single boundary is also excluded when the coasts are adjacent and the outer edge of the continental shelf of the two countries extends beyond 200 miles. In such a case, there might well be a single boundary up to 200 miles from the coast; beyond that distance, the line will delimit only the continental shelf, and the waters to either side of this line will no longer be part of the exclusive economic zone of the two States. Since situations of this sort are rare, the single boundary for the shelf and the exclusive economic zone will remain the general rule.

Finally, one may ask, from the point of view of the single maritime boundary, whether the fifty or so agreements for the delimitation of the continental shelf so far concluded should be regarded as *ipso facto*

---

[95] In 1984 again, the Chamber was able to say that "in a concrete situation where distinctive geological characteristics can be observed in the continental shelf, such as might have special effect in determining the division of that shelf . . . there would in all likelihood be no reason to extend the effect of those characteristics to the division of the superjacent volume of water, in respect of which they would not be relevant" (*Gulf of Maine*, para. 193). One can only add that even in the heyday of natural prolongation, the courts did not hesitate to rely on the equities relating to the water column in delimiting the seabed. So, as we have seen, in delimiting the continental shelf around the Channel Islands, the Court of Arbitration took account of the two countries' fishing zones (*Anglo-French* award, para. 167). Likewise, in *Tunisia/Libya*, the Court relied on a *modus vivendi* over the coastal fisheries for fixing the continental shelf boundary (*Tunisia/Libya*, paras. 93ff). The variety of the equities has never, it is clear, been seen as a serious barrier.

[96] *Libya/Malta*, para. 34.

applicable to the delimitation of the exclusive economic zone between the parties. In view of the preceding remarks, the answer should be in the affirmative. But one cannot exclude the possibility that a continental shelf delimitation agreement concluded at a time when the theory of natural prolongation prevailed, may have been inspired by physical considerations now out of date. Its extension to the exclusive economic zone would in that case no longer be convincingly justifiable.

2. THE SPECIAL NATURE OF TERRITORIAL SEA DELIMITATION

The fact that in the last fifteen years there has been no judicial or arbitration case of any importance on the delimitation of the territorial sea[97] has pushed this problem into the background. Modern writers give it less attention than the delimitation of the continental shelf and the exclusive economic zone, and the question seems to cause few diplomatic problems. But this is a relatively recent development. In the past, before the Second World War, the delimitation of the territorial sea was the subject of intense doctrinal controversy, of difficult discussions at the Codification Conference at The Hague and of several judicial cases the reverberations from which have not completely died away.[98]

There are several explanations for this lack of interest. Clearly, the modest width of the territorial sea, even extended to 12 miles, reduces the number of cases in which the problem of delimitation presents itself between opposing coastlines. On the other hand, the fact that the effect of certain coastal configurations on lines of equidistance is relatively weak at short distances, and increases only as it moves further out to sea, explains why the storm which has raged around equidistance in regard to the lateral delimitation of the exclusive economic zone and continental shelf has scarcely affected the territorial sea. In contrast to the law of continental shelf and exclusive economic zone delimitation, which has been continuously buffeted by violent and contradictory winds, the law of territorial sea

---

[97] The *Guinea/Guinea-Bissau* and *Dubai/Sharjah* cases covered the delimitation of the territorial sea. The *Beagle Channel* case was concerned purely with the delimitation of the territorial sea, but only at a modest level.

[98] For the state of the matter on the eve of the Second World War, see Gidel, vol. III, pp. 746ff, and pp. 765ff, where there is also a detailed examination of the classic *Portland Channel* (pp. 753ff) and *Grisbadarna* (pp. 767ff) cases. See also Rhee.

delimitation has remained sheltered from the storms. It gives the appearance of a calm and uncontroversial area of law.

There is a second, more important, point to be made about territorial sea delimitation, touching on the legal regime. While customary law, as defined by the courts for the delimitation of the shelf and zone, is based on the rule of equitable principles/equitable solution, the delimitation of the territorial sea is governed by the equidistance/special circumstances rule. Established by Article 12 of the 1958 Convention on the Territorial Sea and the Contiguous Zone and incorporated without any difficulty by UNCLOS III in Article 15 of the 1982 Convention, this rule is generally regarded as having become part of customary law for purposes of territorial sea delimitation. There may be a common law for the delimitation of the continental shelf and the exclusive economic zone but there is not, at least at first sight, a common law for the delimitation of these two areas and the territorial sea.

However, this was not always the case. The rules applicable to the delimitation of the territorial sea and to that of the continental shelf have common roots and originally coincided. It was only later that they parted company, leading to the present situation of different legal regimes. The circumstances and reasons for this separation are worth looking at. Is the break beyond repair? This may well not be so, and there are unmistakeable signs of a possible reunification.

The territorial sea: a laboratory for experiments in the law of maritime delimitation

It was the institution of the territorial sea which gave rise to several of the basic principles which underlie the theory of coastal projections, nowadays common to all maritime jurisdictions: the principle that the land dominates the sea, the mediating role of the coastal opening, the idea of the omni-directional projection. Delimitation of the territorial sea also gave birth to many of the concepts which spilt over first into the neighbouring fields of the continental shelf and, later on, the exclusive economic zone, and now constitute what might be called the common heritage of the law of maritime delimitation. The legal writings and arbitral awards from before the Second World War are a clear demonstration of how the major distinctions which were to dominate the controversies over the law of maritime delimitation in the 1950s were for the most part already established in the context of territorial sea delimitation. This is where we first find the distinction between opposite and adjacent coasts—Gidel contrasts ''narrow straits'' with ''adjacent States''—and it is here that the special difficulties posed by delimitation between adjacent coasts were first realized. It is here too that we first come across the geometric method of the median line and that of the thalweg (based on physical facts) for use between opposite coasts. Finally, it is here that, in the case of adjacent States, the advantages and inconveniences of the various available technical methods—prolongation of the land boundary, the perpendicular to this boundary, equidistance, etc.—were compared. The *Grisbadarna* case made it possible, almost in the language of today, to define the need to modify the line dictated by law in order to take into account "factual circumstances".[99] One cannot help being struck by the modern sound of those passages where Gidel, in 1934, said he was in favour of the median line, but added immediately that other methods must be envisaged "as a corrective to the flagrant inequalities which might result from the application of the median line which, in the absence of agreement to the contrary and exceptional physical circumstances, must be considered the rule of common law"; in short, said Gidel, the median line should apply unless there was agreement to the contrary or "exceptional physical conditions" leading to "a line to be determined, taking account of the nature of the area".[100] The main lines of the debate and the elements of the dialectic were all in place from this time: the distinction between equal and equitable division; between the rule and the exceptions to it; between the method of first step and the corrections to be made to take account of special physical circumstances.

In addition to this fundamental approach, there are also certain techniques developed for the delimitation of the territorial sea which have been extended to maritime delimitation in general. Such is the case, for example, with the equidistance method, which was invented for the delimitation of the territorial sea and which draws its inspiration from the envelope of arcs of circles technique, itself developed for drawing the outer limit of the territorial sea.[101]

[99] Permanent Court of Arbitration, Award of 23 October 1909, *UNRIAA*, vol. XI, p. 147 (with a note of the main commentaries); *RGDIP*, vol. 17, 1910, p. 177. In *Gulf of Maine*, the United States relied heavily on the *Grisbadarna* case (United States Memorial, para. 172ff), but the Chamber did not reflect this. It doubtless thought that such an old precedent relating to the delimitation of the territorial sea could scarcely be conclusive for a single maritime boundary delimitation in the 1980s.

[100] Gidel, vol. III, pp. 756-7. The passage quoted refers to opposite coasts. He took the same approach for a lateral delimitation: "The median line solution is, in principle, the one to be preferred to all others. But there are cases where it would involve real disadvantages . . . [and] mean a serious inequality between the two coastal States" (p. 771).

[101] See pp. 68ff above. On the arcs of circles method, see pp. 63ff above.

The unity of the legal regime of the 1958 Conventions

When the International Law Commission turned to the rules governing the delimitation of the territorial sea and the continental shelf, it saw the two problems *pari passu*, taking it for granted that they called for similar, if not identical, solutions. This fact is today largely forgotten, so great has been the divorce between the law of territorial sea delimitation and that of other maritime areas. Without going into the detail of the Commission's work, suffice it to recall that the Committee of Experts, consulted by the Commission in 1953 on the delimitation of the territorial sea, made the point that it had tried to find formulae which could also be used to delimit the continental shelf. Basing itself on this report, the Commission began with the articles relating to the delimitation of the continental shelf, and it was in the context of the continental shelf that the agreement/equidistance/special circumstances triangle was finalized; only later was it to be extended to the delimitation of the territorial sea.[102]

In the mind of the Commission, therefore, there was a close link between territorial sea and continental shelf delimitation regimes, a unity to be reflected in the Geneva Conventions, which applied the same equidistance/special circumstances rule to both delimitations.[103] Thus the Commission and the 1958 Conventions laid the foundations of a common law of maritime delimitation, transcending the different purposes and specific regimes of maritime areas. This made the break, when it came, all the more striking.

The break

Despite their common origin and same underlying principles, ten years after the Geneva Conventions the legal regime for the territorial sea and that for the continental shelf were to take different routes. More precisely, the delimitation of the territorial sea would remain unchanged, unaffected by the theoretical and judicial controversies; UNCLOS III's straightforward adoption of the regime established by the 1958 Convention is evidence of this

---

[102] See *ILCYB*, 1953, vol. I, p. 130, para. 62, and vol. II, pp. 79, 216ff; 1954, vol. II, pp. 6, 157.

[103] There is, however, a difference between the two regimes set up in 1958: "historic title" can be invoked for the delimitation of the territorial sea but not for the continental shelf, this concept being too new for such a concept to have any place in it. On the other hand, nothing is to be made, except by way of an unrealistic exegesis, of the fact that equidistance is displaced in respect of the territorial sea when another delimitation appears "necessary", and for the continental shelf when special circumstances "justify" another delimitation.

continuity. It is the law of continental shelf delimitation—followed, in time, by that for exclusive economic zone delimitation—which was to branch off from this common root, to pursue a path of schism and uncertainty contrasting strongly with the steady orthodoxy which has characterized the delimitation of the territorial sea over the last thirty years.

As we know, it was on the question of the legal role of equidistance in the delimitation process that the Court, in 1969, felt it had to give the signal for separation. Although the Court saw no objection to the equidistance/special circumstances rule governing delimitation of the territorial sea, it was opposed to this rule's becoming the norm of customary law governing delimitation of the continental shelf. As justification for this break-up of a legal regime hitherto homogenous, the Court put forward two explanations, neither of which, it has to be said, is convincing.

The first is based on an observation of fact:

> ... the distorting effects of lateral equidistance lines under certain conditions of coastal configuration are nevertheless comparatively small within the limits of territorial waters, but produce their maximum effect in the localities where the main continental shelf areas lie further out.[104]

The amplification of the effect produced by minor geographical features on an equidistance line the further one goes from the coast is an incontestable fact, as the Federal Republic of Germany graphically illustrated.[105] Was it really necessary, however, to separate so radically the legal regime for delimitation of the shelf and zone from that for territorial sea delimitation? This is where one may have doubts. Far from being unable to correct the amplification effect of minor geographic features as one moves further from the coast, the equidistance/special circumstances rule would itself have allowed the necessary adjustments. In order to obtain the desired equitable effect, all that would have been necessary was to recognize the incriminating geographical feature as having the character of a special circumstance. The separation of the legal regimes served no purpose, and the abandonment of the equidistance/special circumstances rule for the continental shelf and exclusive economic zone cannot be justified on this ground.

---

[104] *North Sea*, para. 59. Likewise, para. 8: "owing to the very close proximity of such waters to the coasts concerned, these effects are much less marked and may be very slight ...".

[105] ICJ *Memorials, North Sea*, vol. II, p. 29.

The second reason put forward by the Court is more subtle:

> There is also a direct correlation between the notion of closest proximity to
> the coast and the sovereign jurisdiction which the coastal State is entitled to
> exercise and must exercise, not only over the seabed underneath the
> territorial waters but over the waters themselves, which does not exist in
> respect of continental shelf areas where there is no jurisdiction over the
> superjacent waters, and over the seabed only for purposes of exploration and
> exploitation.[106]

Why should a legal regime giving equidistance (i.e., proximity) a
special role be more justified in the case of the territorial sea, a multi-
purpose jurisdiction exercised over both the seabed and the superjacent waters, than for the continental shelf, jurisdiction over which
is functional and limited to the seabed?[107] The Court sheds no light
on this point and the statement remains unexplained. In any case,
the distinction has now been overtaken since, in the majority of cases,
the continental shelf has been absorbed into the multi-purpose
jurisdiction of the exclusive economic zone. If, as the Court seems to
suggest, equidistance as a first step is justified when it is a matter of
delimiting a multi-purpose jurisdiction such as the territorial sea,
then it must be the more so for the delimitation of that other multi-
purpose jurisdiction, the 200 mile zone, which nowadays encompasses the continental shelf.

The 1969 divorce was to be confirmed in later cases, and the
explanations offered remained unchanged: on the one hand, the
distinction between delimitation over a short distance from the coast
and delimitation over a long one; on the other, the difference between
the multi-purpose jurisdiction of the territorial sea and the strictly
functional jurisdiction of the continental shelf.[108]

Towards reunification

The divorce between the law of territorial sea delimitation and the
delimitation of the continental shelf and exclusive economic zone
may seem to be final, but there is no overriding reason for the split.
It is conceivable that the gap may soon be breached and the law of
maritime delimitation, at its origin common to both the territorial
sea and the continental shelf and only later suffering disintegration,
may be reunified.

---

[106] *North Sea*, para. 59.
[107] Cf. *North Sea*, para. 42; *Anglo-French* award, paras. 80-1.
[108] *Gulf of Maine*, paras. 120, 160 and 161. Cf. *Tunisia/Libya*, para. 115.

There are already some signs of this, still modest, it is true, but too numerous to be ignored. In the *Beagle Channel* case, the Tribunal, in delimiting the territorial waters in the narrow part of the Channel, took into consideration "mixed factors of appurtenance, coastal configuration, equidistance, and also of convenience, navigability, and the desirability of enabling each party so far as possible to navigate in its own waters".[109] Would the reasoning have been different if it had been a question of delimiting the continental shelves or the exclusive economic zones? No less significant is the absence in *Guinea/Guinea-Bissau* of all suggestion of any distinction between the rules to be applied to that part of the delimitation line relating to the territorial sea and that relating to both the continental shelf and the exclusive economic zone.

The lost unity seems to be reconstituting itself around the rules of customary law developed by the courts rather than on the rule of equidistance/special circumstances, so much so that it would appear to be the legal regime for the delimitation of the territorial sea which is losing its particularity and becoming merged in the legal regime appertaining to the delimitation of the continental shelf and the exclusive economic zone. But, as will be seen, the common regime thus reconstituted is itself in the course of development towards a system in which equidistance will resume the privileged place which, until now, it has held only in the delimitation of the territorial sea.

---

[109] "... the Court has been guided ... by mixed factors of appurtenance, coastal configuration, equidistance, and also of convenience, navigability, and the desirability of enabling each party so far as possible to navigate in its own waters" (para. 110).

III

THE LEGAL REGIME:
TREATY LAW AND CUSTOMARY LAW

THE problem of the legal regime to govern a delimitation (as it happens, of the continental shelf) which was not the subject of any treaty between the two parties arose for the first time in the *North Sea* case. The Court refused to see this as a situation in which "rules are lacking"[110] and accordingly itself undertook to define the applicable norms.[111]

The Court had a simple formula immediately to hand which it could have used for this purpose. On the basis of its own analysis of the relationship between customary and treaty norms, it could have regarded Article 6 of the 1958 Continental Shelf Convention as the written expression of a customary rule, either because it endorsed or crystallized a customary rule which already existed or was in the course of formation, or because it would have led, as a result of the practice it provoked, to the eventual formation of such a rule. Article 6 lent itself particularly well to this mutation from a formally agreed treaty text to a customary norm of general application. Not all treaty provisions, whether bilateral or multilateral, are capable of such an extension, but this one undoubtedly was, first because of the importance of its content, which, in the absence of agreement to the contrary or any special circumstances requiring recourse to another method of delimitation, gave pride of place to equidistance;

---

[110] *North Sea*, para. 83.

[111] The practice has been established, especially in the drafting of special agreements, of referring to the "principles and rules of (or 'of the') international law applicable". In other areas of international law a distinction can be drawn between "principles", which, because of their generality, permit a certain flexibility of interpretation and require gradual translation into practice, and "rules", which are more precise. In maritime delimitation law, however, the two terms are undoubtedly synonymous. The phrase "principles and rules of international law" is intended to refer to the whole body of applicable legal norms, whatever their level of generality. The *Gulf of Maine* judgment, which is the only one to have given thought to this question, rightly says that this is "the use of a dual expression to convey one and the same idea" (*Gulf of Maine*, para. 79).

secondly, because of its flexibility, which allowed the delimitation
line to be adapted to fit the special circumstances of each particular
case; and finally, because of the care with which it had been worked
out over several meetings of the International Law Commission. In
short, everything predisposed this rule, which was both general and
particular, to become the customary norm applicable not only to all
continental shelf delimitations, even between States not party to the
1958 Convention, but also to those of the exclusive economic zone.
Such a development would have had a further justification in that the
regime established by this provision for the delimitation of the
continental shelf was identical in substance to that established by the
1958 Territorial Sea Convention for the delimitation of the territorial
sea. Were there not here the beginnings of a common law of maritime
delimitation?

*The judicial erosion of Article 6 and the fusion of the treaty regime with that of
customary law*

However, as we know only too well, this is not the route the courts
have followed. On the one hand, they have limited the application of
Article 6 to treaty relationships, and to delimitation of the continental
shelf; on the other, they have shown so little sympathy for the
provision as to rob it of its content and equate it with what they have
decided to define as the customary law governing the matter. These
two aspects must be carefully distinguished.

There is hardly any need to mention the responsibility the 1969
judgment carries for its refusal (nowadays almost a legal dogma) to
broaden Article 6 into a rule of general or customary international
law. Although it said it had no difficulty in regarding Articles 1-3 of
the Geneva Convention on the Continental Shelf as stating rules
which were part of general and customary international law, it
refused to see in Article 6 of this same Convention a provision which
could be "of a fundamentally norm-creating character".[112]

The Court put forward several arguments in support of this view.
Article 6, it said, "is so framed as to put second the obligation to
make use of the equidistance method, causing it to come after a
primary obligation to effect delimitation by agreement"; "rules of
international law can, by agreement, be derogated from" in
delimitation cases; the fact that the reference to equidistance in
Article 6 is qualified by that to special circumstances raises "doubts
as to the potentially norm-creating character of the rule"; the 1958

---

[112] *North Sea*, para. 72.

Convention allows reservations to Article 6 and therefore to the "equidistance principle".[113]

The reasoning has obviously gone adrift. In order to justify the non-normative character of Article 6 taken as a whole, with its three component parts, agreement, equidistance and special circumstances, the Court has put forward arguments the sole effect of which is to demonstrate that the equidistance method is not legally obligatory in all cases since international law sometimes allows recourse to other methods. By arguing in this way the Court has chosen the wrong target and, with its caricature reading, has made an innocent victim of Article 6. Far from building equidistance into a legally obligatory method, Article 6 states a rule diametrically the opposite: equidistance, certainly, but with the flexibility to allow a solution which takes account of the particular facts of each specific situation. Even if they had recognized Article 6 as having the character of a norm of customary law, the courts would not have been condemned, either in *North Sea* or in any later case, to adopt a solution based strictly on equidistance: the concept of special circumstances, an integral part of the rule, would have given them all the room for manoeuvre they needed. So the mutilating 1969 reading of Article 6 is not only unjustified. It also serves no purpose.

Confirmed some years later in the *Anglo-French* arbitral award,[114] the refusal to give Article 6 a place in the world of customary international law was to be taken up by the *Gulf of Maine* judgment, which extended it to the exclusive economic zone. The Chamber responded with a veritable barrage to Canadian attempts to see this provision, intended for the delimitation of the continental shelf, as the particular expression of a general rule applicable to all maritime delimitations. Article 6, the Chamber said, constitutes "special international law" governing only continental shelf delimitations and only delimitations between States party to the 1958 Convention; this provision is not "in the process of becoming a norm of general application"; and there is no "argument to justify the attempt to turn the provisions of Article 6 of the 1958 Convention into a general rule applicable as such to every maritime delimitation".[115] The refusal to be drawn into a revision of the doctrine laid down in 1969 could not have been more categoric.

But the Courts did not restrict themselves to the demolition of the treaty regime. Not content with limiting its field of application to the

---

[113] *Ibid.*
[114] *Anglo-French* award, para. 75.
[115] *Gulf of Maine*, paras. 114 and 123-4.

absolute minimum, they had no hesitation in interpreting it in such a way as to deprive it of all content of its own.

It must be said that the *North Sea* judgment is in no way to blame for this. The existence of two different regimes for the delimitation of the continental shelf underlies the whole of the Court's reasoning: on the one hand, Article 6, with its equidistance/special circumstances rule in which equidistance has a privileged place; and on the other, the customary regime, based on equitable principles and the equitable result, in which equidistance has no particular place.[116] The long debate as to whether or not Article 6 was opposable to the Federal Republic would have been no more than a pointless academic exercise had the Court regarded the content of customary international law and that of the treaty regime as identical.

We owe the attack upon the substance of Article 6 to the *Anglo-French* award. There is no doubt, this award proclaims,[117] in the wake of the 1969 judgment, that

> under Article 6 the equidistance principle ultimately possesses an obligatory force which it does not have in the same measure under the rules of customary law; for Article 6 makes the application of the equidistance principle a matter of treaty obligation for Parties to the Convention.

But this recognition of the specific nature of the treaty regime remains a matter of words, since the award spends a great deal of time demonstrating that the content of the two regimes is more or less identical and leads to much the same result. Article 6 is interpreted by the Court of Arbitration as being in substance identical to the rule of customary law, in other words as being based on the equitable and giving no special place to equidistance; thus, it can be presented as giving "particular expression to a general norm"—the customary norm—in which context it has to be read and interpreted.[118]

The 1977 award's reading of Article 6 is not convincing. The Court was certainly right to regard the concepts of equitable principles and equitable result as being incorporated into the treaty regime through the notion of special circumstances. The whole history of Article 6 is there to prove it.[119] But it did not explain why

---

[116] Paras. 25 and 69 of the *North Sea* judgment demonstrate well the Court's view that Article 6 instituted a legal regime different from that of customary international law.

[117] *Anglo-French* award, para. 70.

[118] *Ibid.*, paras. 65, 70, 75 and 97.

[119] See p. 170 below. Cf. the *Anglo-French* award, para. 70.

Article 6 had to be understood, contrary to the natural and ordinary meaning of the words, as refusing any special place to equidistance and, therefore, as identical in its content to the customary rule.[120] Instead of relying, as one would have expected, on the treaty provisions for the definition of the customary regime, the 1977 award followed the opposite course. It used the customary regime it was defining to take the heart out of the treaty regime and force it into the confines of the customary regime.

The *Gulf of Maine* judgment seems to have put a brake on this mutilation of the treaty regime. By observing that, in contrast to the customary regime, which limits itself to prescribing the objective of the equitable result, the Article 6 treaty regime prescribes also the use of equitable criteria and, above all, indicates the method to be used,[121] this judgment restores a certain independence to the Article 6 regime. This is a matter for congratulation even if, elsewhere, the judgment seems to follow in the footsteps of the 1977 award when it says that "[s]uch conventions must ... be seen against the background of customary international law and interpreted in its light".[122]

By refusing to accord the treaty rule of equidistance/special circumstances the status of a general rule, and by interpreting it in such a way as to deprive it of all particularity vis-à-vis customary law, the courts have thrown away the chance, rare when dealing with new subject-matter, of referring, for the definition of the customary regime governing the majority of delimitations, to treaty provisions which were the result of thorough consideration and are rich in content and carefully balanced. Ignoring the 1958 provisions which lend themselves so well to a transformation into general international law, the courts, paradoxically, have preferred to look to Articles 74

---

[120] Unless, of course, the Court of Arbitration, contrary to the interpretation generally given to the *Anglo-French* award, saw customary law as providing for recourse to equidistance as a first step. On this hypothesis, the *Anglo-French* award, far from basing the treaty regime on the customary regime, as is generally thought, would, on the contrary, have assimilated the customary to the conventional. Although the place accorded by the award to equidistance does not rule out this interpretation completely, the argument here will be based on the generally accepted interpretation.

[121] *Gulf of Maine*, paras. 86-9 and 118.

[122] *Ibid.*, para. 83. An example of the amalgam between the treaty regime and the customary regime is provided by the *Dubai/Sharjah* award which, in the context of the customary law governing the case, in order to determine the place of an island in the delimitation, resorted to the concept of "special circumstances" proper to the Article 6 regime (p. 256). The *Gulf of Maine* judgment likewise described the difference of length of the coasts of the parties as a "special circumstance" (*Gulf of Maine*, para. 184; cf. para. 215).

and 83 of the Montego Bay Convention,[123] even though Article 6
has an operative character and Articles 74 and 83 have not.[124] It is,
in fact, well known that these provisions, the text of which was the
result of a last-minute compromise designed to save the Conference,
secured agreement—and even then not unanimous—only at the cost
of maintaining silence on both equidistance and equitable principles,
that is to say, by backing away from the very matter which had been
at issue between two groups of States throughout the Conference.
Equitable principles had disappeared in the turmoil alongside equidistance. All that survived was the harmless mention of an equitable
solution. Need it be pointed out that these neutral provisions, far
from being a legal norm addressed to the judge or arbitrator, are
guidelines for negotiators, without any meaning or sanction? Need
one emphasize yet again that, apart from the requirement for an
equitable solution, Articles 74 and 83, in contrast to Article 6, remain
silent on the path to take, the *modus operandi*, in order to reach this
objective, even though it is on the problem of means—in other
words, on equitable principles and the methods of delimitation—that
the difficulties and controversies are concentrated? The lack of
content in these provisions, so empty of meaning that they are almost
non-provisions, has too often been mentioned, not least by the Court
itself,[125] for them reasonably to be considered a conventional basis
for the customary rules governing the matter.

[123] These articles, according to the *Gulf of Maine* judgment, contain an "identical
definition . . . of the rule of international law respecting delimitation" (*Gulf of Maine*,
para. 95). The *Guinea/Guinea-Bissau* award says that the solution must be sought "by
reference to the terms of Articles 74 . . . and 83 . . ." (*Guinea/Guinea-Bissau*, para. 88).

[124] Cf. Mbaye, *Libya/Malta*, Separate Opinion, p. 96: "Article 6 . . . establishes a
method of delimitation . . . The clause covering delimitation is . . . sufficient in itself to
supply the solution in the event of negotiations or judicial proceedings . . . Article 83 . . .
unlike Article 6 . . . has no self-sufficient existence". The origin and development of
Articles 74 and 83 are traced in detail in Oda, *Tunisia/Libya*, Dissenting Opinion, pp.
234-46. On the circumstances in which the texts were adopted, cf. Oxman, B.H., "The
Third United Nations Conference on the Law of the Sea: The Tenth Session (1981)",
American Journal of International Law, vol. 76, 1982, p. 14. See also Manner, pp. 630ff.

[125] "In the new text, any indication of a specific criterion which could give guidance
to the interested States in their effort to achieve an equitable solution has been excluded"
(*Tunisia/Libya*, para. 50). The definition given in Articles 74 and 83 of the rule of law
for delimitations "is . . . limited to expressing the need for settlement of the problem by
agreement and recalling the obligation to achieve an equitable solution. Although the
text is singularly concise it serves to open the door to continuation of the development
effected in this field by international case law" (*Gulf of Maine*, para. 95). The 1982
Convention "sets a goal to be achieved, but is silent as to the method to be followed to
achieve it. It restricts itself to setting a standard, and it is left to States themselves, or to
the courts, to endow this standard with specific content" (*Libya/Malta*, para. 28). Judge
Oda describes it as "a catchall provision that ought to satisfy both" [schools of thought],

The assimilation of the treaty regime to the customary is based, no doubt, on the laudable intention to avoid a divergence of the legal regimes governing maritime delimitation. It has, however, undoubtedly had regrettable side-effects. By reducing the role of equidistance even in the Article 6 regime, it has encouraged an excessive denigration of this method and has contributed to the concentration of the law of maritime delimitation on the finality of the result, itself dependent upon the actual facts of each particular case. It must therefore bear a part of the responsibility for the impoverishment of the normative density of the law of maritime delimitation.

The alteration of the concept of custom[126]

Once the courts refused to ground the customary rules, now almost supreme in the law of maritime delimitation, in the treaty provisions which were regarded as the written statement of general rules, one would have expected the content of those rules to be defined by reference to the two elements traditionally required for a customary rule: State practice of a certain uniformity and generality, and *opinio juris*, reflecting a conviction on the part of the States concerned that they were under a legal obligation to act in this way.[127]

There already exists a large body of State practice in the matter of maritime delimitation: unilateral practice in some cases, expressed in the various declarations and acts of municipal law; but above all, treaty practice, in a hundred or so delimitation agreements, some in respect of the territorial sea or the continental shelf, others—the frequency of which, as we have seen, has been increasing over the years—in respect of a single maritime boundary separating all the maritime jurisdictions of the States concerned. It should not be forgotten that treaties are usually regarded as a significant part

---

giving each "pleasure that the opposing school has not been expressly vindicated" (*Tunisia/Libya*, Dissenting Opinion, p. 246, para. 143; cf. *Libya/Malta*, Dissenting Opinion, p. 150, para. 48); and as an "empty provision" (*Libya/Malta*, Dissenting Opinion, p. 148, para. 46). Judge Gros called it a "truism", an "empty formula", an "unusable formula" (*Gulf of Maine*, Dissenting Opinion, p. 365, para. 8 and p. 366, para. 10).

[126] The discussion which follows repeats essentially the author's contribution to *Mélanges Ago* (Weil [2]).

[127] Although questioned by some writers, the doctrine of the two elements of customary law, adopted by Article 38 of the Statute of the Court and by the PCIJ in the *Lotus* case (PCIJ, *Series A*, No. 10, pp. 18, 28), has been confirmed several times by the ICJ (*North Sea*, para. 77; *Libya/Malta*, para. 27; *Military and Paramilitary Activities in and against Nicaragua (Nicaragua v. United States)*, ICJ *Reports*, 1986, pp. 97-8, paras. 183-4, and pp. 108-9, paras. 206-7; *ILR*, vol. 76, pp. 431-2, 442-3).

of State practice. Treaties not only determine the law between the parties, but are also a manifestation of the conduct of States and, as such, are just as capable of contributing to the formation of a customary rule as any other State conduct.[128] In every case so far brought before an international tribunal, the parties have, in fact, invoked State practice, each seeking to interpret it in a manner to support its views. In *Gulf of Maine*, Canada submitted to the Court, as an annex to its written pleadings, a volume containing the texts of all delimitation agreements previously concluded, with maps in support. Libya took the same step in its case against Malta.

It is therefore somewhat surprising that in one judgment after another, the courts, in defining the content of the applicable norms of customary law, appear to have turned their backs on State practice. When they do refer to it, it is to confirm a conclusion arrived at by other means, or to reject an argument put forward by one of the parties, rather than as direct evidence of the content of the customary rule. Thus the Anglo-French Court of Arbitration, *after* stating its views on the subject of equidistance, says that "[t]he truth of these observations is certainly borne out by State practice";[129] and it is *after* rejecting the British argument about the Hurd Deep and the Hurd Deep Fault Zone that the Court adds:

> Moreover, to attach critical significance to a physical feature [of this kind] ... would run counter to the whole tendency of State practice in the continental shelf in recent years.[130]

Likewise, it is *after* deciding that it was appropriate to attribute a certain effect to the Kerkennah Islands that the *Libya/Tunisia* judgment states: "The Court would recall, however, that a number of examples are to be found in State practice of delimitations"[131] attributing a partial effect to islands near to the coasts. In the same spirit, the *Gulf of Maine* decision refers to the Franco-Spanish

---

[128] On this point, cf. D'Amato, A.A., "The Concept of Custom in International Law", Ithaca, Cornell University Press, 1971, pp. 104, 113-4. In the *Nottebohm* case, the Court, with a view to establishing the customary rule of effective nationality, referred to the treaty practice of States, in particular treaties between States not party to the case (ICJ *Reports*, 1955, pp. 22-3). The courts similarly attach importance, for defining the customary law in the matter of compensation for the nationalization or expropriation of foreign property, to "the bilateral investment treaty practice of States, which much more often than not reflects the traditional international law standard of compensation for expropriation" (Iran-US Claims Tribunal, *SEDCO* case, interlocutory award of 27 March 1986, 10 IRAN-U.S. C.T.R. 180 at 185).

[129] *Anglo-French* award, para. 85.

[130] *Ibid.*, para. 107.

[131] *Tunisia/Libya*, para. 129.

agreement in the Gulf of Gascony to confirm its view, *previously* expressed, about whether respective coastal lengths should be taken into account.[132] In *Libya/Malta* the Court rejects the Libyan thesis that the landmass stretching behind the coast should be taken into consideration, observing[133] that "such a proposition finds no support in the practice of States, in the jurisprudence, in doctrine, or indeed in the work of the Third United Nations Conference on the Law of the Sea", and it is only *after* rejecting the theory of proportionality, for reasons of principle, as a method of delimitation that the Court adds:[134]

> Its weakness as a basis of argument, however, is that the use of proportionality as a method in its own right is wanting of support in the practice of States, in the public expression of their views at (in particular) the Third United Nations Conference on the Law of the Sea, or in the jurisprudence.

But it is on the most hotly disputed problem of maritime delimitation, that of the place of equidistance in the delimitation process, that the courts have shown the greatest reluctance to give State practice a decisive role. It cannot be seriously contested that the great majority of agreements concluded between States have used this method or one of its variants.[135] The Anglo-French Court of Arbitration, however, seems to have been alone in drawing certain direct consequences from this practice for a statement of the applicable law.[136] Other judgments have sought rather to minimize it. The attitude of the courts is in fact somewhat variable, if not, indeed, contradictory.

In some cases the courts take a position of negative principle: State practice is not decisive or even relevant in the formulation of a customary rule. Three reasons are put forward in support of this position. The first is the meagreness of the practice which, "owing to the relative newness of the question", is not yet "sufficiently extensive and convincing" to generate a customary rule.[137] The second is that, since each situation is *sui generis*, no legal conclusions can be drawn from the precedents, however many there may be. The

---

[132] *Gulf of Maine*, para. 184.

[133] *Libya/Malta*, para. 49.

[134] *Ibid.*, para. 58.

[135] See p. 269 below.

[136] *Anglo-French* award, paras. 85 and 249 (regarding the "variants of equidistance"). The text of these passages is quoted below, pp. 270ff.

[137] *Gulf of Maine*, paras. 81 and 111.

Gulf of Maine judgment is particularly firm in this respect. "The practice . . . is there", it says, "to demonstrate that each specific case is, in the final analysis, different from all the others, that it is monotypic . . .", so that "statistical considerations afford no indication either of the greater or lesser degree of appropriateness of any particular method, or of any trend in favour thereof discernible in international customary law".[138] Finally, the third reason for denying State practice any relevance is that when States resort to the equidistance method, they do not do so because they feel themselves "legally compelled . . . by reason of a rule of customary law";[139] what, therefore, is missing is *opinio juris*.

In other cases, by contrast, the courts, far from denying any role to State practice, deduce from it a precise but negative legal conclusion: since some treaty delimitations reject equidistance, customary law cannot accord this method a privileged position. Agreements based on non-equidistance weigh heavier in the eyes of the courts than equidistance agreements and have greater evidentiary power. State practice is not rejected *en bloc*, but only to the extent that it would favour equidistance. This double standard— that, although equidistance is often used the fact that it is not *always* proves that it has no more value than any other method—is more or less a constant in the case-law.[140]

It is, however, arguable that the Court is losing some of its reluctance to take account of State practice. In *Libya/Malta*, it states that "[i]t is of course axiomatic that the material of customary international law is to be looked for primarily in the actual practice and *opinio juris* of States",[141] and explains that it has "no doubt about the importance of State practice in this matter".[142] A more careful reading, however, gives the lie to this impression: it is only because in this case "there has . . . been much debate between the Parties as to the significance . . . of State practice in the matter" that the Court[143] thought it useful to pronounce on the problem. Malta had presented State practice from a new point of view. Practice,

---

[138] *Ibid.*, para. 159.

[139] *North Sea*, para. 78.

[140] *Ibid.*; *Tunisia/Libya*, paras. 109-10 (although the formulation, in this passage, is quite a balanced one); *Gulf of Maine*, paras. 107 and 162-3; *Libya/Malta*, para. 43.

[141] *Libya/Malta*, para. 27.

[142] *Ibid.*, para. 44. Several separate opinions give an important place to State practice (Sette-Camara, Separate Opinion, pp. 61-2; Ruda, Bedjaoui, Jiménez de Aréchaga, Joint Separate Opinion, pp. 78-80, paras. 7-14; Valticos, Separate Opinion, pp. 107-8, paras. 10-11).

[143] *Libya/Malta*, para. 27.

according to Malta,[144] "need not be seen as evidence of a particular rule of customary law, but must provide significant and reliable evidence of normal standards of equity". The Court rejects this approach and confirms its previous position: even if practice offers "impressive evidence that the equidistance method can in many different situations yield an equitable result", it "falls short of proving the existence of a rule prescribing the use of equidistance, or indeed of any method", even at the start of the delimitation process and with the reservation of a final adjustment in the light of the relevant circumstances.[145] The tone may have changed but the substance remains the same.

To be fair, this judicial caution is in many ways understandable. It has already been noted that treaty delimitations—whether based on equidistance or not—are not necessarily inspired by a sense of legal obligation. Some are intended to fall within a legal framework; others have much more to do with considerations of expediency and are based on political or economic concerns remote from the law.[146] The courts are therefore justified in refusing to see the precedents drawn from State practice as the expression of an *opinio juris* creative of a customary rule. The courts are also right to emphasize that, because of the specific nature of each particular situation, the formation of a customary rule on the basis of treaty delimitations must be approached with extreme caution. That said, the justifications put forward in the various judgments are not always absolutely decisive. It will not be possible for much longer to speak of the poverty of practice given that already, as the Court pointed out in *Libya/Malta*, "[o]ver seventy such agreements have been identified and produced to the Court",[147] and that this number is growing year by year.[148] Nor is the argument about the particularity of each case entirely convincing. It could be put forward in all fields, not just that of maritime delimitation, and, taken to extremes, would prevent the formation of any new customary rule on the basis of repeated practice. Nor is it clear why the minority of non-equidistant precedents should have a greater power to create custom than the equidistant majority. As to the lack of *opinio juris*, how can it be

[144] *Ibid.*, para. 44.

[145] *Ibid.*

[146] See pp. 111ff above.

[147] *Libya/Malta*, para. 44.

[148] There is, as yet, no study, or even an exhaustive compilation of all maritime delimitation agreements. Apart from the two volumes produced for the Court in *Gulf of Maine* and *Libya/Malta*, (p. 150 above), reference may be made to *Limits in the Seas, New Directions*, Conforti and Francalanci, Jagota [1] and [2], Prescott.

denied that repeated usage can, by that very repetition, lead to the presumption of the existence of the psychological element necessary for customary law?

However, the most serious objection to the position taken by the courts lies elsewhere. It would be wrong to think of *opinio juris* fixing necessarily on a prescriptive or prohibitive rule. It may also consist in the conviction of States that on a given point there is a permissive rule. The exclusive economic zone became an institution of customary law because States came to the view that it had become legally *possible* to proclaim such a zone, without there being the least suggestion that they regarded this proclamation as *obligatory*. In the same way, treaty practice in respect of equidistance at least establishes an *opinio juris* according to which recourse to this method is legally indicated in various situations because in these situations it leads to an equitable result. To pick up a comment from *Gulf of Maine*: ''The absence of an obligation to do something must not be confused with an obligation not to do it''.[149] Treaty practice on equidistance ought to be able to play a part in the formation of the customary law of delimitation as much as the first declarations or domestic legislation did in the formation of the customary concept of the continental shelf.

Since, according to reliable testimony, governments always begin the negotiation of a maritime delimitation by considering an equidistance line, while at liberty subsequently to modify it,[150] there is no reason why this practice should not be taken into account in the development of the customary law governing the delimitation process. What is true of the process of delimitation is equally true of the substantive solutions. It cannot be denied that a delimitation on which two States agree reflects their view of the equity of both the method of delimitation and the result, since governments are hardly likely to subscribe to a solution which they would consider inequitable. The moment one finds that, in the great majority of cases, States regard as equitable delimitations based on equidistance or one of its variants, it is difficult to see why international tribunals should refuse to integrate this element of State conduct into the determination of the customary rules governing the matter. This conduct certainly does not show that States regard equidistance as a legally obligatory method, but it does show that they often, indeed usually, regard it as the appropriate method. Why is this massive and

---

[149] *Gulf of Maine*, para. 180.
[150] On this practice, see p. 206 below.

impressive fact given no place in the definition of the customary law? In this area, where equity can so easily slide into subjectivity, it would seem that State practice should at the very least be regarded as an *objective yardstick of equity*.

In other fields, a customary rule has been founded on sometimes the most skeletal of practice, and there has even been talk of the possibility of "instant custom". Is it not paradoxical that in the matter of maritime delimitation, where there is a wealth of practice, the content of customary law has been determined by the courts, if not by completely ignoring that practice, at least by according it only a modest supporting role? Is it not regrettable that it should thus have been possible for "a divorce . . . to set in between the treaty practice of States, to which Article 38 of the Statute of the Court refers, and the Court's jurisprudence" on the important question of the role of equidistance in the law of maritime delimitation?[151] We have here a first indication that in speaking of customary law in this context, it is perhaps not quite the same custom as elsewhere.

There is a further indication that this impression is correct. Once the courts decide they can, or must, decide customary norms independently of State usage, they are forced, in the absence of any other basis, to decide these norms themselves, directly. It is, of course, generally accepted that international courts always have an important role in deciding what the custom is. The formation of customary law is too fluid and diffuse a process for the intervention of an authority with the task of certifying, in some way, the maturation of this process to be avoided. Usually, it is a case of certifying something which predates the certification and has an existence with or without that certification. Here, in contrast, the customary norm has no existence until the judge determines its content. It is this determination which gives it life and identity. Custom is here defined without reference to any State conduct. It is disembodied custom. The content of the customary law no longer derives from a combination of State practice and *opinio juris* but directly from the law-making power of the international courts. In short, customary law is none other than judge-made law.

If this observation is correct, it means that customary law does not here show the specific characteristics attributed to it in other areas. No longer is it that "fruit of spontaneous germination" which Professor Ago contrasted with the *jus positum* produced by a "source", i.e. by the act of a competent authority set in time and

---

[151] Valticos, *Libya/Malta*, Separate Opinion, p. 108, para. 11.

space.[152] The legal force of the customary norm in this case does not derive from a spontaneous process but from the will of an identifiable human authority which has effected its *"positio"*, its "establishment", in an act creative of law and itself easily identifiable. The law of maritime delimitation no longer falls (other than as a matter of mere words) under Article 38(b) of the Statute of the Court—"international custom, as evidence of a general practice accepted as law"—but rather under 38(d), "judicial decisions". In a word, customary law is here no longer "spontaneous law" but "positive law". It is no longer custom in anything but name.

This is perhaps the underlying explanation for certain features of the case-law on maritime delimitation: the difficulty the courts have in moving from the particular of the given case to the general inherent in every legal norm; their problems in defining the relationship between law and equity; the doubts which assail them when they have to choose between the concept of a customary law which limits itself to prescribing an equitable result and one which also lays down the rules for reaching such a result. The importance attributed by the law of maritime delimitation to a customary law, which is largely detached from practice, and in reality the product of the law-making power of the courts, raises the question of the normative density of the law.

---

[152] Ago, R., "Droit positif et droit international", *Annuaire français de droit international*, 1977, pp. 14ff, *passim*.

PART III

THE NORMATIVE DENSITY OF THE LAW OF MARITIME DELIMITATION

PART III

THE NORMATIVE DENSITY
OF THE LAW OF
MARITIME DELIMITATION

I

THE THREE LEVELS OF NORMATIVITY
AND THE PROBLEM OF EQUITY

As we have just seen, the courts, in determining the law governing maritime delimitation, have chosen not to rely on either the 1958 Treaty provisions or State practice. Nor have they found much help in the rather hollow 1982 Law of the Sea Convention provisions on the delimitation of the continental shelf and the exclusive economic zone. Instead, they have looked to their own imagination for the essentials of the rules which form what they have called the customary or general international law of maritime delimitation.

It is to this sort of spontaneous generation that the customary law of maritime delimitation owes one of its distinguishing features, its continuing relative lack of legal rules. Basing themselves on the *sui generis* nature of each particular situation and the novelty of the subject-matter, the courts have always stressed the rudimentary character of maritime delimitation law which is limited to providing a few relatively abstract guidelines, without any detailed rules. It is, the courts say, for them to adapt these guidelines to the various situations which come before them, without their freedom of judgment being hampered by pre-existing norms of general application. This theme of the poverty of the law of maritime delimitation was developed furthest in the *Gulf of Maine* judgment. Customary international law, it says,

... can of its nature only provide a few basic legal principles, which lay down guidelines to be followed with a view to an essential objective. It cannot also be expected to specify the equitable criteria to be applied or the practical, often technical, methods to be used for attaining that objective ...

A body of detailed rules is not to be looked for in customary international law ... it is therefore unrewarding, especially in a new and still unconsolidated field ... to look to general international law to provide a ready-made set of rules that can be used for solving any delimitation problems that arise.[1]

The low profile assigned to the regulatory content of customary law would be acceptable if this were fixed at a well-defined level. Unfortunately, this is not the case, and it is the ups and downs within this area of low normative content that makes the description of the law of maritime delimitation particularly difficult.

The "fundamental norm"

The only uncontested element, on which all the judgments agree, is the celebrated "fundamental norm" for which the *Gulf of Maine* judgment provided a "better formulation" or "reformulation" and "whose existence ... is apparent from an examination of the realities of international legal relations".[2] This common denominator of "every maritime delimitation" prescribes that

... delimitation is to be effected by the application of equitable criteria and by the use of practical methods capable of ensuring, with regard to the geographical configuration of the area and other relevant circumstances, an equitable result.[3]

However helpful it may be, this fundamental norm is not enough to determine how much normative content there is in the law of maritime delimitation. It is still necessary to know whether this norm is the sole element or whether it is just one among others. This is precisely the point on which there is uncertainty. Apart from the hard and indisputable core of this fundamental norm, what the courts offer for analysis is an ill-defined haze.

Equitable solution, equitable principles, methods

To simplify matters, one can say that three concepts are present in

[1] *Gulf of Maine*, paras. 81 and 111.
[2] *Ibid.*, paras. 111-12.
[3] *Ibid.*

the case-law, each corresponding to a different level of normative density.

In the first concept, the law of maritime delimitation contains no rule of law other than the fundamental norm; it is limited to this one norm which alone forms the legal corpus of maritime delimitation. According to this approach, neither equitable principles nor the methods of delimitation are part of this corpus. The law is silent on them and it is for the courts to decide in full freedom what they are *on a case by case basis*. What this means, to put it bluntly, is that the equitable principles which in a way make up the philosophy of the law of maritime delimitation do not derive from a legal definition and that the law is indifferent to them. A court can decide in one case that equity implies equality and in another that it does not; in one case that it is right to bend to nature's whims, in another that it is incumbent on the court to correct them; in one case, that equity requires a division of the resources of the region, in another that this consideration has no part to play. More justifiably, the methods of delimitation also escape legal regulation; any method, or combination of methods, is legally acceptable provided it leads to an equitable result.

With this approach, the normativity is at its lowest. The law prescribes an equitable outcome, but goes no further. What is equitable, what inequitable, and, as a corollary, what circumstances should be considered relevant, are all outside the legal domain, as also is the choice of practical methods of delimitation. True enough, international law is not entirely silent on the issue, but all it actually has to offer is the fundamental norm of the equitable result. Essential as the requirement of an equitable result may be, without legal guidance on how to achieve that result, we are still left floundering. One cannot but agree with the disillusioned remark of three members of the Court that a delimitation process "dominated by a 'fundamental norm' . . . is as uninstructive as it is all-embracing".[4]

A little higher on the scale of normative density is the approach which includes the definition of equitable principles within the legal framework. Here, the law is not content to prescribe an equitable result; it also takes a view on what is to be understood by equitable and inequitable, and, to this end, it includes a criterion allowing a distinction to be made, in each case, between those facts which are legally relevant and those which are not. But the law still does not

---

[4] Ruda, Bedjaoui, Jiménez de Aréchaga, *Libya/Malta*, Joint Separate Opinion, p. 90, para. 37.

prescribe methods; whether at the start of the delimitation process or in its final stage, the court can choose any method it likes.

At the highest level of all, the legal field is broadened to include, in addition to the definition of equitable principles and relevant circumstances, the methods themselves. The law no longer leaves the courts free reign; it decides the method to be used at the start of the operation, and it may even intervene to determine the choice of methods for adjusting the line resulting from this starting method to meet the exigencies of equity.

Law, equity, ex aequo et bono

Equity and its associated problems are at the heart of this uncertainty. Depending on the place and content accorded it, the idea of equity allows the level of normativity to rise and fall. A law which required the delimitation to be equitable, but specified neither the content of equity nor the methods of delimitation, would be placed at zero on the scale of normativity. A law which required an equitable result and also had something to say about the equitable criteria, but not about methods, would rise to what one might call the first degree of normativity. And finally, a law which, not content with requiring an equitable result and defining what equity means, also included legal rules regarding methods, would reach the second degree of normativity. From the very first stumblings of the law of maritime delimitation, equity has occupied a central place in the body of legal norms relating to it. Though not mentioned in the 1958 Conventions, all that went before, from the pre-Second World War work up to the International Law Commission's discussions and commentaries, by way of the Truman Proclamation and the 1953 report of the Committee of Experts, shows that the equidistance/special circumstances rule incorporated in the 1958 Conventions was intended precisely for the purpose of avoiding inequitable solutions and reaching equitable results.[5] The courts have rightly regarded the requirement of equity as "logically underlying" the Geneva provisions.[6] Included by implication in the 1958 Conventions, the idea of equity dominates the case-law. There is not a single judgment, not a single award, which does not see it as a major axis of the law of maritime delimitation. And it is scarcely necessary to recall that an equitable result is the only legal element of any substance in the 1982 Convention relating to the delimitation of the continental shelf and the exclusive economic zone. It should

---

[5] Cf. pp. 169ff below.
[6] *Gulf of Maine*, para. 89. Cf. *Anglo-French* award, para. 70.

be noted that, in parallel with this terminology of the "equitable" and "inequitable", the *North Sea* judgment also used the words "reasonable" and "unreasonable".[7] This variation of language persists in the subsequent cases.[8] Taken as a whole, however, the terminology based on reason and the reasonable has retreated to the wings, leaving the centre-stage to the ideas of equity and the equitable. A semantic quarrel? Perhaps it is something more, a point to which we shall return.

Equity is defined by the courts both negatively—it does not mean a decision *ex aequo et bono*—and positively—it is a part of the law.

The courts have been careful to distinguish between equity and *ex aequo et bono*. The solution arrived at must certainly be equitable, but that does not mean that it must necessarily be the same as if the court had been asked by the parties to decide *ex aequo et bono*. The courts obviously attach a good deal of importance to this distinction since they come back to it in case after case.[9] This probably explains the long legal expositions with which the majority of judgments open.

If equity is regarded by the courts as different from *ex aequo et bono*, it is because, looked at from a positive point of view, it must be seen as being part of the law. The courts know they must decide on the basis of law and they say, loud and clear "The Chamber is . . . bound . . . to achieve a result on the basis of law";[10] "A delimitation is a legal operation . . . [which] must . . . be based on considerations of law".[11] In applying equitable principles with a view to reaching an

---

[7] ". . . the use of this method [equidistance] . . . can under certain circumstances produce results that appear on the face of them to be extraordinary, unnatural or unreasonable" (*North Sea*, para. 24); ". . . provided that, by the application of equitable principles, a reasonable result is arrived at" (*ibid.*, para. 90); unity of deposit is "a factual element which it is reasonable to take into consideration in the course of the negotiations" (*ibid.*, para. 97). Cf. Salmon, J., "Le concept de raisonnable en droit international public", *Mélanges offerts à Paul Reuter*, Paris, Pedone, 1981, p. 447.

[8] ". . . the reasonable or unreasonable—the equitable or inequitable—effects . . ." (*Anglo-French* award, para. 100); "[w]hat is reasonable and equitable in any given case must depend on its particular circumstances . . ." (*Tunisia/Libya*, para. 72); special circumstances can make an equal division of overlapping areas "unreasonable" (*Gulf of Maine*, para. 115); corrections must be made to the "unreasonable" effects of such a division (*ibid.*, para. 196); an uncorrected median line would risk producing an "unreasonable effect" (*ibid.*, para. 220).

[9] "There is . . . no question . . . of any decision *ex aequo et bono*" (*North Sea*, para. 88); "[a]pplication of equitable principles is to be distinguished from a decision *ex aequo et bono* . . . . this is very far from being an exercise of discretion or conciliation" (*Tunisia/Libya*, para. 71); "[t]he Chamber is bound . . . not to take a decision *ex aequo et bono* . . ." (*Gulf of Maine*, para. 59); the international arbitrator is neither "endowed with discretionary powers", nor "authorized to decide *ex aequo et bono*" (*Guinea/Guinea-Bissau*, para. 88).

[10] *Gulf of Maine*, para. 59.

[11] *Guinea/Guinea-Bissau*, para. 120.

equitable result, it is, they like to repeat, law which they are deciding, because equity is part of the law and because it is law. There is no clash of opposites between law and equity, but rather an integration of the two. There is virtual synonymy between them. The formulae expressing this legal doctrine are well-known but merit repetition.

> It is not a question of applying equity simply as a matter of abstract justice, but of applying a rule of law which itself requires the application of equitable principles . . . *the decision finds its objective justification in considerations lying not outside but within the rules*, and . . . it is precisely a rule of law that calls for the application of equitable principles.[12]

> The legal concept of equity is a general principle directly applicable as law . . . the Court . . . is bound to apply equitable principles *as part of international law*.[13]

> The justice of which equity is an emanation, is not abstract justice but justice according to the rule of law . . . the normative character of equitable principles applied *as a part of general international law* is important . . . .[14]

To explain why the law has made equity its own, and perhaps to give it greater force, the judgments emphasize that law and equity are close because they start from and give expression to the same idea, the idea of justice.[15] This is true enough but goes too far. If law and equity are the twin daughters of justice, *ex aequo et bono* is a third. From law to *ex aequo et bono* by way of equity is a seamless continuum. So much is this the case, that, however much the courts assimilate equity to the law, they have sometimes given the impression of leaning rather in the direction of *ex aequo et bono*. The very emphasis in the repeated pronouncements on the subject of

---

[12] *North Sea*, paras. 85 and 88.

[13] *Tunisia/Libya*, para. 71.

[14] *Libya/Malta*, paras. 45-6. The Court took a similar position in respect of land boundaries. The Chamber said, in the *Frontier Dispute (Burkina Faso/Mali)* case, that it was not its task, unless the parties asked it to do so, to decide *ex aequo et bono*, in other words to carry out "an adjustment of their respective interests". It must avoid any use of equity *contra legem* or *praeter legem* and stick strictly to "equity *infra legem*, that is, that form of equity which constitutes a method of interpretation of the law in force and is one of its attributes" (ICJ *Reports*, 1986, pp. 567-8, para. 28). Since the courts have not used the terminology *contra, praeter* and *infra legem* in maritime delimitation matters, it has not been used in this book.

[15] "Whatever the legal reasoning of a court of justice, its decisions must by definition be just, and therefore in that sense equitable" (*North Sea*, para. 88); "equity as a legal concept is a direct emanation of the idea of justice" (*Tunisia/Libya*, para. 71; the phrase was quoted in the *Frontier Dispute*, ICJ *Reports*, 1986, p. 633, para. 149); "the justice of which equity is an emanation" (*Libya/Malta*, para. 45).

equity "as a legal concept"[16] cannot but arouse the suspicion that it is necessary, from time to time, to retrieve the position.

This is all the more so since the courts are far from unanimous on the nature of the links between equity and the law. There is no need to enter into the doctrinal argument over the relationship between the two concepts in general or in public international law:[17] for our purposes, it suffices to say that two trends have emerged, one or other of which predominates according to which judgment one is reading. Sometimes they co-exist within the same judgment.

Equity as a corrective and autonomous equity

According to one view, equity is a corrective, intended to remedy the inequity produced, in some circumstances, by the application of the rule of law. This concept is based on the idea that the legal norm, which is by nature general and therefore capable of application to a range of cases, can sometimes produce an inequitable result. The rule of law itself prescribes that it can then be modified. From this point of view, equity is a rule of substitution which, in cases where the application of the general rule leads to an inequity, allows a more flexible rule to be applied, one more appropriate to that particular

---

[16] *Tunisia/Libya*, para. 71.

[17] There is a vast literature on the subject. Among recent works, for example, are: Degan, V.D., "L'équité et le droit international", La Haye, Nijhoff, 1970; Visscher, Ch. de, "De l'équité dans le règlement arbitral ou judiciaire de droit international public", Paris, Pedone, 1972; Pirotte, O., "La notion d'équité dans la jurisprudence de la Cour internationale de Justice", *Revue générale de droit international public*, vol. 69, 1973, p. 92; Akehurst, M., "Equity and General Principles of Law", *International and Comparative Law Quarterly,* vol. 25, 1976, p. 801; Lauterpacht, E., "Equity, Evasion, Equivocation and Evolution in International Law", Proceedings and Committee Reports of the American Branch of the ILA, 1977-8, p. 33; Reuter, P., "Quelques réflexions sur l'équité en droit international", *Revue belge de droit international*, vol. 15, 1980, p. 165; Bilge, S., 'Le nouveau rôle des principes équitables en droit international", *Festschrift für Rudolf Bindschedler*, Berne, Stämfli, 1980, p. 105; Rosenne, S., "Equitable principles and the Compulsory Jurisdiction of International Tribunals", *ibid.*, p. 410; Bardonnet, D., "Equité et frontières terrestres", *Mélanges offerts à Paul Reuter*, Paris, Pedone, 1981, p. 35; Chemillier-Gendreau, M., "La signification des principes équitables dans le droit international contemporain", *Revue belge de droit international*, vol. 16, 1981-82, p. 509; Sohn, L.B., "The role of Equity in the Jurisprudence of the International Court of Justice", *Mélanges Georges Perrin*, Lausanne, Payot, 1984, p. 303. There are references to equity in maritime delimitation matters in many of the works mentioned in the bibliography, notably the majority of the commentaries on judgments and awards. For recent works on the subject as a whole, see in particular Degan, Jiménez de Aréchaga (who takes a position firmly against the corrective role of equity advocated here) and Virally.

case. One could say that the law has two irons in the fire: one for the majority of cases, for those situations which might be described as normal, the other for certain abnormal and exceptional cases. Equity thus conceived does not derogate from the law, it is *within* the law on the same basis as the general rule which it supports and completes. In the words of one judge, "Equity is ... achieved, not merely by a singular decision of justice, but by the justice of that singular decision".[18]

Interpreted thus, equity comes into play only after the inequity of the result produced by the application of the general law has been established. It does not appear as a primary element, but only at a second stage. One is tempted to say that its role is not so much the positive assurance of an equitable result as the negative avoidance of an inequitable one.

Seen in this corrective role, equity tends to have a degree of objectivity. It is not a desire for moral justice which leads to the preference for the rule of the particular over that of the normal, but the objective finding that, on the face of it, a result is inappropriate. It is manifest, obvious inequity, indisputable by any normally enlightened mind, that calls for the correction. To the extent that the idea of *reasonable* is more objective than *equitable*, the terminology of *reason* will be more appropriate than that of *equity*. Equity, on this basis, is an affair of the head rather than the heart.

According to the second approach, equity is no longer an alternative norm, but is viewed as an independent factor in delimitation, in the sense that the court will derive the solution it deems equitable directly and without intermediary from its apprehension of the facts of the case. Looked at in this way, there are no longer normal situations and abnormal, but only specific situations, each of them different from the others. This is taking the *unicum* theory to extremes. Instead of trying, negatively, to avoid an inequitable result, it is a question of searching, positively, for an equitable one. This conception gives pride of place to the facts. Avoiding any general norm, it seeks to fashion each solution to its particular circumstances. This means that the legal quality of equity hangs by a tenuous thread. In a way, the law half-opens the door for an instant of reason, the time it takes to prescribe recourse to equity, after which it withdraws on tip-toe, leaving equity in command. In theory, equity plays its role under the law, as its proxy, one might say, rather on the *renvoi* principle, but this connection is more verbal than real. It is a little as if municipal law simply provided that the

---

[18] Jiménez de Aréchaga, *Tunisia/Libya*, Separate Opinion, p. 106, para. 25.

courts should apply equitable penalties to the facts which they regard as delictual. Would the principles *nullum crimen sine lege* and *nulla poena sine lege* still be respected? No longer just a corrective to the legal norm, but with direct and independent effect, equity, with this approach, ends up replacing the norm and taking the place of the law. It is no use saying that equity remains a legal concept because it is the law which determines when it is to be applied. Equity thus conceived inevitably drifts from the objectivity of the reasonable and the unreasonable into the subjectivity of the just and the unjust. The distinction between this equity which is theoretically legal and the pure equity of *ex aequo et bono* is a fine one.

II

JUDICIAL HESITATIONS

THE courts seem to have had difficulty in making up their minds between the three degrees of normativity and the two conceptions of equity. It is easy enough to find the minimal normativity option set out in one judgment or another, but the courts' choices between the second level, where the rules cover equitable principles but not methods, and the third, where methods are also covered, remain unclear. The choice between equity as a corrective and equity as an independent force seems even more muddled. A number of combinations between these two sets of variables have been tried and it is sometimes difficult to grasp quite what the courts have in mind. To put it at its simplest, one could say that the *North Sea* case and the *Anglo-French* case in essence adopted the intermediate view of normativity—the *Anglo-French* award even leant towards an assumption that methods were included in the rules—and inclined towards a corrective view of equity. *Tunisia/Libya, Gulf of Maine* and, to a lesser extent, *Guinea/Guinea-Bissau*, inclined towards a minimal normativity and autonomous equity. With *Libya/Malta*, the conception of equity simply as a corrective returned in full strength, but, at the same time, the normative content was seen as extending to principles and even, albeit tentatively, to methods.

The antecedents

It is not surprising that it was the corrective approach which tempted the courts at the beginning. This concept had put down solid roots in both practice and theory well before the Court had to tackle the problem of equity in 1969. The idea of correcting the inequity which sometimes results from the inflexibility of the normal method dates from before the Second World War. This, of course, was the approach adopted by the *Grisbadarna* arbitral award and, more systematically, by Gidel,[19] for the delimitation of the territorial sea.

---

[19] See p. 137 above.

The work of the International Law Commission had been dominated by the same idea for both the territorial sea and the continental shelf. After a period of wavering, when fears were expressed that there might not be any rule of law in the matter and that the only way out, in the case of a dispute, might be through an *ex aequo et bono* arbitration,[20] the rapporteur had suggested putting forward the median line as the rule, at least between opposite coasts, adding that "this solution, however, would not be applicable if the special configuration of the coastline necessitated modifications".[21] At a technical level, the Committee of Experts consulted by the Commission had proposed the median line as the normal method for both the territorial sea and the continental shelf, adding that, in the case of opposite coasts, "There may, however, be special reasons . . . which may divert the boundary from the median line", and that, in the case of adjacent coasts, "In a number of cases this may not lead to an equitable solution . . . ".[22] It was against this background that the idea of a general formula, equidistance, to be corrected in particular cases where it led to inequitable results, had found its way onto the Commission's desk.[23] To give expression to this idea, a member of the Commission, Mr. Spiropoulos, had suggested following the mention of equidistance with the formula "unless another boundary line is justified by special circumstances",[24] a formula which, as we know, was to be a resounding success.

The Commission had clearly set out the significance of this solution in the commentary on its draft articles: to make of equidistance a "rule" endowed with "elasticity", "flexibility". One would depart from the "general rule, based on the principle of equidistance" when this was "necessitated by any exceptional configuration of the coast, as well as the presence of islands or navigable channels". In this case, one would proceed to make "reasonable modifications".[25] In short, equidistance, but with safety-valves.

The Geneva Conference took the same line. In the course of debate, Commander Kennedy of the United Kingdom delegation gave some examples of special circumstances which would justify a deviation from the median line, namely, the presence of islands,

[20] See pp. 103-4 above.

[21] *ILCYB*, 1952, vol. II, p. 38.

[22] *ILCYB*, 1953, vol. II, p. 79.

[23] See, for example, *ILCYB*, 1953, vol. I, p. 106, para. 39; p. 126, para. 14; p. 127, para. 35; p. 128, paras. 37-8.

[24] *Ibid.*, p. 130, para. 62.

[25] *ILCYB*, 1953, vol. II, p. 216, para. 82; 1956, vol. II, pp. 272 and 300.

navigation channels, certain coastal configurations.[26] The 1958 Conventions endorsed this equidistance/special circumstances rule for both the territorial sea and the continental shelf.[27]

The passing supremacy of maximal normativity and of equity as a corrective

The *North Sea* judgment and the *Anglo-French* award were in the direct line of this concept of equity as a corrective. Both saw equity as a means of remedying the inequitable effects produced by the equidistance method in certain geographical situations. This approach, applied in the context of both conventional and customary law, was to give rise, as we shall see, to the two-stage approach and to the theory of particular configurations.[28] Neither the *North Sea* judgment nor the *Anglo-French* award treated equity on an *ad hoc* basis. Both saw its content as being determined by the law in the form of equitable principles which have legal validity and are applicable in individual cases in a way extending beyond the special features of any one of them. It was as normative elements transcending the specific case in question that the 1969 and 1977 decisions enunciated certain principles which have ever since characterized the courts' concept of equity: equity does not necessarily imply equality; it does not consist in distributing resources or allocating shares; it requires adherence to geography, except for some correction where insignificant features have a disproportionate effect; it forbids the cut-off of maritime areas just in front of a State's coasts, etc.

The extension of normativity to the methods of delimitation also dates from this period. The *North Sea* judgment may have been undemanding as to the choice of method (it must not be forgotten that the Court was addressing itself to governments and did not mean to state rules applicable in a judicial delimitation), but the *Anglo-French* judgment did extend legal regulation to methods. In a famous dictum, it said that the Court does not have "carte blanche to employ any method that it chooses in order to effect an equitable delimitation".[29] This is true for both the method of departure, conceived by the Court of Arbitration as that of equidistance, and for the method to be substituted when the court considers it necessary to make an adjustment to the provisional, equidistant line in order to

---

[26] UNCLOS I, *Official Documents*, vol. VI, p. 93 (French text, vol. VI, p. 112).

[27] Equidistance was adopted for the delimitation of the contiguous zone without the special circumstances reservation; cf. p. 105 n. 6 above.

[28] See pp. 191ff and 225ff below.

[29] *Anglo-French* award, para. 245.

achieve an equitable solution. No court since then has pushed the legal nature of the process of delimitation so far.[30]

This coherent and balanced conception of equity, which could be supported by respectable antecedents, seemed to be firmly established when, in 1982, in a volte-face, the Court threw its 1969 ideas overboard and abandoned the concept of equity as a corrective in favour of autonomous equity. In this respect, the *Tunisia/Libya* judgment well and truly marks what Judge Gros called, as a matter for regret, a "sudden turn" in the case-law.[31]

The 1982 volte-face: the victory of minimal normativity and autonomous equity

With *Tunisia/Libya* the Court was set on a path diametrically opposed to that which had been followed in 1969 and 1977. Henceforth, the law was to limit itself to prescribing that equity be used. This was the sum total of its task. The prescription once made, the law had nothing more to say and judges were given total freedom to decide both the content of equity and the means of achieving it. Everything which the judges might decide was equitable was, *ipso facto*, legal. Equity no longer served to correct the undesirable result *sometimes* produced by the legal rule, but was the immediate and only source of the solution. The Court has put its cards on the table. Far from trying to obscure the fact of the U-turn, it has rejected, in the clearest of terms, the previous concept of equity as a corrective in favour of equity as directly generating the outcome:

> [Equity] was often contrasted with the rigid rules of positive law, the severity of which had to be mitigated in order to do justice. In general, this contrast has no parallel in the development of international law; the legal concept of equity is a general principle *directly applicable* as law.[32]

Equity dictates only the search for an equitable result, not the means of reaching it. As for the criteria of equity, they fade into the background:

> The equitableness of a principle must be assessed in the light of its usefulness for the purpose of arriving at an equitable result. It is not every such principle which is in itself equitable; it may acquire this quality by reference to the equitableness of the solution.[33]

---

[30] Cf. pp. 271ff below.
[31] *Gulf of Maine*, Dissenting Opinion, p. 360, para. 2.
[32] *Tunisia/Libya*, para. 71.
[33] *Ibid.*, para. 70.

Although the Court adds that "this was the view of the Court" in its 1969 judgment, what we in fact have is the complete opposite. The concept of equitable principles is now deprived of any specific content. A principle, for example, such as "no refashioning of nature", or of non-encroachment, might be regarded as equitable by the judges in one case and not in another. All that matters is the result as the judges see it in each separate situation. Equitable principles are no longer part of the law.

Methods are even more determinedly chased from the legal field. The law is indifferent as to which is chosen, and accords none of them any greater validity than any other. All methods are valid, all are possible, as also any combination of them, provided that they lead to an equitable solution:

> ... in international law there is no single obligatory method of delimitation and ... several methods may be applied to one and the same delimitation.[34]

The judges have to extract the solution, at their discretion, directly from the facts of each case, and since the facts are never the same from one case to the next, each solution is *sui generis*:

> It is clear that what is reasonable and equitable in any given case must depend on its particular circumstances ... Each continental shelf case in dispute should be considered and judged on its own merits, having regard to its peculiar circumstances; therefore, no attempt should be made here to overconceptualize the application of the principles and rules relating to the continental shelf.[35]

It might seem difficult to take the reduction of the normative density of the law of maritime delimitation any further. Two years later, however, the *Gulf of Maine* judgment, while making no substantial innovations in the 1982 legal theory, emphasized its essential features still further.

Although it once again insisted on the legal nature of equity, the judgment, as the passages previously quoted show,[36] pushes the doctrine of the poverty of the law to its extreme. The legal content is reduced to the requirement of an equitable result. Equitable principles—"criteria" in the language of the *Gulf of Maine* judgment—and methods of delimitation, lie beyond the law, in the world of non-law:

[34] *Ibid.*, para. 111.
[35] *Ibid.*, paras. 72 and 132.
[36] See pp. 159-60 above.

... general customary international law is not the proper place in which to seek rules specifically prescribing the application of any particular equitable criteria, or the use of any particular practical methods . . . .[37]

Even those principles, such as non-encroachment, thought of as firmly established in the law do not rise to the level of legal norms: "the criteria in question are not themselves rules of law"; "for one and the same criterion it is quite possible to arrive at different, or even opposite, conclusions in different cases". As to methods, none has any "intrinsic merits" which would allow it to be accorded a special legal value, and there must therefore always be a "willingness to adopt a combination of different methods".[38]

It is not surprising that within this context of poverty of legal content, the generality inherent in the rule of law gives way to the individualization of specific situations. "[E]ach specific case is, in the final analysis, different from all the others . . . it is monotypic"—a *unicum*, as the authentic French text has it—so much so that, resistant to all generalization, criteria and methods must be "determined in relation to each particular case and its specific characteristics".[39] There are no rules, only particular cases. In these conditions, "to achieve a result on the basis of law" is not too demanding a prescription.[40]

The *Guinea/Guinea-Bissau* award took up the same theme:

> The factors [i.e., the equitable principles] and methods . . . result from legal rules . . . However . . . none of them is obligatory for the Tribunal since each case of delimitation is a *unicum* . . . .[41]

Some members of the Court had already in 1982 expressed their disagreement with a concept of equity which was so invasive and had so little legal content. Judge Oda regretted that the delimitation line adopted by the Court

---

[37] *Gulf of Maine*, para. 114.

[38] *Ibid.*, paras. 110 and 157-63. These statements about the lack of rules in the law of maritime delimitation should not lead us to overlook the fact that, because of the "increasingly general demand for single delimitation" of a "multi-purpose" kind, the same judgment (though without according them legal status) shows at least a "preference" for "neutral" and "geometrical" methods (*ibid.*, paras. 194 and 199).

[39] *Ibid.*, para. 81. Cf. para. 158 (for equitable criteria) and para. 163 (for the method of delimitation).

[40] *Ibid.*, para. 59.

[41] *Guinea/Guinea-Bissau*, para. 89.

does not exemplify any principle or rule of international law ... The qualified equidistance method is ... the equitable method *par excellence*, and for this reason alone should be tried before all others.[42]

Judge Evensen also deplored the fact that the concept of equity as a corrective had been abandoned by the Court: "[Equity] cannot operate in a vacuum", he wrote; the Court should have examined "whether the equidistance principle could be fruitfully used".[43] But the strongest attack on the doctrine behind the 1982 judgment came from Judge Gros. As a supporter of the corrective concept and the two-stage delimitation process which characterize the previous decisions, he considered

The Court's first task was ... to see what an equidistance line would produce in order to identify the 'extraordinary, unnatural or unreasonable' result to which, it is said, this method might lead.

This task, according to Judge Gros, the Court had not fulfilled: it had not made any "strict verification of the equity of the results", or "crosscheck", as it should have done by reference to the equidistance line. Judge Gros rejected the idea of equity as leading directly to the solution: "Equity is not a sort of independent and subjective vision that takes the place of law", he wrote. By choosing to draw "lines of direction which no principle dictates", the judgment, Judge Gros concluded, has "strayed into subjectivism", but the Court's task is to "declare the law, not attempt a conciliation by persuasion which does not belong to [its] judicial role ...".[44]

In his dissenting opinion in *Gulf of Maine*, Judge Gros renewed and amplified his criticism of the substitution of "controlled equity" by a "system of equity erected into a doctrine separate from law". He deplored the triumph of "an equity which lacks all general doctrine and varies from case to case" and reproached the Chamber for having "gone in search of a line equitable in itself", taking the view that "the end having first been established, the means follow". By rendering a judgment which "can be summed up in four words: the result is equitable", the Chamber has, whatever it says, placed itself outside the law, for "[e]quity discovered by an exercise of discretion is not a form of application of law" but "a law unto itself, where each case is exposed to the application of any imaginable criteria, methods

[42] *Tunisia/Libya*, Dissenting Opinion, pp. 269-70, paras. 180-1.
[43] *Ibid.*, Dissenting Opinion, pp. 290 and 297.
[44] *Ibid.*, Dissenting Opinion, p. 149, para. 12; p. 151, para. 15; p. 152, para. 17; p. 153, para. 19; p. 156, para. 24.

and corrections conducive to a result which the disappearance of rules leaves to the discretion of each tribunal''. He saw equity as now ''a matter of each judge's opinion'' and doubted that ''international justice can long survive an equity measured by the judge's eye''.[45]

The pendulum swings back

Having reached the limit of ''delegalization'', the courts were, no doubt, bound to suffer what the stock-market would call ''a technical reaction''. This is what happened in *Libya/Malta*. On the basis of *Tunisia/Libya* and *Gulf of Maine*, Libya relied on the concept of autonomous equity, arising out of the facts and leading directly to an equitable solution without going through, as a preliminary, any method dictated by the law. ''Libya examines the facts, opening up the map, observing the coasts of the Parties ... and all the geographical, geomorphological and geological features'', and asked the Court, by balancing up all the factual circumstances, to extract, *de plano*, the appropriate solution.[46] This time, the Court rejected this approach, saying that ''the courts have, from the beginning, elaborated equitable principles as being, at the same time, means to an equitable result in a particular case, yet also having a more general validity and hence expressible in general terms''.[47] A rule of law requires a certain generality and a certain consistency, otherwise it will not fulfill the essential functions of the law: certainty and predictability. The application of justice, said the Court in a memorable phrase, ''should display consistency and a degree of predictability''.[48] This enrichment of the legal content of equity was accompanied by a noticeable retreat from the *unicum* theory:

> Even though it looks with particularity to the peculiar circumstances of an instant case ... [equity] also looks beyond it to principles of more general application.[49]

> While every case of maritime delimitation is different in its circumstances from the next, only a clear body of equitable principles can permit such circumstances to be properly weighed, and the objective of an equitable result, as required by general international law, to be attained.[50]

---

[45] *Gulf of Maine*, Dissenting Opinion, p. 378, para. 30; p. 379, para. 32; p. 382, para. 37; p. 385, para. 41; p. 386, para. 42; p. 388, para. 47.
[46] Libyan Reply, p. 96, para. 8.09.
[47] *Libya/Malta*, para. 45.
[48] *Ibid.*
[49] *Ibid.*
[50] *Ibid.*, para. 76.

After being eclipsed in *Tunisia/Libya* and *Gulf of Maine*, equitable principles thus enjoyed legal rehabilitation in the *Libya/Malta* judgment, and now possess a *"normative character"*.[51] As if to make itself better understood, the Court immediately cited "some well-known examples" of these principles. On this point, the tone of the *Libya/Malta* judgment departs strongly from that of *Tunisia/Libya* and *Gulf of Maine*.[52] If 1982 saw one U-turn, 1985 saw another.

The *Libya/Malta* breakthrough on equitable principles did not extend quite so clearly to methods. On this point, as already noted, the judgment is not without ambiguity. On the one hand, the Court refers to "the choice of ... the method which it is to employ" in order for the delimitation to be carried out "in a manner consistent with the concepts underlying the attribution of legal title". On the other, it claims that judges are free to use whatever method they wish, even as a starting point. This split approach translates into an equilibrium too unstable to be durable. Now that equitable principles have been integrated into the field of legal norms, it seems inevitable that methods will, to some extent, follow.

---

[51] *Ibid.*, para. 46.

[52] One of the principles mentioned (that of non-encroachment) figures amongst those which the *Gulf of Maine* judgment refused to accept as legally binding (*Gulf of Maine*, para. 110).

III

AN ASSESSMENT

THIS has been a discursive account. It is time to take stock of the ground covered and try to see the way things are likely to go. Certainly, the *Libya/Malta* judgment has not seen the end of the development of the law of maritime delimitation. The present state of the law is too full of contradictions for there not to be new variations the moment the next case comes before the courts. Where have we got to? Where are we going?

What is at stake?

The choice as to the degree of normative density is fundamental to most of the crucial aspects of the matter.

In the first place, it will determine how much freedom is left to the courts, and therefore, the degree of predictability and legal certainty. A loose-knit law will leave the courts almost total latitude while one that is tightly woven will force them to remain on the beaten track and protect the parties from an unforeseeable outcome.

The choice will also determine the degree of generality of the rule of law. If the normative content is deemed to be at zero level, this will mean an emphasis on the peculiarity of the particular situation to the detriment of pre-existing norms of general application. A degree or two highter and the courts will be forced to play down the specific to the advantage of the general and thus avoid an excessive individualization of the legal rules.

But it is above all in respect of the delimitation process itself that the level of normativity and the conception of equity are decisive. A low level of normativity and an autonomous role for equity will justify a delimitation dominated by the facts. The courts will draw the line which seems to them appropriate directly on the basis of their appreciation of the facts of each particular case. A high legal content and an equity which is seen simply as a corrective will mean a more complicated process in which legal considerations will come into play, though differently, at each stage of the operation. The choice is therefore of immense importance. In a law with few precise rules, relevant circumstances will play a predominant, even exclusive role. In a law where there is a high level of precise rules, relevant circumstances will have only a modest part, to check the equity of a result obtained on the basis of considerations of a legal nature, and the adjustments which may have to be made to this result will themselves be caught by the legal norms.

This leads to a fundamental difference, perhaps the most important of all. With a loosely-woven legal fabric, a large, almost unlimited, number of delimitation lines is conceivable. As many lines are legally possible as the courts can imagine as being equitable. The closer the normative fabric, the narrower the range of possible lines. In short, on this central option will depend the size of the gap between the legal reasoning of the judgment and the line it actually decides.

A tale of contrasts

Unfortunately, the case-law is more divided on this issue than on any other. The waverings of view just described occur not only over time but are to be found also at the very heart of each judgment. Which of the innumerable judicial dicta relating to the normative density of the matter is the scholar to regard as making law? Which of the many concepts co-existing side by side in the cases must the commentator regard as authoritative? Is the present state of the law determined by those decisions which exclude both principles and methods from the field of law, or by those decisions which accept the principles as law, but not the methods, or by those decisions which regard both principles and methods as part of the law? Which of these three versions is to be considered authentic? As for equity, although the judgments are unanimous in distinguishing it from *ex aequo et bono*, there remains a considerable difference between the approach which assigns to it the task of *avoiding inequitable results* and that which expects it to *produce an equitable result*. Where is the legal truth?

Equitable principles: their normative character part of the acquis

One thing is certain, that, with the *Libya/Malta* judgment, the Court turned its back on the theory of the inherent poverty of international law, and gave the rule of law a content going beyond the simple prescription of the equitable result. Henceforth, it is not enough for the courts simply to draw a line which they think is equitable. They must justify it in the light of equitable principles, which themselves have a normative character. The delimitation process, therefore, cannnot be reduced to a simple consideration of the facts. To start from the facts and never to leave them, as some judgments seem to have suggested doing, would be to decide *ex aequo et bono*. Raw facts cannot, by the wave of a magic wand, bring forth a legal solution, like Venus rising from the waves. Facts can only produce law if they have a pre-existing legal norm applied to them. By themselves, they are powerless to create law. This is always true. For example, particular actions are liable to incur legal responsibility only if there is a pre-existing legal rule covering the principle of responsibility, the conditions in which it comes into play and its effects. Otherwise, it is a decision in equity, and nothing else. In the same way, a court does not reach a delimitation line based on law by opening the map and drawing on it lines which it then bends, modifies, and displaces at will in a groping search for a satisfactory solution. It must start with a set of rules against which to gauge the geographical and other facts of the case and which will give it some indication of what conclusions to draw.

As a corollary, it is nowadays recognized that in this matter as in any other, the rule of law must necessarily have a certain degree of generality. It may be true that the same water never flows twice under the same bridge, but the law of maritime delimitation should not be seen as made up of a series of particular solutions, or it would inevitably drift towards the subjective and unpredictable. This means that it is not enough for the law of maritime delimitation to reject all generalities, as does Talleyrand: ''There are no principles, only events; there are no laws, only circumstances''. The application of any general rule is, of course, bound to lead to inequity in certain specific situations, which is why no legal system limits itself to general rules the blind application of which would fail to take proper account of the special features of particular cases. But no more would a satisfactory legal system push the search for equity to the extreme individualization of the rule of law, since a totally individualized rule would be a rule in no more than name. The path between these two extremes is a narrow one.[53]

The infinite variety of circumstances has, from the beginning, led to the incorporation of a certain amount of flexibility into the law itself. This was precisely the role of the special circumstances

---

[53] Judge Jiménez de Aréchaga speaks of the "fundamental dilemma arising in all cases of continental shelf delimitation: the need to maintain consistency and uniformity in the legal principles and rules applicable to a series of situations which are characterized by their multiple diversity" (*Tunisia/Libya*, Separate Opinion, p. 106, para. 26).

concept; it is also the role of equity: to allow the general norm to be individually fashioned so as to avoid unreasonable results. But, if the law of delimitation has always managed to avoid the trap of automaticity and excessive generality, it has not been so good at escaping the opposite one, that of excessive individualization. From one judgment to the next, the balance tipped more and more towards the individualizing characteristic of equity and the elevation of the *unicum* theory. Instead of correcting the inequitable effects of a general rule, equity has led to a direct solution for each particular problem, so much so that the law of maritime delimitation, instead of being formed from a system of norms definable *ex ante*, was to dissolve into a collection of solutions reached on a case by case basis, without any thread running through them. The normativity of the law of maritime delimitation was to be pared down to the point where it succumbed to the courts' discretionary power.

This course was fraught with danger. It had serious implications for the courts whose subjectivity was open to criticism on all sides. If "the decision . . . must reflect the deep-seated convictions of the Arbitrators and their sense of justice",[54] it was only to be expected that others—for example, governments or academic writers—would have different "deep-seated convictions" or "sense of justice". This development was also serious from the point of view of the good functioning of international justice and the pacific settlement of disputes in general. A law individualized to excess encouraged each State to maintain from the start of negotiations that unique factual circumstances existed which justified a delimitation favourable to it. The unpredictability of the result—"equity is now a matter of each judge's opinion", to quote Judge Gros—[55] risked frightening governments off the game of chance which judicial or arbitral settlement threatened to become, except in those cases where their main preoccupation was to clear themselves vis-à-vis internal oppositions ready to condemn any negotiated concession. The choice of judges and arbitrators took on an exaggerated importance, with each party seeking to obtain the appointment of those whose views they might hope would be sympathetic. To set up an arbitral tribunal or Chamber of the Court became almost the most difficult procedural hurdle. States were liable finally to become discouraged from committing themselves to such uncertain routes, or at least found it in their interests to maximize their claims in the hope that the

---

[54] *Guinea/Guinea-Bissau*, para. 90.
[55] *Gulf of Maine*, Dissenting Opinion, p. 386, para. 42.

eventual solution would consist, more or less, in "splitting the difference".[56]

By insisting in *Libya/Malta* on the necessity of a rule of law marked by "consistency and a degree of predictability", by demanding a norm which, though capable of attaching to the circumstances of a given case, "looks beyond it to principles of more general application", by proclaiming the "normative character" of principles of equity enjoying a "global validity ... and thus expressible in general terms", the Court thwarted the law of maritime delimitation's disintegration into a boundless collection of parts and gave it back its normative function. From then on, a solution which seemed equitable to the judges would not, *simply for this reason*, equate to equity "as a legal concept". Now that it has a content determined by the law, equity no longer fluctuates at judicial will. The 1985 *Libya/Malta* judgment has undoubtedly been far and away the most innovatory since the 1969 *North Sea* case.

Methods of delimitation: their normative character in the making

Although the *Libya/Malta* judgment marked undeniable progress in giving a greater legal content to the law of maritime delimitation, it has to be admitted that this undertaking has not yet been completed. The attempt to integrate principles of equity into the law has not been extended to methods of delimitation, since, as we have seen, the Court limited itself, in this judgment, to the doctrine that all methods were equal in the eyes of the law. The law does not prescribe any method, even for the start of the process, permitting any method or combination of methods from the very beginning. The Court in *Libya/Malta* did not budge a single inch on this crucial point from the preceding cases. The courts still consider themselves no less free than before, as far as the law is concerned, to juggle with methods, to move lines in any direction, to play with angles and degrees of latitude and longitude, to refuse to give any effect to this island, to give half-effect to another, and full effect to yet another. It is true that the time has passed when an equitable outcome was enough to justify cartographic acrobatics. At least, these days, the equity of the result has to be measured by the standard of equitable principles, defined in advance because they are part of the law.

As far as methods are concerned, the normativity of the law of maritime delimitation remains, therefore, even after the *Libya/Malta* judgment, extremely meagre. There is no doubt that the final

[56] By coincidence or not, it may be observed that so far all judicial and arbitral decisions have opted for a line intermediate between those claimed by the parties.

responsibility for this lies with States who failed, at UNCLOS III, to reach agreement on any rule whatsoever for delimitation, however imprecise. After all, why should the courts try to mitigate the powerlessness of governments? But *noblesse oblige*, and it is the essence of the judicial function to define the law where States have not done so. As Judge Mosler said, ''The judicial task is to make the law more determinable by objective criteria, and thus more predictable to potential parties''.[57] The law-making power of the courts is not just a matter of empty words, and in many cases it is for the courts themselves to determine the legal framework restraining the power which the failure of States to make rules has left them.

The law's relative silence so far on methods of delimitation is as fraught with danger as was its silence on equitable principles before 1985. In *Libya/Malta*, the Court took the view that the law could not be confined to the result but must also be present in the process leading to it. The reasons which forced the Court to weave a closer legal cloth with respect to equitable principles militates with just as much force in favour of a parallel development for methods of delimitation. To define the philosophy of equity in terms of legal rules should produce the same result for the choice of methods. All things considered, it is, at the end of the day, the method of delimitation which determines the boundary line, the ultimate purpose of the delimitation exercise. Now that the Court has brought the philosophy of equity within the legal field, it would be difficult to understand why it should stop half-way, and long persist in excluding from the ambit of the law the methods permitting equity to be put into practice.

The reluctance shown in the *Libya/Malta* judgment to take the submission of maritime delimitation to the law to its logical conclusion may perhaps be explained by the judges' traditional hostility to equidistance. The fear of according equidistance the character of a legally obligatory method rises like a ghost in one case after another. It was in vain that Canada in *Gulf of Maine*, then Libya in *Libya/Malta* said that they did not in any way advocate equidistance as an obligatory or unique method of delimitation but only as a point of departure and provisional solution. The Court would seem in both cases to have feared a return to the Danish and Netherlands theses of 1969.[58] There are apparently ghosts which the Court feels it necessary to lay again at every chance. Nonetheless, the progress marked in the ''legalization'' of equitable principles in

---

[57] *Libya/Malta*, Dissenting Opinion, p. 114.
[58] Cf. *Gulf of Maine*, paras. 106-7, and *Libya/Malta*, para. 77.

Libya/Malta would be a Pyrrhic victory if the Court were to sick to its present refusal to see the rules of law as relating also to methods. Fortunately, in *Libya/Malta*, the Court already has the ingredients for repairing the crack it has for the moment chosen to leave open, probably so as not to go too far too fast.

It would, however, be a mistake to think that the argument about the "legalization" of methods boils down to the question of equidistance as the starting point for the delimitation operation. However important it may be, this question does not exhaust the debate. There is no reason why there should not be rules for every stage of the operation. As we shall see, this is already the case for deciding the relevant circumstances which, put into the balance, provide a check on the equity of the provisional, first-stage result, and confirm the equity of the result which the judges are preparing to make final. At an earlier stage in the process, the law ought also to play a role in the choice of methods for any necessary adjustment to the provisional line. For the moment, the legal content of this ultimate step is still at the drafting stage, but that is the direction in which matters are pointing.

As we see, the law still has some way to go before it covers the whole process of delimitation from beginning to end, but the seeds of development are already there, and it would seem that the loosening of the normative density of the law of maritime delimitation has now, at last, been put into reverse.

PART IV

THE DELIMITATION PROCESS

PART IV

THE DELIMITATION PROCESS

THE point has now been reached where it is possible to tackle the ultimate questions of the law of maritime delimitation. How is delimitation to be carried out in practice?[1] What is the structure and content of the delimitation process? It must again be emphasized that these questions are looked at here only from the legal point of view. It is the rules of law governing the delimitation process which interest us, not the techniques, which are the scientists' business. These questions, it must also be emphasized, concern only delimitations decided by judge or arbitrator. Governments negotiating a delimitation agreement may follow whatever route they choose, just as they may agree whatever solution they wish.

Of all the problems considered so far, it is the process of delimitation itself which presents the greatest uncertainties. Clearly, the courts are still feeling their way. However, their judgments give a good inkling of the way things are going and allow us, with only some slight measure of anticipation, to draw the outlines of an ordered legal schema.

---

[1] To describe the legal route to a delimitation according to international law, it is current practice to refer to the delimitation process or operation. The Court spoke in the *North Sea* case, and again in *Tunisia/Libya*, of the "delimitation process" (*North Sea*, paras. 18 and 20, and *Tunisia/Libya*, paras. 44 and 106). In the *North Sea* case, the term was translated into French as "*opération de délimitation*", in *Tunisia/Libya*, by "*processus de délimitation*", but the idea was the same. In *Gulf of Maine*, the Chamber went back to "*opération de délimitation*" (for example, paras. 115, 215, etc.), and the Court used it in *Libya/Malta* (for example, para. 65).

I

THE COURTS IN SEARCH OF THE
DELIMITATION PROCESS

Two trends

A CAREFUL reading of the cases shows that there are two trends at work, sometimes side by side in the same judgment. Each has several elements which are to be found in inverse form in the other. We have come across most of them in previous chapters. It is now a question of putting them into some kind of order.

According to one approach, the delimitation process is a single operation which starts from relevant circumstances and, applying equitable principles, arrives immediately at an equitable line. The delimitation exercise rests on the autonomous concept of equity and looks only to the final outcome: the facts lead straight to the desired result. Legal considerations relating to title, and more particularly to the distance criterion, have scarcely any place in this operation, which goes from start to finish without pause. Seen in this way, the delimitation process is centred on the facts and teleological in nature. According to this view, the path which leads from the relevant circumstances to the result remains outside the law's field of interest. This means that the stress is laid on the unique and specific character of each factual situation, and the legal content rests at a relatively low level: prescription of an equitable result, yes, certainly; legal principles of equity, perhaps; regulation of methods, definitely not. In the eyes of the courts all methods are legally interchangeable, and at no matter what stage of the process they are lawfully at liberty to combine them in whatever proportions they find appropriate.

This philosophy appears in almost all the judgments, including the most recent. However, another ideology has appeared in parallel. According to this second concept, the delimitation process is bipolar in character. At its origin, it is rooted in the legal title to the area in question; in its result, it is dominated by equity. To translate this bipolarity into practice, a two-stage approach is required. At the first stage, the method used is that of equidistance, as dictated by the legal nature of title and inherent in the concept of maritime delimitation. However, this first step produces only a provisional line, and it still remains to check that the line thus obtained on the basis of legal considerations also meets the requirements of equity. It is only at the second stage that relevant circumstances, specific to the case in question, will come into the picture, and, looked at in the light of equitable principles which are themselves defined by law, make it possible to assess the result of the first stage from the point of view of equity. It is only if it comes through this test successfully that the provisional equidistance line can become final. Otherwise, it will have to undergo appropriate adjustments in order to produce an equitable solution.

This second approach thus accords a privileged place to equidistance, the priority use of which is required for reasons of law relating to the legal nature of title and the link between title and delimitation. As for relevant circumstances, they have no independent role, but only come into the picture as a sort of litmus test to check the equity of the provisional result dictated by the legal title. This approach, which rests on a conception of equity as a corrective, gives a greater place to the legal content than does the previous one, not only because it incorporates legal considerations relating to title, but also because it implies the extension of the law to methods. In this approach, methods are not a matter of legal indifference.

Even if the *Libya/Malta* judgment in 1985 marked a turning point for certain crucial aspects of this complex issue, it would be wrong to think that the first concept dominated exclusively up to 1985 and the second equally exclusively thereafter. Case-law lends itself badly to sharp breaks or spectacular U-turns. Just as the courts for some time kept natural prolongation and distance alive side by side, so the two concepts of the delimitation process will co-exist in the case-law until such time as the second prevails. Signs of change appeared even before *Libya/Malta*, but this case represented more a transition than a definite break, and the judgment still retains traces of the opposite philosophy.

Theme and variations

Various judicial and arbitral decisions have dwelt at some length on the basic option just described, but it has to be acknowledged that the actual structure of the delimitation process has rarely been considered clearly and directly.

The idea of taking a given line as the point of departure, and then correcting it to take account of the particular circumstances of the case, appeared at the very beginnings of the law of maritime delimitation, but it was more implied than express. It was not accepted in all judgments, nor was it always conceived in the same way.

Although the *North Sea* judgment has the reputation of marking the beginning of a toning down of equidistance, the Court actually took equidistance as its starting point. "The Court", one reads,[2] "must examine the question of how the continental shelf can be delimited when it is in fact the case that the equidistance principle does not provide an equitable solution". How are we to know that equidistance "does not provide an equitable solution" if we do not at least start by trying it? The *Anglo-French* arbitral award raised[3] "the question whether the effect of individual geographical features is to render an equidistance delimitation 'unjustified' or 'inequitable' ...". The theory of special geographical configurations was conceived in the context of the use of the provisional equidistance line as a point of departure.[4] As Judge Evensen was later to write, "[T]he equidistance principle was applied [in this case] as a juridical starting point for the application of equity".[5]

The 1969 judgment and the *Anglo-French* arbitral award thus both imply a two-stage operation. The first stage consists in drawing a provisional line of equidistance, and the second in making any necessary correction to this line in the light of the specific circumstances of the case. Neither decision, however, makes this explicit, and their reservations about the value of equidistance in the case under consideration managed to obscure the fact that both took it for granted as the first stage of the operation.

The trouble really starts with the 1982 *Tunisia/Libya* judgment. The rejection of a two-stage process seems to be total:

> Nor does the Court consider that it is in the present case required, as a first step, to examine the effects of a delimitation by application of the equidistance method, and to reject that method in favour of some other only if it considers the results of an equidistance line to be inequitable ... equidistance is not, in the view of the Court, either a mandatory legal principle, or a method having some privileged status in relation to other methods.[6]

[2] *North Sea*, para. 92.
[3] *Anglo-French* award, para. 240.
[4] Cf. pp. 225ff below.
[5] *Tunisia/Libya*, Dissenting Opinion, p. 291.
[6] *Tunisia/Libya*, para. 110.

The rejection of the two-stage process seems absolute, but such an interpretation would go too far. The Court makes the point that it must not, *"in the present case"*, turn to equidistance in the first place. In this case, in fact, the two parties were agreed that the equidistance line was inequitable. Although, as the Court itself indicates, this did not mean that it was impossible for the Court to come up with an equidistance line, the hostility of the two sides to such a solution would have made it very difficult: "The Court must take this firmly expressed view of the Parties into account".[7] All the same, says the Court[8] in a much-quoted statement of principle:

> ... equidistance may be applied if it leads to an equitable solution; *if not*, other methods should be employed.

The rejection of equidistance if it does not lead to an equitable solution implies that one starts by considering it.

However, that is not how the *Tunisia/Libya* judgment proceeds. Instead of starting with equidistance and checking at a second stage whether it is equitable in the light of relevant circumstances, it extracts the equitable line direct from those circumstances. Although the Court implicitly advocates the two-stage process as a general rule, this is not the course it follows, a fact which some judges were quick to point out with regret.[9] The most the judgment does, *in fine*, was to test the line derived from the facts of the case for proportionality,[10] and thus introduce the embryo of a two-stage operation in another form, the final check being carried out not on an equidistance line, but on a line drawn directly from the relevant circumstances.

In *Gulf of Maine*, the structure of the delimitation operation becomes more complex and harder to grasp. At first sight, the Chamber seems, in its turn, to be rejecting all idea of a two-stage operation. Refusing to regard equidistance as "a method to be given priority or preference", or as having "intrinsic merits which would make it preferable to another",[11] the Chamber says:

---

[7] *Ibid.* Cf. Jiménez de Aréchaga, *Tunisia/Libya*, Dissenting Opinion, p. 135, paras. 109-10.

[8] *Tunisia/Libya*, para. 109.

[9] See, for example, Gros, *Tunisia/Libya*, Dissenting Opinion, p. 149, para. 12 and p. 151, para. 15; Oda, Dissenting Opinion, p. 270, para. 181; Evensen, Dissenting Opinion, p. 319.

[10] *Tunisia/Libya*, paras. 130-1.

[11] *Gulf of Maine*, paras. 107 and 162.

Nor is there any method of which it can be said that it must receive priority, a method with whose application every delimitation operation could begin, albeit subject to its effects being subsequently corrected or it being even discarded in favour of another, if those effects turned out to be clearly unsatisfactory in relation to the case.[12]

However strongly this statement of principle may have been put, the Chamber did not apply it to the letter. The line of one of the three segments of the maritime boundary was, in fact, drawn after a two-stage process, the first stage of which used the equidistance method. For the central segment, as the judgment clearly states, the Chamber:

> ... has *first* to make its choice of an appropriate practical method for use in *provisionally* establishing a basic delimitation, and ... must *then* ascertain what corrections to it are rendered indispensable by the *special circumstances* of the case. *A two-stage operation is therefore entailed.*[13]

As a result, the Chamber begins by drawing a median line; then, finding in a "second stage" that this provisional line might "produce an unreasonable effect if uncorrected", engages in the "specific task of correction", which, by taking into account the position of the land boundary and the comparative length of the two coastal fronts, will result in a "corrected median line".[14] Even for those segments where it refused to take equidistance as the point of departure, the Chamber adopts a two-stage process, but in a slightly different form. The first stage consists in the equal division of the areas of overlap. This "basic criterion", however, may in certain geographical conditions prove inequitable and will then, at a second stage, have to be "adjusted or flexibly applied" in order to make it "genuinely equitable ... in relation to the varying requirements of a reality that takes many shapes and forms". This is why, in certain cases, the starting point of an equal division of zones of overlap must be "combined" with "appropriate auxiliary criteria".[15] The originality of this approach lies in the fact that the two stages are defined less by relation to a method than to an equitable principle: the first stage, in particular, is characterized more by the equitable principle of the equal division of zones of overlap than by use of the equidistance method.[16]

[12] *Ibid.*, para. 163.
[13] *Ibid.*, para. 215.
[14] *Ibid.*, paras. 217 and 220-3.
[15] *Ibid.*, paras. 195-7.
[16] For the use of methods other than equidistance to satisfy the equitable principle of the equal division of overlapping zones, see pp. 59ff above.

The Chamber does not, however, bring the delimitation process to an end with these two stages. It also proposes checking whether the line reached on the basis of the coastal configuration is equitable in the light of the facts of human and economic geography, "circumstances which, though . . . ineligible for consideration as criteria to be applied in the delimitation process itself, may . . . be relevant to assessment of the equitable character of a delimitation first established on the basis of criteria borrowed from physical and political geography"; and it is only when this final check has led to the conviction that there are no "conditions of an exceptional kind which might justify any correction of the delimitation line it has drawn" that this line will be regarded as final.[17] In the end, therefore, the *Gulf of Maine* judgment adopts a three-stage approach.

The *Guinea/Guinea-Bissau* award, delivered some months later, shows the same ambivalent approach. Once again, it states that "the equidistance method is just one among many and that there is no obligation to use it or give it priority"[18] in the pursuit of the "essential objective"[19] of the equitable solution. But, as in *Gulf of Maine*, the award resorts to a complicated process. The Tribunal first examines "characteristics peculiar to the region", in particular the geographical configuration of the coasts and other delimitations already made or still to be made in the region; this, it says, "opens the possibility of an equitable delimitation". However, before regarding this delimitation as final, it intends to "establish whether the chosen line effectively leads to an equitable result". This is why, after referring in the first stage to "circumstances which it considers relevant in the present case", it will consider, at a second stage, "other circumstances", described as "additional": the structure and nature of the continental shelf; the proportionality between the maritime areas in relation to the landmass and to the length of coastline of the two States; economic circumstances; security. It is only after the Tribunal finds that none of these additional circumstances "is such as to affect its decision concerning the delimitation line" that the line is finally adopted.[20] The Tribunal may, indeed, have adopted a two-stage process, but this is not based on equidistance as the first step, followed by consideration of the relevant circumstances. Instead, a hierarchy is established between the most important relevant circumstances, allowing the delimitation line to

---

[17] *Gulf of Maine*, paras. 230ff.
[18] *Guinea/Guinea-Bissau*, para. 102.
[19] *Ibid.*, para. 88.
[20] *Ibid.*, paras. 111, 112 and 125.

be drawn, and the "additional circumstances", for checking the equity of the result. In this respect, *Guinea/Guinea-Bissau* is closer to *Tunisia/Libya* than to *Gulf of Maine*. The courts, in all three cases, are obviously tempted by the two-stage process, but of the three, it is *Gulf of Maine* which makes the clearest use of it, at least for one segment of the line. Despite appearances, *Gulf of Maine*, in this respect, is closer to the 1969 and 1977 cases than the other two decisions.

As to the 1985 *Libya/Malta* judgment, although, as already pointed out, it perpetuates the tradition, started in 1982, of refusing to recognize equidistance as having a privileged or priority character, its theory is belied by the practical steps it takes to resolve the problem facing it. The moment it moves to action, the Court forgets what it has just written and, in effect, resorts to a two-stage operation.[21] However, by comparison with the *Gulf of Maine* judgment, *Libya/Malta* contains an important innovation. In *Gulf of Maine*, the Chamber attached no importance to the link between title and delimitation, and thus did not consider that the distance criterion could have any influence on the method to be followed.[22] In *Libya/Malta*, however, the Court says the opposite:

> [it is] logical . . . that the choice of the criterion and the method which it is to employ in the first place to arrive at a provisional result should be made in a manner consistent with the concepts underlying the attribution of legal title;[23]

and it is as a result of this "logical" (i.e., legal) necessity that it adopts the median line "by way of a provisional step in a process to be continued by other operations".[24] But immediately to accept this line as definitive would mean conferring on equidistance an obligatory character it does not possess. This is why there has to be a second operation:

> . . . under existing law, it must be demonstrated that the equidistance method leads to an equitable result in the case in question. To achieve this purpose, the result to which the distance criterion leads must be examined in the context of applying equitable principles to the relevant circumstances.[25]

---

[21] See pp. 81-2 above.
[22] *Gulf of Maine*, paras. 104-6.
[23] *Libya/Malta*, para. 61.
[24] *Ibid.*, para. 62.
[25] *Ibid.*, para. 63.

This time, the relevant circumstances are clearly seen as a means of checking, in the light of equitable principles, whether the equidistance line adopted "as the first stage in the delimitation process . . . as the provisional delimitation line"[26] produces an equitable solution. In contrast to the approach in *Tunisia/Libya* or *Guinea/Guinea-Bissau*, they are not seen as giving rise directly to an equitable line. They have lost their autonomous and primary character and resumed their mission, accorded to them in the *North Sea* judgment and the *Anglo-French* award, as a test of equity. This is the perspective from which the judgment considers the comparative length of the two coastlines and the general geographical framework in which the delimitation is to take place, and concludes that it is necessary,

> in order to ensure the achievement of an equitable solution, that the delimitation line . . . be adjusted so as to lie closer to the coasts of Malta.[27]

The result thus achieved will in its turn be submitted, in a final, complementary stage, to the test of proportionality.[28]

Basically, the *Libya/Malta* judgment once again proceeds in three stages, but the resemblance to the *Gulf of Maine* judgment is limited to this arithmetical aspect. Each of these stages, and the order in which they occur, appears differently in *Libya/Malta* than in *Gulf of Maine*. This time the Court begins with an "initial" equidistance line,[29] regarded as "the result to which the distance criterion leads". At the second stage, this provisional line is checked against the relevant circumstances and any necessary adjustments made; at the third stage, the line thus obtained is submitted to the final proportionality test. As already pointed out, however, the Court added a caveat on the same lines as in previous judgments. Although it proceeded in this way in this particular case, where it was dealing with a situation of opposite coasts, it should not be inferred that it would regard itself as legally bound to do the same in all cases, or even in all cases of opposite coasts.[30] The two trends in the post-1969 case-law continue cheek by jowl, in *Libya/Malta* as in previous judgments.

The picture emerging from the cases on this important problem

---

[26] *Ibid.*, para. 65.
[27] *Ibid.*, para. 71.
[28] *Ibid.*, paras. 74-5.
[29] *Ibid.*, para. 78.
[30] *Ibid.*, para. 77.

of the process of maritime delimitation is confused and contradictory. Each judgment has its own view of the process—one, two or
three stages depending on the case—and each of these stages is seen
differently from one judgment to the next. Order clearly needs to be
restored. If "the impact of distance considerations on the actual
delimiting"[31] led the Court to begin with equidistance, the same
logic should lead to the same result in all future cases. Since *Libya/
Malta*, the principle, rejected in case after case, according to which
equidistance has no privileged or priority role in the delimitation
process, has lost all *raison d'être* and all justification. Recognition of
the distance criterion, once the death warrant of natural physical
prolongation in continental shelf delimitation, should lead logically
to the adoption of a two-stage operation. The final development,
which would make equidistance the first step, to be tested against
relevant circumstances in the light of equitable principles, would
seem to be written into the *Libya/Malta* judgment, waiting to be
brought to life. Taking those elements which have already been
established, and without ignoring the gaps which still have to be
filled, some attempt can now be made to describe the process now
under way.

[31] *Ibid.*, para. 62.

II

RESTORING ORDER

The legal nature of the process

ACCORDING to one theory, much repeated before international tribunals and finding some echo in judicial statements, the law ought to concentrate on the goal of an equitable result, accepting as legal any method or combination of methods capable of producing such a result.

As demonstrated in preceding chapters, such a theory is today no longer tenable: the method of arriving at a delimitation line is as important from the law's point of view as the result. If there were no rule determining the path which leads from the facts to the delimitation line, that would mean not only that the end justifies the means but also that each case must be treated as *sui generis*. Excluding the law from the actual process of delimitation and concentrating it entirely on the result would cause the delimitation of maritime areas to lose all predictability and certainty. Governments, in resorting to judicial or arbitral settlement of their maritime delimitation disputes, would embark on the risky route to decisions no longer founded in law. When two States decide to go to court or arbitration, it is not to obtain a sort of compulsory conciliation, but to be judged by the standards of the law. To meet this requirement, it is not enough to proclaim the necessity of an equitable result without considering how to achieve it. Any confusion over this could be fatal for international justice. It is the function of judicial settlement which is at stake in deciding the legal definition of the delimitation process. At a time when there are hundreds of delimitations still to be made, such a risk should not be taken lightly.[32]

A multiple process

The concept of the process of delimitation suggests a multiple operation, made up of several elements or phases, as opposed to a

---

[32] See p. 182 above.

single act which produces the boundary line at a stroke. Why a multiple process and not a single act of delimitation? The answer is to be found in the remarks made previously about the bipolar character of maritime delimitation.[33] Delimitation, it must be remembered, has to satisfy two conditions: it must be founded in the law, that is to say, it must be carried out according to a schema connected with the legal nature of the title to the maritime area in question; and it must produce an equitable line, for which purpose it must comply with principles of equity. The reason for this duality is the need to satisfy two essential but contradictory requirements. On the one hand, the delimitation must be in accordance with general, objectively identifiable norms. On the other, there must be scope for modifying the law in response to the particular features of a given situation. A delimitation made entirely on the basis of legal considerations relating to title would be fine as far as objective, general norms were concerned, but possibly at the expense of equity, since such a delimitation might not be sufficiently responsive to the diversity of the real world. By contrast, a delimitation based entirely on equity would lack the necessary generality and objectivity that every legal norm must have; a delimitation without legal basis would dissolve into legal impressionism. Here as elsewhere, "it is necessary that the law be applied reasonably",[34] i.e. "adapted to the diverse facts in question".[35] "It is not a matter of finding simply an equitable solution, but an equitable solution derived from the applicable law."[36]

If it is to satisfy both these requirements, the law of maritime delimitation must have two elements. To go straight from the facts of the case to the equitable line would be to leapfrog the legal basis for the delimitation and veer towards the subjective and arbitrary. But to stick solely to legal considerations would put the requirement of equity at risk. Legal title without the facts of the case would be bones without flesh; the facts of the case without legal title would be flesh without bones.

How, then, is one to begin? With title and the general norm, or with equity and respect for actual situations? The answer to this question has been clearly demonstrated. Equity cannot be judged *in vacuo*; it is only the equity of a given line which can be checked. One has to begin, therefore, with a line drawn on the basis of a general and objective norm. This line will constitute the point of reference for

[33] See p. 49 above.

[34] *Barcelona Traction* case, ICJ *Reports*, 1970, p. 48, para. 93.

[35] *Fisheries* case, ICJ *Reports*, 1951, p. 133; cf. *North Sea*, para. 94.

[36] *Fisheries Jurisdiction*, ICJ *Reports*, 1974, p. 33, para. 78.

assessing the equity of the outcome, an assessment to be made only at the second stage, when relevant circumstances and equitable principles come into play. First, delimitation based on legal title; then, a check to see whether, when the relevant circumstances of the case are taken into account, the line conforms with equitable principles. Methods, equitable principles and relevant circumstances are all elements subject to the law and each has its proper place: methods in the first phase for the provisional line and in the second for the final line; equitable principles and relevant circumstances only in the second phase.

It should be added that, although the delimitation process has two aspects, which for reasons of logic and convenience are presented as chronologically distinct, it is a single operation. The exercise has several elements, but it remains a whole, a totality, with no presumption in favour of equidistance, any more than there is any burden of proof on a State party wishing to reject it. One might compare it to the interpretation of international treaties, governed, according to the Vienna Convention, by a ''single rule'', itself composed of several elements and accompanied by ''supplementary means of interpretation''. As the International Law Commission explains, this is to be seen as ''a single complex operation''. In both cases, it is only ''logic'' which makes a distinction. This logic must not be allowed to put the ''unity of the process'' at risk.[37]

The process of delimitation will thus begin with a provisional line based on law. This line, as shown above, cannot be anything other than a line of equidistance. Then comes a check on the equity of this line, on the basis of which check it will be possible to arrive at the definitive line. The starting line will always be a line of equidistance: the finishing line not necessarily so.

1. THE STARTING LINE: A LINE OF EQUIDISTANCE

The crusade against equidistance

The reason the courts seem to have found it so difficult to accept the use of equidistance other than as a first step is almost certainly the disrepute into which this method fell after 1969. The International Law Commission and the Geneva Conventions made it the preferred solution, to be rejected only in ''special circumstances''. The *North Sea* judgment, however, gave the signal for a fierce attack on the method. In fact, the judgment was more subtle and balanced than is

[37] *ILCYB*, 1956, vol. II, pp. 239-40.

usually thought. The Court noted the advantages of this method and added only as a limitation or exception[38] that "[i]t would however be ignoring realities if it were not noted at the same time that the use of this method . . . can *under certain circumstances* produce results that appear on the face of them to be extraordinary, unnatural or unreasonable". Of these two elements—the obvious advantages and the inequity "under certain circumstances"—the second has been remembered, the first forgotten. The received wisdom now is not that equidistance can in *some* cases lead to an inequitable result but that *only* in some is it capable of producing an equitable one. The exception has become the rule, the rule the exception.

The debates at UNCLOS III fuelled this crusade against equidistance. The Conference was divided into two schools of thought over the delimitation of the continental shelf and exclusive economic zone. One side wanted to introduce a mention of equidistance into the provisions under discussion, the other was opposed to any reference to equidistance and sought to put the emphasis on equitable principles. An artificial contrast was thus implanted in the legal mind between the generous flexibility of equitable principles and the blind rigidity of mathematical equidistance. The end result of setting equitable principles against equidistance was a belief—or implication—that equidistance excludes equity and that equity is incompatible with equidistance.

Even the courts, it must be admitted, were sometimes led astray. As we shall see, the judgments are unanimous in recognizing that equidistance has advantages and that there are frequent examples of it in State practice. But this is simply lip service. In spite of their careful language, the judgments show a steady drift from the idea of equidistance as sometimes inequitable to equidistance as sometimes equitable. It is true that they always keep open the possibility of equidistance, but since the circumstances are never suitable, this has become an empty formula, a rhetorical question, a courtesy clause. It was this which, until the *Libya/Malta* judgment, encouraged the courts' fidelity to those hallowed phrases which denied equidistance any privileged position as a matter of principle, even for a provisional line or as a first step.

It is not surprising in these circumstances that States have indulged in overkill. They have not hesitated, in various judicial proceedings, to go beyond specific criticism of the equidistance line in the case at issue and to launch a major attack against the method itself, presenting it as an almost unmitigated evil.

[38] *North Sea*, paras. 22-4.

It goes without saying that, in this kind of holy war against equidistance, waged under the banner of equitable principles, the arguments are taken to unwarranted extremes. Equidistance and equity may not be synonymous, but nor are they antonyms. The fact that equidistance does not always produce an equitable result does not mean that it never does so. Equidistance can be equitable. The relationship between equidistance and equity, clouded by an opposition to equidistance that is almost pathological, and informed more by passion than reason, is, in fact, extremely simple. Equidistance and equity may coincide but need not; they may diverge but do not have to.

The conflict between equidistance and equity, which arises from an erroneous reading of the 1969 judgment, is artificial. It is a false dilemma.

> There is no . . . dilemma as between equidistance and equity, but a goal, the equitable solution, which has to be attained by applying the legal rule whereby equidistance is to be corrected in the light of special circumstances.[39]

This campaign against equidistance should not prevent its value being recognized by international law as a method of departure, given its advantages and its inherent link with legal title and the very concept of maritime delimitation.

The practical advantages of equidistance

The campaign against equidistance is the more surprising in that the merits of this method have often been recognized, even for a definitive line, in those judgments which elsewhere have shown themselves most hostile to its use as a provisional line. This is not the least of paradoxes in an area where passion has too often overcome reason.

The convenience, simplicity and scientific character of equidistance have never been disputed. One could say of it what Boggs said of the arcs of circles method for determining the outer limit of the territorial sea: "It is as simple as the use of litmus paper to determine whether a solution is acid or alkali."[40] Everything there was to be said about it was said in the *North Sea* case:

> It has never been doubted that the equidistance method of delimitation is a very convenient one, the use of which is indicated in a considerable number

[39] Guillaume [2], p. 280.
[40] Boggs [4], p. 248.

of cases. It ... has the virtue that ... [the lines] traced by competent cartographers will for all practical purposes agree ... [N]o other method of delimitation has the same combination of practical convenience and certainty of application.[41]

To the simplicity and objectivity of the method must be added the fact that, even though it does not always lead to an equitable result in itself, it *does* produce a line which is *prima facie* equitable. A method which divides the overlapping areas more or less equally respects, *prima facie*, the equal right of the two countries to a certain physical area of maritime jurisdiction and thus, again *prima facie*, avoids an unreasonable encroachment of one State upon the other. A line of equidistance is especially to be recommended as a starting point in that it lends itself particularly well to any adjustments which may prove necessary in order to meet the requirement of an equitable result.[42]

There is thus a striking contrast between, on the one hand, the destructive criticisms sometimes levelled against the equidistance method and, on the other, its advantages, demonstrated by an impressive accumulation of practice and by the praises lavished on it by those very judgments which deny it any privileged status even as a starting point.

Equidistance, long since an accepted point of departure

When two governments are seeking to effect a delimitation by treaty, they nearly always take a line of equidistance as their starting point. This was pointed out by Commander Kennedy in 1958, during the Geneva Conference: even if, in a given situation, there are special circumstances justifying a line other than that of equidistance, this "would still provide the best starting point for negotiations".[43] There is no lack of authoritative evidence for this practice.[44]

---

[41] *North Sea*, paras. 22-3. The courts have continued to take the same line: *Anglo-French* award, para. 85; *Tunisia/Libya*, para. 109; *Gulf of Maine*, para. 195; *Guinea/Guinea-Bissau*, para. 102 ("... a certain intrinsic value because of its scientific character and the relative ease with which it can be applied"); *Libya/Malta*, para. 19 ("... any given set of basepoints will generate only one possible equidistance line"); cf. Boggs' observation: "There is one and only one such line which can be drawn in front of any coast" (Boggs [1], p. 545). On the technique for constructing a line of equidistance, see the references given above, p. 69 n. 160.

[42] Cf. pp. 272-6 below.

[43] UNCLOS I, *Official Documents*, vol. VI, p. 93.

[44] For example, see, Gutteridge, p. 120; Guillaume [2], p. 282; Pearcy, quoted by Whiteman [1], p. 329; Smith [1], p. 402; Voelckel [2], p. 707. M. Guillaume, who, as Legal Affairs Director at the French Ministry for Foreign Affairs, negotiated several

If one is to believe Judge Jiménez de Aréchaga, the courts proceed in the same way. While refusing to give equidistance any priority or privileged status, the former president of the Court says that:

> Naturally, in all cases the decision-maker looks at the line of equidistance, even if none of the parties has invoked it.[45]

In effect, the majority of judgments have taken an equidistance line as their point of departure, and either accepted it as it was because it seemed to them equitable in the particular circumstances of the case, or rejected or modified it because it seemed inequitable.[46]

Equidistance, a legally necessary point of departure

Whether in a negotiated or third-party delimitation, the first step has long been to see what a line of equidistance would produce, simply because a start has to be made somewhere. But, although the equidistance method may have been more convenient than others for beginning the delimitation process, it was not legally necessary. In this sense, the courts' insistence that equidistance had no priority or privileged validity was justified.[47] With the development of the law of maritime delimitation set out in the *Libya/Malta* judgment, the situation changed completely. The practical advantages of the method certainly remain, but now there is a legal reason for requiring—not just recommending—equidistance as a first step: the need to divide the overlapping areas of two coastal projections according to a criterion connected to the legal basis of title to those projections. It is worth recalling that when the maritime areas created by two opposite or adjacent coasts partly overlap, the equidistance method does more than any other to ensure that the two coasts each project over as great a distance as respect for the other allows. The equidistance method, besides reflecting the coastal

---

French maritime delimitation agreements, wrote of equidistance: "Its advantages are obvious ...: it accommodates easily the modifications and corrections necessary to reach the ultimate goal, equity; it is an excellent point of departure for a first, objective, delimitation line which makes it possible for the negotiations to start from something concrete."

[45] *Tunisia/Libya*, p. 105, para. 18. This evidence is all the more significant in that Judge Jiménez de Aréchaga has recently argued against a two-stage process, against equidistance as a legally obligatory point of departure, against the corrective concept, and in favour of a line drawn directly from what he calls the *"factual matrix"* of each case (Jiménez de Aréchaga, p. 232).

[46] *Anglo-French* award, para. 249; *Gulf of Maine*, para. 216; *Libya/Malta*, paras. 61-2.

[47] Except, of course, for the delimitation of the continental shelf between States party to the 1958 Convention, and therefore bound by Article 6 (cf. *Gulf of Maine*, para. 115).

geography, incorporates to a remarkable degree the double parameter of coast and distance which lies at the very heart of the legal concept that States are entitled to maritime areas adjacent to their shores. It takes account of the concept of maritime delimitation as presently provided for by the law. It respects the principle of non-encroachment both in its negative aspect—not to cut off one of the States from "areas situated directly before [its coastal] front"[48]—and its positive aspect—to give each State a boundary line which is sufficiently far from its coasts. The link between title and delimitation, the legal nature of title and the modern concept of delimitation all lead, as we have seen above, to equidistance as a first step. *The law now requires what was originally no more than a matter of convenience.*[49]

2. CHECKING THE EQUITY OF THE RESULT: THE FINISHING LINE

The delimitation process may begin with a line of equidistance but it does not necessarily end with one. Otherwise, one would fall into the trap of regarding equidistance as a principle of law, that is, a legally binding rule, and not simply a method. This trap was avoided, as far as treaty law is concerned, by the International Law Commission and the 1958 Conventions, and by the courts in respect of customary law. The law of maritime delimitation accords a place not only to the legal concept of title, but to the no less legal concept of equity. Equidistance for title purposes, however, does not always satisfy the demands of equity: an equidistant line, even if *prima facie* equitable, may turn out to be inequitable in the light of the particular circumstances of the case in question. The provisional line and the definitive line have to be seen from different perspectives. Each corresponds to one side of the operation. Equidistance must be seen as a point of departure because it is an inherent expression of legal title, and not because it will always and inevitably be equitable—this is not the case. This preliminary line once drawn, it is possible to appreciate "the appropriateness of the equidistance method as a means of effecting a 'just' or 'equitable' delimitation";[50] it is only when one comes to "cross-check"[51] the equity of the results that the fate of the original line of equidistance will be determined. Legal title

---

[48] *North Sea*, para. 44.
[49] Cf. pp. 79ff above.
[50] *Anglo-French* award, para. 242.
[51] Gros, *Tunisia/Libya*, Dissenting Opinion, p. 151, para. 15.

is the starting point, but only if it is found to be equitable can the line of equidistance survive. If it passes this test it will become the definitive boundary line; otherwise, it will have to be adjusted.

It is in this second phase of the delimitation operation, which ought to end in an equitable solution, that equitable principles and relevant circumstances come into play. The original equidistance line, determined on the basis of legal title, is tested against the relevant circumstances of the case. It is this test, using equity in a corrective role, which makes an equitable result possible.

The second phase of the delimitation operation is thus dominated by the equitable principles-relevant circumstances-equitable solution trilogy:

> Judicial decisions are at one . . . in holding that the delimitation . . . must be effected by the application of *equitable principles* in all the *relevant circumstances* in order to achieve an *equitable result.*[52]

The third element relates to the outcome of the exercise, the first two to the means of achieving it.

As in any relationship between means and ends, it is obviously the end which dominates, since it determines both the choice and the implementation of the means. The Court explained in the *Tunisia/Libya* case: "It is . . . the result which is predominant; the principles are subordinate to the goal."[53] It repeated this in *Libya/Malta*: "It is . . . the goal—the equitable result—and not the means used to achieve it, that must be the primary element . . . ."[54] There is, however, an important difference betwen these two statements. In the 1982 approach, as already indicated,[55] the primacy of the end was such as to attract all the legal content; the means were left outside the law for the court to decide on a case by case basis. In the 1985 approach, in contrast, the goal was only "the *primary* element" and the Court was careful to explain that it is for the law to determine both equitable principles and relevant circumstances.[56] Thus, the legal nature of the second phase of the maritime delimitation process is affirmed. This second phase is neither more nor less subject to the law than the first. It is a serious mistake to see a legal phase as being in opposition to an equitable one. One question, however, remains: whether the choice of methods to modify, if necessary, the original

[52] *Libya/Malta*, para. 45.
[53] *Tunisia/Libya*, para. 70.
[54] *Libya/Malta*, para. 45.
[55] See pp. 172-3 above.
[56] See pp. 176-7 above.

line so that it produces an equitable solution, itself has a legal character. We shall need to consider this when we come to the question of possible adjustments to the starting line. For the moment it is the concepts of equitable principles and relevant circumstances which must be examined since it is they which will decide the necessity or usefulness of such an adjustment.

A. Checking the Equity of the Starting Line: Equitable Principles and Relevant Circumstances

The concept of relevant circumstances

The concept of relevant circumstances, introduced into the vocabulary of the law of the sea by the Court in the *North Sea* judgment in 1969, has shown so much vitality that, after absorbing the idea of special circumstances in the 1977 *Anglo-French* award, it has become an integral part of the language of the courts.[57] Even though it does not figure in Articles 74 and 83 of the 1982 Convention, its importance in the maritime delimitation operation remains intact. The function of relevant circumstances is to ascertain that the particular facts of the situation do not render inequitable the line dictated by legal considerations related to title, and do not call for a correction of this line. Their role, let us remind ourselves, is to test the equity of equidistance.[58] It is by taking relevant circumstances into consideration that the individualizing and corrective function of equity expresses itself.[59] Relevant circumstances form a

---

[57] In theory, the two concepts are different: the "special circumstances" of the Geneva Convention only arise in certain situations, whereas the "relevant circumstances" of the courts ("the delimitation is to be effected . . . taking account of all the relevant circumstances" (*North Sea*, para. 101)) exist in all cases. In practice, even in the context of the equidistance-special circumstances rule, it is only after looking at all the "relevant" circumstances that one knows whether or not, in the given case, there are "special" circumstances justifying a delimitation other than an equidistant one. The difference between "special" circumstances and "relevant" circumstances reflects more a difference of approach and terminology than one of substance (cf. *Anglo-French* award, para. 148).

[58] Evensen, *Tunisia/Libya*, Dissenting Opinion, p. 297. Looking at the relevant circumstances makes it possible not only to check the equity of the provisional equidistance line but also to see that any substitution line is equitable. Their function as a test operates in respect of the definitive line just as much as for the provisional line.

[59] Cf. *Anglo-French* award, para. 195 ("Any ground of equity . . . is rather to be looked for in the particular circumstances of the present case") and Jiménez de Aréchaga, *Tunisia/Libya*, Dissenting Opinion, p. 106, para. 24 ("To resort to equity means . . . to appreciate and balance the relevant circumstances of the case").

kind of bridge between the starting line of equidistance, which is not always equitable, and the finishing line of delimitation, which must be.

It follows from this that relevant circumstances must always be taken into consideration. But it also follows that, although relevant circumstances always have to be taken into consideration, they can never be the sole determinant of a delimitation and thus, as we have already seen, do not constitute a self-sufficient factor in delimitation. That is precisely the reason for having a two-stage process.

It is important to note that the facts do not dictate the solution, at either the first or the second stage of the delimitation process. Facts are just as unsuitable for correcting a line already established on the basis of other criteria as for drawing a line *ab initio*. In both cases, the facts are silent. In order to check the equity of the provisional equidistance line, they must be marshalled and evaluated, in themselves and by reference one to another, in the light and from the perspective of a certain conception of equity. What is equitable? What is not? By themselves, the facts have no answer to these questions. Only human judgment can fulfil this task. The consideration and balancing-up of relevant circumstances are deliberate legal acts. They presuppose what might be called a philosophy of equity.

The concept of equitable principles

This philosophy is expressed by equitable principles;[60] and these are the filter through which the court passes the factual aspects of the situations in order to assess the equitable character of a delimitation.

Theoretically, equitable principles and relevant circumstances are different in kind. The concept of relevant circumstances relates to raw facts, such as the concavity of a coast, the presence of an island, or the difference in length of coastal fronts. The concept of equitable principles implies a judgment on these elements of fact and a particular view of the purpose of the delimitation. Relevant circumstances are nature's gift. Equitable principles exist on the level of value judgments. They are man-made.

In practice, however, relevant circumstances and equitable principles go hand in hand, the first never without the second, the second never without the first. Without the help of equitable principles, relevant circumstances would be powerless to produce any assessment of the equity of a situation. It is equitable principles

---

[60] These "principles" are called "criteria" in *Gulf of Maine* (paras. 156ff) and "factors" in *Guinea/Guinea-Bissau* (paras. 87-8); these terms may lead to confusion since they are also used by the judgments for the final proportionality test (cf. p. 236 below).

which make it possible to accord, or deny, legal relevance to the facts and to draw useful conclusions from them for assessing the equity of a delimitation line. The concavity of a coast, or the presence of an island, for example, makes it possible to form a judgment on the provisional delimitation only in the light of a principle according to which equity requires the rectification of excessive deviations in the equidistance line caused by a minor geographic feature. This equitable principle does not arise from any natural or logical necessity; it is the result of a legal choice. At the same time, however, equitable principles would be nothing without relevant circumstances, for they would then form a conceptual framework devoid of content. The principle of non-encroachment, for example, has meaning only by reference to the actual geographical circumstances which cause the line of equidistance to move further towards or away from the coasts of the two parties. In short, equitable principles acquire substance only by reference to the relevant circumstances in the case, and the relevant circumstances in the case operate only with the help and in the context of equitable principles.

To apply equitable principles and to take account of relevant circumstances are, in the end, just two ways of saying the same thing. Nowhere has the link between the two concepts appeared more strikingly than in the passage in the *Libya/Malta* judgment where the Court, giving some examples of equitable principles, cites exactly ''the principle of respect due to all such relevant circumstances''.[61] Equitable principles and relevant circumstances are two sides of the same coin. It is their coming together which produces ''equity as a legal concept''. Logically, equitable principles come before relevant circumstances since it is in the light of principles that circumstances are defined and weighed up. But in practice, the opposite is the case. It is relevant circumstances that give life and body to equitable principles and the courts will often prefer to consider the weight to be given to such and such a fact rather than to formulate equitable principles in the abstract. So, it is *a posteriori*, in the light of relevant circumstances and by implication, that equitable principles can best be understood.

The still unsettled state of the law

It would be nice to make an inventory of the present state of the law and to draw up a list of the equitable principles and relevant circumstances currently applied by the courts. Such a task, however, is fraught with difficulty. As we know, the courts have not always been

---

[61] *Libya/Malta*, para. 46.

persuaded that equitable principles and relevant circumstances have the character of rules of law. They have sometimes suggested that it is on a case by case basis, and according to the actual situation, that a particular principle ought to be considered as equitable, or not, and a particular circumstance as relevant, or not.[62] It is only since *Libya/ Malta* that the legal nature of relevant circumstances and relevant principles has been unambiguously recognized. Therefore, caution must be exercised in extrapolating the position taken in previous judgments into the new legal environment initiated by the *Libya/ Malta* judgment. These judgments offer interesting ideas but not binding precedent.

In *Libya/Malta* the Court provides what it called "some well-known examples" of equitable principles of a normative character. It quotes

> the principle that there is to be no question of refashioning geography, or compensating for the inequalities of nature; the related principle of non-encroachment by one party on the natural prolongation of the other . . . the principle of respect due to all such relevant circumstances; the principle that although all States are equal before the law and are entitled to equal treatment, "equity does not necessarily imply equality" . . . nor does it seek to make equal what nature has made unequal; and the principle that there can be no question of distributive justice.[63]

But these are only examples, formulated, moreover, in a general fashion and at a fairly high level of abstraction. Other principles may be adopted in the future, and the principles cited by the Court formulated differently, in more detail, and in more practical terms.

Relevant circumstances and, through them, equitable principles, constitute at present one of the least precise chapters of the law of maritime delimitation, and on some aspects it is possible to do no more than venture some suggestions on the basis of a rather rough and undeveloped case-law.

The identification of relevant circumstances

In a famous passage in the *North Sea* judgment, the Court declared:

> In fact, there is no legal limit to the considerations which States may take account of for the purpose of making sure that they apply equitable procedures . . . .[64]

[62] Cf. pp. 172ff above.
[63] *Libya/Malta*, para. 46.
[64] *North Sea*, para. 93.

The observation is perfectly true in the context of a negotiated delimitation. In order to decide on the equitable character of the line of equidistance which has served as the starting point for their discussions, two governments can take into consideration any fact they wish without asking themselves whether a court would regard it as relevant. This is why the siting of resources or how to share them—circumstances which, it will be seen, are not relevant in legal terms—are at the root of many treaty delimitations.

There are some who have assumed from the *North Sea* dictum that any circumstance whatsoever may be taken into consideration by the courts. According to this view there is no circumstance which could be rejected as legally irrelevant. If this were so, it would be possible at a given moment to draw up a list of circumstances which had been accepted by the courts, but one would look in vain for any rhyme or reason in it. Relevant circumstances could be described. They could not be defined.

This pragmatic approach has encouraged an almost anarchic proliferation of relevant circumstances. Already in 1977, the *Anglo-French* arbitral award, while putting the emphasis on circumstances of a geographical nature, added "and others".[65] Among these "others" figure "the limits of the territorial seas and coastal fisheries" of the two countries as well as "their respective navigational defence and security interests in the region".[66] In 1982, with *Tunisia/Libya*, the list seemed to grow still longer. To "the facts of geography or geomorphology", the Court added factors as diverse as "the existence and interests of other States in the area, and the existing or potential delimitations between each of the Parties and such States", "the position of the land frontier", "the conduct of the States concerned", "historic rights" and "a number of economic considerations".[67]

A more careful study of the cases, however, shows that the almost limitless interpretation of the *North Sea* dictum has always come up against certain barriers. In almost every case, certain circumstances have been rejected as not legally relevant. Economic facts, for example, as will be seen, have always been treated in a very restrictive fashion. There was, however, no precise criterion governing the judgments, and we had to wait until 1985 for a definition of what circumstances are legally relevant. After repeating the "much-

[65] *Anglo-French* award, paras. 69, 70, 181 and 232.
[66] *Ibid.*, paras. 187-8.
[67] *Tunisia/Libya*, para. 81.

quoted dictum of the Court in its 1969 Judgment'', the *Libya/Malta* judgment goes on:

> Yet although there may be no legal limit to the considerations which States may take account of, this can hardly be true for a court applying equitable procedures. For a court, although there is assuredly no closed list of considerations, it is evident that *only those that are pertinent to the institution of the continental shelf as it has developed within the law*, and to the application of equitable principles to its delimitation, will qualify for inclusion. Otherwise, the legal concept of continental shelf could itself be fundamentally changed by the introduction of considerations strange to its nature.[68]

There can be no doubt. Some circumstances are legally relevant and can play a role in a judicial or arbitral delimitation; others are of no legal interest, and there is no need for the judge or arbitrator to take them into consideration. As for the criterion of relevance, it is now clearly established: those circumstances are relevant which ''are pertinent to the institution'' of the maritime jurisdiction in question ''as it has developed within the law'', that is to say, which play a role in title. Those circumstances which are ''strange to its nature'' and which do not affect the title are not.

The existence of a criterion of legal relevance ensures that the choice of relevant circumstances taken into account by the court in each case no longer rests upon a constant reassessment of equity. The courts remain free, nonetheless, to confer legal relevance upon a factor which has previously been denied it, or, conversely, to refuse legal relevance to a consideration previously accorded it. Moreover, new facts may arise in the future, the relevance of which the courts will decide at the time. Although a degree of stability has been written into the concept of legal relevance, the matter, inevitably, remains in a state of development.

The *Libya/Malta* definition of relevant circumstances is too recent for the courts yet to have developed jurisprudentially. This makes it all the more difficult at present to draw up a list of circumstances which are, or are not, relevant in law for testing equidistance. Judgments prior to *Libya/Malta*, it is true, also accepted or rejected the relevance of circumstances, but they did so at a time when no legal criterion had been established and when the courts were inclined to think that relevance could vary from one situation to another. Moreover, it was not always in relation to a line of equidistance as a first step that relevant circumstances were taken into account, but, more often, in the context of a direct search for an

---

[68] *Libya/Malta*, para. 48.

equitable solution starting from the facts of the case. Solutions prior to 1985 must, therefore, be treated with caution. Some well-established ones are part of the judicial *acquis* and will, no doubt, be followed. Others, sometimes imprecise and contradictory, are unlikely to survive a more rigorous approach. As a result, the subject remains somewhat uncertain, and there is every reason to suppose that, for some time to come, States will remain tempted, as they are at present, to invoke before the courts any fact whatsoever which they think may tilt equity in their favour. This does not help the process of disentangling the legal web of arguments competing for the courts' attention.

In these circumstances, it is possible to offer no more than a few brief comments on some of the circumstances most frequently put forward and on which the courts have given a precise answer or, at least, a fairly detailed legal examination. The nature of the matter means that the discussion of these disparate examples is inevitably fragmentary and illustrative.

Circumstances of a physical nature: the coastal geography

Of the vast range of factual elements which might be taken into account, it is those of a physical nature which are the best established.

It need hardly be recalled that *Libya/Malta* put an end to the legal relevance of the *geological and geophysical characteristics* of the seabed in the delimitation of the continental shelf.[69] The refusal in *Gulf of Maine* to rely on *bio-geographical considerations* for the delimitation of fishery zones, and therefore of the exclusive economic zone, appears just as definitive.[70] It may also be considered as established that considerations relating to the *landmass* extending behind the coasts are irrelevant: "The Court is unable to accept this as a relevant consideration".[71]

There is, on the other hand, one circumstance which the courts are agreed *is* relevant: the *coastal geography*. This has a political as well as a physical aspect.[72] This is why the location of the land frontier—more precisely, its intersection with the shore-line—was regarded as "a circumstance of considerable relevance" in *Tunisia/Libya*[73] and was taken into consideration, although with less emphasis, in *Gulf of*

---

[69] *Libya/Malta*, para. 40.
[70] *Gulf of Maine*, paras. 54-5.
[71] *Libya/Malta*, para. 49.
[72] Cf. *Gulf of Maine*, para. 195.
[73] *Tunisia/Libya*, para. 82.

Maine[74] and *Guinea/Guinea-Bissau.*[75] But it is, of course, the physical aspect which has held the attention of the courts, to the point of becoming the most important relevant circumstance.[76] This essentially, is what the *Gulf of Maine* judgment is referring to when it says that equitable principles and delimitation methods must be chosen "against a background of geography".[77] Looked at more closely, the concept of coastal geography in the physical sense, far from being monolithic, has itself several different aspects which will not necessarily all be accorded the same legal relevance. The relevance of the configuration of the coasts as such has long been recognized and is hardly likely to be challenged in the future, but the relevance of coastal lengths and the geographical relationship (opposition or adjacency) between the two coasts remains controversial and uncertain. These various aspects of the concept of coastal geography must therefore be considered separately.

The dual function of the coastal geography

As shown above,[78] it is because of the decisive role of coasts in the theory of maritime projections that the delimitation process starts with the method which reflects the coastal fronts of the two countries most faithfully. The role of the coastal geography does not, however, stop at this first stage of the delimitation operation. It is likely to come into play also in the second phase, this time as a circumstance relevant to the decision as to whether or not the provisional line is equitable. The facts of the coastal geography thus constitute the "dominant parameters"[79] in the two phases of the delimitation process: at the first stage, its role as an element in the legal basis of title means that coastal geography dictates the original equidistance line; at the second stage, when it comes to the definitive delimitation, it is the parameter of reference *par excellence* for determining the equity of the line. In other words, having generated the original line of

[74] *Gulf of Maine*, paras. 217-18.

[75] *Guinea/Guinea-Bissau*, para. 106.

[76] Occasionally, the Courts have taken notice of geographical aspects unconnected with the coastal geography properly speaking, such as the general geographical context or the distance between the coasts of the parties. (On these problems, see pp. 248ff below.)

[77] *Gulf of Maine*, para. 199. Human geography, with its socio-economic aspects, in contrast to physical geography, has been rejected as a relevant circumstance (see pp. 260ff below).

[78] See pp. 72ff above.

[79] *Gulf of Maine*, para. 231.

equidistance, the coastal geography will provide the means of criticizing and possibly modifying it.

If one is to believe the courts, the need to correct the equidistance line in certain geographical situations arises out of inherent defects in the equidistance method, defects which justify modification of the line. In certain configurations, inequitable effects appear which, according to the Court in the *North Sea* case, ''are directly attributable to the use of the equidistance method''.[80] The Court has never gone back on its reasoning in this case,[81] when it blamed equidistance for the inequity produced in certain geographical contexts. In *Libya/ Malta*, the Court denounced ''the use of a method inapt to take adequate account of some kinds of coastal configuration'' and which causes ''distortion—disproportion''. It went on to explain the nature of this inherent vice:

> . . . since an equidistance line is based on a principle of proximity and is therefore controlled only by salient coastal points, it may yield a disproportionate result where a coast is markedly irregular or markedly concave or convex. In such cases, the raw equidistance method may leave out of the calculation appreciable lengths of coast, whilst at the same time giving undue influence to others . . . .[82]

The circumstance causing the inequity of the provisional line of equidistance is thus to be found, according to the Court's perception, not in the geographical situation but in a ''technical quirk'' of the equidistance method.[83]

Although this language, by force of repetition, may seem to have become a statement of the obvious, it is nonetheless vitiated by a fundamental error. The need to make corrections to the initial equidistance line is not in the least attributable to the need to remedy some intrinsic defect in the equidistance method, but rather to the judges' feeling that the consequences of geography as it is are not equitable and should not be accepted. Thus, in particular, the cut-off or encroachment effect noted in some judgments is not the perverse result of the equidistance method, but entirely due to the shore-line, to the actual geographical facts. It is not the defects of the method which would have caused a line equidistant between France and the

---

[80] *North Sea*, para. 8.

[81] Cf. *ibid.*, paras. 24 and 89 (''. . . in certain geographical circumstances which are quite frequently met with, the equidistance method, despite its known advantages, leads unquestionably to inequity'').

[82] *Libya/Malta*, para. 56.

[83] *Ibid.*

United Kingdom to project towards France in the Atlantic region, but the combined geographical facts that the English landmass stretches further westwards than the French and that the Scillies are situated further seawards than Ushant.[84] The fact that a line equidistant between Guinea and Guinea-Bissau produced a cut-off effect at the expense of Guinea is not the fault of the method but of the geographical circumstance that the coast of Guinea-Bissau projects further seaward than that of Guinea.[85] The equidistance method is no more responsible for the inequity of delimitation in certain geographical configurations than is the thermometer for the temperature. The culprit is the geographical configuration itself, whose whims and eccentricities the equidistance method simply translates. And the real purpose of correcting the equidistance line is to establish a delimitation corresponding to a reconstituted geography, more equitable in the judges' eyes than the actual geography—a geography in which the Scillies would have been located closer to the English coast than they are, and in which the Bijagos Islands would have benefited Guinea-Bissau less than in fact they do.

It would thus appear that, under cover of testing the equity of equidistance, it is the equity of the geography which the courts are to assess. In condemning the method, the courts have once again mistaken the target and found an innocent victim. The culprit in all the cases of alleged "distortion", "disproportion", "deviation", is not the equidistance method but nature and the courts determine the equity of this nature in the light of an equitable principle according to which a maritime boundary must always, *whatever the geographical facts*, be at a sufficient distance from each of the coasts.[86] It is this equitable principle of an eminently political character which constitutes the ultimate justification for any adjustment of the original line of equidistance, and not the baleful capacity imputed to the equidistance method for generating inequities in certain geographical contexts.

The all-purpose "relevant circumstances of geographical character" gives expression to the complex and ambiguous conception which the law of maritime delimitation has of the relationship between nature and the law.[87] First, respect for nature leading to equidistance, then an adjustment of geography in the light of equity

---

[84] See the *Anglo-French* award, paras. 243ff.

[85] See *Guinea/Guinea-Bissau*, para. 103.

[86] See pp. 60ff above and pp. 265-6, 285 below.

[87] See pp. 85-90 above.

tested against the relevant circumstances. Thus is clearly demonstrated the double function of geography, on the one hand, as an element in the legal title and a factor determining the original line of delimitation, and on the other, as a relevant circumstance which may lead to an adjustment of this line.

The general configuration of the coasts

Ever since 1969, it has been a point of principle that a delimitation must take account of "the general configuration of the coasts of the Parties".[88] To the extent that this rule forms part of the theory of coastal projections, it is sufficient to refer to previous discussion of the function of the coasts in the concept of maritime delimitation.[89] We have seen, in particular, that once it has been decided which segments of the two coasts are relevant for the delimitation, it is their configuration, through the medium of the equidistance method, which will determine the first-stage delimitation line. At this point, it is the first of the two functions of coastal geography which the general configuration is called on to fulfil. This has already been sufficiently explained. What now needs to be considered is the role assigned by the courts to the coastal configuration at the second stage of the process, when it is a question of the equity of the line which has emerged from the coastal projection theory. To what extent, and in what circumstances, can the general configuration of the coasts of the parties give rise to inequity in an equidistance line? This is the question now for consideration.

In 1969 the Court denounced the inequitable character of the equidistance method in the case of a State whose coasts were strongly concave or convex in comparison with those of two neighbouring States:

> . . . where two such lines are drawn at different points on a concave coast, they will, if the curvature is pronounced, inevitably meet at a relatively short distance from the coast . . . . In contrast to this, the effect of coastal projections, or of convex or outwardly curving coasts . . . is to cause boundary lines drawn on an equidistance basis to leave the coast on divergent courses . . . .[90]

Since then, a concavity and a convexity, a "recessing" or "projecting"[91] coast, have been the principal examples of configurations

[88] *North Sea*, para. 101D1.
[89] See pp. 71ff above.
[90] *North Sea*, para. 8.
[91] *Ibid.*

regarded as causing inequities in the context of the equidistance method. In *Gulf of Maine*, for example, the United States based an important part of its criticism of the equidistance line advocated by Canada on the concavity of the Gulf as a whole.[92] The Chamber, however, did not endorse this view. It was not the concavity of the Gulf which caught its attention but rather its more or less rectangular appearance.[93] Although it rejected the Canadian equidistance line, this was for reasons other than the concavity of the Gulf.[94] It is true that this case lacked the characterizing feature of the *North Sea* case, i.e., a recessing coast situated between the protruding coasts of two adjacent countries, but it was less the concavity of the German coast which was at issue in 1969 than the result of two equidistance lines, between three States, taken conjointly.[95] In the *Guinea/Guinea-Bissau* case, the concave or convex configuration again played an important role. "When ... there are three adjacent States along a concave coastline", said the Tribunal "the equidistance method has the other drawback of resulting in the middle country being enclaved by the other two and thus prevented from extending its maritime territory as far seaward as international law permits".[96]

Concavity and convexity are not, however, the only configurations capable of causing inequity in an equidistance line. The Court has noticeably enlarged the bill of indictment, and in fact suggests that any markedly irregular coastline renders an equidistance line inequitable.[97] The charge thus levelled at equidistance is as excessive as it is unjustified. If equidistance, by definition, were inappropriate wherever the coast was irregular, there would remain very few situations in which it would be appropriate. The majority practice in negotiated delimitations is enough to give the lie to such an extreme point of view, which would make equidistance the rarest of exceptions, a veritable museum piece. Moreover, as already demonstrated, because of the technique used, equidistance gives a faithful reflection of the configuration of even the most irregular

---

[92] "The distortion inherent in the application of the equidistance method to concavities is well established" (United States Memorial, para. 328).

[93] *Gulf of Maine*, paras. 29, 184, 213 and 218.

[94] *Ibid.*, paras. 178ff.

[95] *North Sea*, paras. 8 and 91.

[96] *Guinea/Guinea-Bissau*, para. 104.

[97] The degree of irregularity which a coast must show to produce the unwanted effect imputed to equidistance varies from one judgment to another. In the *North Sea* case, the Court thought that "[t]he slightest irregularity in a coastline is automatically magnified by the equidistance line" and "leads unquestionably to inequity" (*North Sea*, para. 89). In *Libya/Malta* (para. 56) it accuses the method of yielding "a disproportionate result where a coast is *markedly irregular* or *markedly concave or convex*".

coasts,[98] so faithful indeed that, in order to avoid too tortuous a delimitation line, a simplified version of equidistance is sometimes used.[99]

Other geographical circumstances, besides the concavity (or convexity) of the coast and its irregularity, often said to be liable to produce inequity in an equidistance line, are the length of the coasts and their relationship of opposition or adjacency one to another. In view of the arguments to which these ideas have given rise, it is best to consider them separately.[100]

Before going any further, it is worth pointing out the extent to which the apparently simple idea of the general configuration of the coasts is subject to interpretation. For example, when there is an island formation near to the shore of one of the parties, the coast of the latter will appear convex or not depending on whether this formation is or is not incorporated in the description of the shore-line. In *Guinea/Guinea-Bissau*, for example, the coast of Guinea-Bissau could only be described by the Tribunal as convex because the Bijagos Islands were included. If it had taken only the mainland coast into consideration, it would have been dealing with a concave shore-line.[101] The scale of the map being used is another highly influential factor. A recession or a salient takes on different proportions depending on whether the map is small or large scale. Finally, apart from any cartographic distortions, the assessment of the configuration of the coast will inevitably be a function of the micro- or macrogeographic view which is taken. The *Guinea/Guinea-Bissau* award is particularly revealing in this respect:

> If the coasts of each country are examined separately, it can be seen that the Guinea-Bissau coastline is convex, when the Bijagos are taken into account, and that of Guinea is concave. However, if they are considered together, it can be seen that the coastline of both countries is concave and this characteristic is accentuated if we consider the presence of Sierra Leone further south .... However, while the continuous coastline of the two Guineas—or of the three countries when Sierra Leone is included—is generally concave, that of West Africa in general is undoubtedly convex.[102]

Nor can the regularity or irregularity of a coast be regarded as a scientific fact. There is no need of long explanation to be persuaded

---

[98] See pp. 72ff above.
[99] See pp. 272-3 below.
[100] See pp. 235ff and 244ff below.
[101] *Guinea/Guinea-Bissau*, para. 103.
[102] *Ibid.*, paras. 103 and 108.

that a coast will seem more or less regular according to the scale of the map, or the size of the segment taken into account. As with concavity, one's spectacles determine what one sees.

The idea of the general direction of the coasts has sometimes been put forward as a way of mitigating the allegedly harmful effects of equidistance, the thought being that by relying on this, rather than the actual, tortuous shoreline, one would avoid the inconveniences inherent in the equidistance method. The idea of general direction has cropped up in several cases, in different guises. In the *Anglo-French* case, France maintained that the configuration to be adopted for the Atlantic region should be determined by the prolongation into the Atlantic of straight lines reflecting the general direction of the coasts of the two countries in the Channel.[103] In *Tunisia/Libya*, the Court took into consideration as a relevant circumstance "the radical change in the general direction of the Tunisian coastline marked by the Gulf of Gabes": "no delimitation . . . could be regarded as equitable which failed to take account of that feature".[104] In *Gulf of Maine*, the United States maintained that a line of equidistance would not take account of the general direction of the eastern coast of the North American continent.[105] In *Guinea/Guinea-Bissau*, the Tribunal took into consideration the "general direction of the coastline" and "the overall configuration of the West African coastline".[106]

But the cure is worse than the disease. Of all the aspects of the general configuration of the shoreline, the concept of the general direction of the coasts is one of the hardest to pin down, and one of the most debatable. To draw straight lines between given points on the coast in order to determine the length of a coastal front is permissible. Although the method may always be tainted by a certain arbitrariness, this is acceptable, as we shall see later,[107] when the calculation does not have a direct influence on the delimitation, but comes into play only as an *a posteriori* check—and a very rough one at that—on the reasonable proportionality between the coastal lengths and the areas in question. When, by contrast, it is a matter of making the general direction of the coast a relevant circumstance for the purpose of a possible adjustment to a line of delimitation, the subjectivity of the concept makes it hard to accept. This subjectivity has been very conspicuous in all the cases. The reason the Anglo-French Tribunal did not pronounce on the British argument that the

[103] *Anglo-French* award, paras. 207ff.
[104] *Tunisia/Libya*, para. 122.
[105] *Gulf of Maine*, paras. 170-1.
[106] *Guinea/Guinea-Bissau*, para. 110.
[107] Cf. pp. 78ff above and pp. 236ff below.

method of *"lignes de lissage"* proposed by the French was "purely arbitrary"[108] was that it rejected the French thesis on another ground. It nonetheless noted[109] "the difficulties which the application of that method would involve in determining the precise lines that should be considered as the appropriate representation of the general directions of the two coasts". In *Tunisia/Libya*, the Court made no secret of the differences of opinion geographers might have "as to the 'direction' . . . of any coast which does not run straight for an extensive distance on each side of the point at which a perpendicular is to be drawn", and it acknowledged that the point where the direction of the coast changes "cannot be objectively determined".[110] In *Gulf of Maine*, the Chamber refused to base itself on the "abstract concept" of the "general direction" of the coast, above all because, in the area to be delimited, "the real geographical configuration differs so markedly from such general direction".[111] It must be said that with coasts changing direction as often as do coasts within a gulf, the idea of a *single* general direction seems a little artificial.[112] In fact, only in *Guinea/Guinea-Bissau* has this concept been used to the full. Rejecting the "short coastline" in favour of the "facade", the Tribunal took as its reference not only the totality of the "continuous coast" of the two countries concerned but the "general configuration of the West African coastline", and it was by reference to the general direction expressing this "overall configuration" that it drew the boundary in the form of a perpendicular to the straight line connecting a point in Senegal to a point in Sierra Leone.[113] An odd idea, one might say, of the general direction of the coast of two States, a line joining two points located in third countries, crossing islands and even encroaching on the mainland.[114] Rarely can the concept of the general direction of the coast have seemed so arbitrary.

---

[108] *Anglo-French* award, para. 230.

[109] *Ibid.*, para. 247.

[110] *Tunisia/Libya*, paras. 120 and 123.

[111] *Gulf of Maine*, para. 176.

[112] The Chamber nonetheless turned to the idea of the general direction of the coasts to represent the tortuous shoreline of the Gulf of Maine, made up of headlands and bays, dotted with islets and rocks, in the form of an "elongated rectangle" (*Gulf of Maine*, paras. 29 and 184). Judge Gros strongly criticized this "mythical rectangle", the fourth side of which was an "unreal closing line of the Gulf" (*Gulf of Maine*, Dissenting Opinion, p. 378, para. 32).

[113] *Guinea/Guinea-Bissau*, paras. 109-10.

[114] The 800 kilometre line from Pointe des Almadies to Cape Shilling, which the award took as representing the general direction of the coast, crosses the land territory of the two States for nearly 350 kilometres and, at places, is nearly 70 kilometres inland. The line adopted by the Court in *Tunisia/Libya* to represent the general direction of the

These few remarks suffice to reveal the falsely objective nature of the concept of the general direction of the coasts. Like beauty, "general direction" lies in the eye of the beholder. This is obvious so as far as the general direction of the coast is concerned. It is no less true of other aspects of the coastal configuration such as concavity and regularity. One always comes back to the same observation: since a line of equidistance, by its very nature, reflects the direction of the two coasts and their changes of direction, together with the irregularities of the shoreline as a whole, any adjustment to this line on the grounds of the general configuration of the coast amounts, in the end, to a correction of geography. The court substitutes for the real configuration another which it finds more equitable. Under cover of relevant geographical circumstances, geography is, in fact, refashioned. Here, a salient is reduced or wiped out, there, an indentation corrected, elsewhere, an irregular shoreline replaced by an imaginary general direction. The statement made earlier[115] is borne out; the alleged inequity of the equidistance method serves as a scapegoat. Nature, not equidistance, should be the target. The revisionism which characterizes the concept of the general configuration of the coast as a relevant circumstance is magnified when accompanied by a macrogeographical approach,[116] and Judge Koretsky's warning in 1969 has lost none of its force: "All macrogeographical considerations are entirely irrelevant, except in the improbable framework of a desire to redraw the political map of one or more regions of the world".[117]

General configuration and special features

In 1969, the Court, taking up ideas previously developed in connection with the delimitation of the territorial sea, and extended by the International Law Commission and the Geneva Conference to the delimitation of the continental shelf,[118] tackled the problem of how to take account of geographical facts by drawing on a distinction which we have met already.[119] The delimitation, says the Court, must take account of "the *general configuration* of the coasts of the

---

Tunisian coast north of the Gulf of Gabès also runs inland, to about 11 kilometres from the coast. (*Tunisia/Libya*, para. 128, with the map at p. 90; cf. Judge Evensen's criticism; p. 303, para. 19).

[115] See p. 219 above.

[116] See below, pp. 249ff on the question of taking the "general geographical context" into account.

[117] *North Sea*, Dissenting Opinion, p. 162.

[118] Cf. pp. 170ff above.

[119] See pp. 89ff above.

Parties as well as the presence of any *special or unusual features*".[120] At
first sight, these two concepts seem to derive from the same source.
Delimitation must be modelled on nature in all its aspects, both its
general lines and its "pronounced configurations".[121] Looked at
more closely, the two concepts serve completely different purposes:
the line must reflect the general geographical configuration; it need
not reflect the special geographical features. This guideline to States
in respect of a negotiated delimitation was elevated by the *Anglo-
French* arbitral award into a rule of law to be applied by the courts
in any delimitation carried out in conformity with international law.

This approach is based on the idea, mentioned above, that in some
geographical contexts equidistance has perverse side-effects. The
Court and the Anglo-French Court of Arbitration started from the
idea that certain minor coastal irregularities cause the equidistance
method to lead to "results that appear on the face of them to be
extraordinary, unnatural or unreasonable",[122] in the sense that the
boundary may find itself shifted too far towards one of the coasts,
thus cutting off the other State from "areas situated directly before
[its] front".[123] The Court and the Court of Arbitration saw in the
explosive effect of the conjunction of equidistance and a certain
geographical situation an anomaly which equity required to be
corrected. It is important, said the Court, to find a way "of abating
the effects of an incidental special feature from which an unjustifiable
difference of treatment could result".[124] "The function of equity",
explained the Anglo-French Court of Arbitration, "is ... an
appropriate abatement of the inequitable effects of the distorting
geographical feature".[125]

The method of achieving this is extremely simple. The equidistance line is to be drawn as if the special feature does not exist or
is less important than in fact is the case. The equidistance method,
although carrying the blame for the situation to be corrected, is not
abandoned. It is applied to a geographical reality which has first been
adjusted to meet the needs of the case. More precisely, the courts will
seek to ascertain whether a minor geographical feature, which is out
of line with the general configuration of the coast, has a disproportionate effect on the equidistance line, by comparison with the line
which would have been produced had this feature not existed, and is

[120] *North Sea*, para. 101D.
[121] *Ibid.*, para. 96.
[122] *Ibid.*, para. 24.
[123] *Ibid.*, para. 44.
[124] *Ibid.*, para. 91.
[125] *Anglo-French* award, para. 251.

therefore unreasonable and inequitable. As the *Guinea/Guinea-Bissau* award was later to say, one must not give "exaggerated importance to certain insignificant features of the coastline" in order to avoid either State suffering "a cut-off effect which would satisfy no equitable principle".[126]

According to this theory, the courts do not intend every geographical feature to be taken into account for correcting the original line of equidistance, but only those which are special, unusual, non-essential, insignificant. Nor does every deviation, however minimal, have to be corrected because it produces an inequity, but only those which, by a kind of multiplier effect, cause a "disproportionately distorting effect", an "unjustifiable difference of treatment", or "results which are on the face of them extraordinary, unnatural or unreasonable".[127] The aim is not to correct all inequities, whatever their importance; ". . . it is not the function of equity . . . to create a situation of complete equity where nature and geography have created an inequity"[128] but, more modestly, to erase the most flagrant and most obvious ones. Insignificant distortions do not call for any correction: *de minimis non curat delimitator*.

It will be recalled that, when the International Law Commission and the 1958 Geneva Conference began work on the concept of special circumstances, three examples were given: islands, navigation channels and certain exceptional coastal configurations. Navigation channels seem to have been forgotten,[129] but the other two remain topical even if the courts have thrown out the equidistance/special circumstances rule as a rule of general international law. Operating on the basis of customary law, the Court suggested in the *North Sea* case that no account be taken of "islets, rocks and minor coastal projections, the disproportionally distorting effect of which can be eliminated by other means".[130] The Court was no doubt impressed by the Federal Republic of Germany's demonstration that an almost insignificant salient on one of the coasts (or the presence of an island off one of the coasts) causes a displacement of the equidistance line to the benefit of the State with this geographical feature, a displacement becoming more marked the further one goes

---

[126] *Guinea/Guinea-Bissau*, para. 103.

[127] It will be seen later (pp. 237ff below) that the excessive and unreasonable character of the distortion will be assessed by reference to the proportionality criterion.

[128] *Anglo-French* award, para. 249.

[129] This consideration played a role in the *Beagle Channel* case (see p. 141 n. 109 above), particularly in the vicinity of Gable Island "where the habitually used navigable track has been followed" (para. 110).

[130] *North Sea*, para. 57.

from the coast and being greater in the case of adjacent than opposite coasts.[131] Twenty years later, salients and islands still form the bulk of the category of unimportant geographical features liable to cause inequitable results.

Which, more precisely, are the salients whose effects warrant correction? Whereas the *North Sea* judgment spoke of "minor coastal projections", the *Anglo-French* award referred, in contrast, to an "exceptionally long promontory".[132] Should the effect of a salient be discounted or attenuated when it is negligible—in which case, the correction is pointless—or, on the contrary, when it is particularly pronounced—in which case there is no question but that it is a case of rectifying nature? The concept is far from clear.

It is therefore understandable that the courts have not found it easy to ignore this or that protrusion of the coast of one of the parties. The Anglo-French Court of Arbitration did, indeed, note that the landmass of the United Kingdom projects further westward than the landmass of France, but in the end it did not draw any conclusions from this, and it was the position of the Scilly Islands compared to that of Ushant which was taken as the special feature calling for correction.[133] In the *Dubai/Sharjah* case, full effect was given to the port installations of the two countries which both projected into the sea.[134] In *Gulf of Maine*, Canada maintained that the salient formed by the Cape Cod peninsula constitutes a "particular geographical configuration",[135] the effect of which should be eliminated. It also constructed its line of equidistance starting from the base of the Cape, acting thus as if the Cape did not exist. The United States, for its part, presented the whole of the Canadian Province of Nova Scotia[136] as an aberrant protrusion in relation to the general direction of the coast of the American mainland and, although it did not demand that it be completely ignored, argued that at least its coastline should be treated as a "secondary coast", whose projection must be effaced by the "primary coast" of the United States. The Chamber wasted no time in rejecting both the Canadian demand for

[131] Cf. p. 139 above and p. 245 below.

[132] *Anglo-French* award, para. 244.

[133] *Ibid.*, paras. 235, 244 and 245.

[134] *Dubai/Sharjah*, p. 235.

[135] A hundred kilometres long, the Cape Cod peninsular carries the United States coast almost 50 kilometres eastward. Taking this peninsular into account, Canada argued, would mean a loss to it of an area 8 times the size of the peninsular itself. Canada saw this as an inequity it was necessary to correct. (Canadian Counter-Memorial, para. 137; Canadian Reply, para. 138).

[136] The area of Nova Scotia is 45,000 square kilometres.

the removal of "these alleged geographical anomalies",[137] and the American demand for "ignoring even the existence of real coasts, and disregarding them on account of their allegedly 'secondary' character".[138]

Strictly speaking, the Chamber's decision goes beyond the case in question. It rejects in principle "the idea ... that certain geographical features are to be deemed aberrant by reference to the presumed dominant characteristics of an area, coast or even continent". Geographical features, it states, cannot be the object of a value judgment, positive or negative. They are "the result of natural phenomena, so that they can only be taken as they are".[139] Such a far-reaching pronouncement ought to sound the death knell of the whole theory of insignificant features. Perhaps it will have this effect in relation to coastal salients. The same can hardly be hoped for as far as islands are concerned (even though the problem in principle is the same),[140] given that the application of this dialectic to island formations is now firmly established.

Islands

Islands are, indeed, the principal example of the theory of non-essential geographical features. Numerous studies have been devoted to the role of islands in maritime delimitation, among them several recent works setting out the present state of the subject.[141] There is no need, therefore, to go over the whole ground again, and a few general remarks will suffice. It is hardly necessary to point out that we are dealing here only with dependent islands, i.e. islands under the sovereignty of one or other of the parties. The problem, fundamentally different, of island States has been mentioned earlier[142] and will not be reverted to.

Although the 1958 and 1982 Conventions do not provide any special rule on the subject, it has always been accepted, in State practice as in legal theory, that the effect given to islands by

---

[137] *Gulf of Maine*, para. 182.

[138] *Ibid.*, para. 177.

[139] *Ibid.*, paras. 36 and 37.

[140] The *Gulf of Maine* judgment itself applies the theory of minor features to Seal Island (cf. p. 231 below).

[141] See in particular Bowett [2], Delin, Dipla, Dupuy, Gounaris [1], Hodgson [1], Karl, Laveissière, Marín López, Symmons.

[142] See p. 52 above. We are speaking here, of course, only about the role of dependent islands for delimitation purposes. The problem of the title of islands to maritime areas proper (territorial sea, continental shelf or exclusive economic zone) will not be considered.

international law for delimitation purposes differs from one island to another. Reference is often made, on this point, to Commander Kennedy's intervention at the 1958 Geneva Conference. After noting, as mentioned previously, that "among the special circumstances which might exist there was, for example, the presence of a small or large island in the area to be apportioned", the United Kingdom representative suggested that "for purposes of drawing a boundary, islands should be treated on their merits".[143] The "merits" to be taken into consideration are various: the size of the island, its population, its economy, its position on the "good" or "bad" side of the median line or nearer to or further from one of the coasts. Depending on the circumstances, the island will be given full or partial effect. In certain cases it will be ignored. In others it will be enclaved, which means that the delimitation will be carried out between the mainlands as if the island did not exist, and it will be given its own maritime space around its coasts. These various approaches have been dealt with extensively in the literature, and there are many examples in State practice.

The courts apply the theory of special geographical features to islands. If the island appears as an integral part of the general coastal configuration, it is treated for the purposes of delimitation on the same footing as the mainland and given full effect. If, on the other hand, it seems to be an aberrant geographical feature in relation to the general configuration or an insignificant feature, it is given partial effect or ignored. The result is that the courts, in adopting the general configuration/special features theory, and relying on much the same "merits" as scholars and State practice, have arrived at the same diversity as they. In the *Anglo-French* case, the geographical situation of the Channel Islands, their size, population and political status, led the Court of Arbitration to an enclave solution: first, a median line was drawn between the two countries, as a "primary boundary", without taking the islands into account; then, in a second stage, the islands were given their own belt of continental shelf, 12 miles in width.[144] As for the Scillies, the fact that they are situated twice as far westwards from the landmass of the United Kingdom as is the Isle of Ushant from the landmass of France, seemed to the Court of Arbitration a special geographical feature which could not be completely ignored. The Scillies are, in effect, like Ushant, "islands of a certain size and populated".[145] But it would

[143] See p. 171 n. 26 above.
[144] *Anglo-French* award, paras. 201-2.
[145] *Ibid.*, para. 248.

not have been possible, because of the general equality which characterizes the coasts of the two countries, to give them full effect. The Court of Arbitration therefore decided to give these islands half-effect which, it said,

> ... consists in delimiting the line equidistant between the two coasts, first, without the use of the offshore island as a basepoint and, secondly, with its use as a basepoint; a boundary giving half-effect to the island is then the line drawn mid-way between those two equidistance lines.[146]

For the same reasons, the Court thought it necessary, in *Tunisia/Libya*, to "attribute some effect" to the Kerkennah Islands because of "their size and position".[147] The solution adopted was again that of the half-effect.[148] Despite its size and population, the island of Jerba, in contrast, had no influence on the delimitation line.[149]

The *Dubai/Sharjah* arbitral award allowed no effect to the island of Abu Musa for the delimitation of the continental shelf, according it only a twelve-mile belt of territorial waters.[150]

In *Gulf of Maine*, the Chamber decided to discount certain "minor geographical features", in particular "tiny islands, uninhabited rocks or low-tide elevations, sometimes lying at a considerable distance from terra firma".[151] On the other hand, it considered that it could not discount Seal Island "by reason both of its dimensions and, more particularly, of its geographical position", as well as the fact that it is "inhabited all the year round". It therefore gave it half-effect.[152]

---

[146] *Ibid.*, para. 251.

[147] *Tunisia/Libya*, para. 128.

[148] The *Tunisia/Libya* judgment gives a different definition of half-effect from that which figures in the *Anglo-French* award. This difference is explained by the fact that the half-effect is applied here without any reference to equidistance, while in the *Anglo-French* award, the question was raised in the context of the determination of the basepoints before being used for drawing a line of equidistance. The definition in the *Tunisia/Libya* judgment is as follows: "Briefly, the technique involves drawing two delimitation lines, one giving to the island the full effect attributed to it by the delimitation method in use, and the other disregarding the island totally, as though it did not exist. The delimitation line actually adopted is then drawn between the first two lines, either in such a way as to divide equally the area between them, or as bisector of the angle which they make with each other, or possibly by treating the island as displaced toward the mainland by half its actual distance therefrom" (*Tunisia/Libya*, para. 129).

[149] *Ibid.*, para. 120 (though the Court had previously said that "the presence of the island of Jerba ... is a circumstance which clearly calls for consideration" (*ibid.*, para. 79)).

[150] *Dubai/Sharjah*, pp. 264-5.

[151] *Gulf of Maine*, para. 201.

[152] *Ibid.*, para. 222.

In *Guinea/Guinea-Bissau*, the minuscule, deserted island of Alcatraz played a more important role in defining the line than the larger Bijagos Islands, most of which are inhabited.[153]

Finally, in *Libya/Malta*, the Court thought it equitable not to take the uninhabited islet of Filfa into account in calculating the median line between Malta and Libya.[154]

This deliberately stark account demonstrates that the rule of law developed by the courts within the framework of customary law roughly corresponds to the guidance given to the States by the Court in the *North Sea* case for negotiation purposes: take no account of "rocks" and "islets", but *do* take account, in varying degrees, of the most important island formations.

This rule is simple only in appearance. It must first be noted that the theory of the graduated effect of islands in delimitation crops up in different contexts. In the majority of examples quoted from the case-law, the question arises for the purpose of determining base-points for a line of equidistance. Is this line to be drawn from the island, or from the mainland, or, perhaps, from a fictitious point between the island and the mainland? In two cases, however, equidistance was rejected from the outset and so the theory of the graduated effect had nothing to do with determining the basepoints for a line of equidistance. The island of Jerba had no effect on the delimitation line in *Tunisia/Libya* because this line was drawn as a perpendicular to the general direction of the shore ignoring "coastal configurations found at more than a comparatively short distance" from the land boundary, "for example the island of Jerba".[155] And the half-effect given in this same case to the Kerkennah Islands was seen by the Court from the point of view of determining the angle which the second segment of the line should form with the meridian, so this too was unconnected with the drawing of an equidistance line.[156] Nor was it a question in *Guinea/Guinea-Bissau* of taking, or not taking, this or that island as a basepoint for a line of equidistance: it was for quite different reasons, specific to the case, that the islet of Alcatraz had an influence on the drawing of the maritime boundary.[157]

Another source of complication: the question of taking islands into account arises not only for the purpose of drawing the delimitation line, but also for determining the general configuration of the shore-

---

[153] *Guinea/Guinea-Bissau*, para. 107.
[154] *Libya/Malta*, para. 64.
[155] *Tunisia/Libya*, para. 120.
[156] *Ibid.*, paras. 127-9.
[157] *Guinea/Guinea-Bissau*, paras. 106-7 and 111.

line and calculating the coastal length. These three functions do not coincide, so that an island may be taken into consideration for one or other of them and yet not for all. Two examples illustrate this somewhat surprising phenomenon. In *Tunisia/Libya*, the island of Jerba, as we have seen, was not taken into account in establishing the general direction by reference to which was drawn the perpendicular which was to constitute the line of delimitation, but it was taken into account when the Court came to calculate the length of coastal fronts for purposes of the ultimate test of proportionality. As to the Kerkennah Islands, although they were given half-effect for drawing the line, they were ignored in one of the calculations of proportionality.[158] Taking sophistication still further, the *Guinea/Guinea-Bissau* award made a distinction between three sorts of islands, and thus subtly modulated their impact on the delimitation.[159] Coastal islands, close to the mainland and often connected to it at low tide, were considered part of the mainland in all respects, i.e., for purposes of determining the general shape of the shore-line, calculating the coastal length, drawing the boundary. The Bijagos Islands, which extend between 2 and 37 nautical miles from the mainland, were used by the Tribunal to establish the convexity of the coast of Guinea-Bissau, but played hardly any role in drawing the boundary. As for the scattered islets further to the south, these were quite simply ignored when it was a question of determining the shape of the shore-line and measuring its length, but one of them, the islet of Alcatraz, as previously noted, played a decisive role in the drawing of a segment of the boundary. It may be added that, in this same case, a long segment of the boundary was defined as a perpendicular to a line of general direction of the coast which ignored the islands altogether. This kaleidoscopic role of islands in delimitation, scarcely explained in the case-law, is one of the most difficult aspects of the subject.

Despite its apparent attraction, this dialectic between non-essential characteristics and the general configuration is undoubtedly somewhat confusing. It would, of course, be possible, at the cost of a somewhat tedious recitation, to draw up a list of solutions adopted by successive judgments, but it would be impossible to put them into any sort of order. Why has this geographical fact been thought to give rise to inequity and not another? Why has this island been considered insignificant, and not that one? Why has this line been regarded as the intangible result of a natural fact, while that one has called for

---

[158] *Tunisia/Libya*, para. 131.
[159] *Guinea/Guinea-Bissau*, para. 95.

correction? Why has this island been taken into account for this
function but not that, while another has been given diametrically
opposite treatment? It is not always easy to find a convincing answer
to these questions.

The unusual or non-essential geographical feature, the disproportion between a given geographical feature and the distortion
which it causes, unjustifiable differences of treatment, all these
concepts which form part of judicial thinking in fact lack objectivity.
Certainly there have been cases where a litigant State has tried to give
one or other of these ideas a firm basis or mathematical expression,
but not once have the courts committed themselves to this course.
The assessment of proportionality or the determination of the nature
of the frontal or adjacent relationship between coasts,[160] is no more a
matter of nice calculation than is its corollary, the correction of so-
called inequities caused by non-essential geographical configurations. In both cases international courts have shown themselves
resistant to any attempt at more than an approximate and global
quantification.

The significant or particular character of a salient or an island
depends (just as does the convex or concave, regular or irregular,
configuration of a shore-line) largely on the micro- or macrogeographical view which happens to be taken and on the scale of the
map. This being so, the court's decision is, in the end, based on an
intuitive value judgment, and so inevitably open to criticism.

These observations aside, it is in actual fact the very basis of the
courts' theory which seems precarious in the extreme. It is difficult
to see how a line of equidistance, given that it is supposed to be based
on respect for nature and geography, can require correction on that
same basis. Nature and geography cannot both dictate the line and
then require its rectification. Nature and geography have completed
their task once the line of equidistance is established at the first stage.
They have no place at the second stage. One can understand that the
provisional equidistant line may need adjustment in the light of
relevant circumstances of a non-geographical nature. What is not
understandable is that it can be amended on the basis of geographical
circumstances, given that it is itself the product of geography. Nature
and geography are neither equitable nor inequitable, neither normal
or abnormal. There are no major or minor features, general or
special configurations, usual or unusual situations, significant or
insignificant features. There are no geographical aberrations any
more than there is geographical normality. The case-law is so well

[160] Cf. pp. 237ff, 246 below.

established that it would be wishful thinking to hope that it might be abandoned, but these criticisms needed to be set out.

Coastal lengths, maritime areas, proportionality

The role of coastal lengths, maritime areas and proportionality has been mentioned previously in the context of the theory of coastal projections and the concept of delimitation.[161] As already pointed out, since the length of the coast has no direct and independent role in determining the areas over which the coastal State has legal title, it cannot play a direct and independent role in determining the maritime areas which must be left to each of the States at the end of the delimitation process. Moreover, as delimitation does not consist in sharing out or allocating resources or areas, its purpose cannot be the allocation to the parties of areas proportional to the length of their coastal fronts. In this sense, the conclusion reached was that there is no principle of proportionality. This, however, does not exclude considerations of coastal lengths, areas and proportionality, from coming into play in the second stage of the delimitation operation as considerations of equity. It is from this point of view that it is now convenient to look at them.

Reduced to essentials, the question can be put very simply: to what extent are considerations based on a comparison of coastal lengths or maritime areas legally relevant for assessing the equitable character of a provisional line of equidistance, and justifying, if necessary, its correction?

Behind this general question lie, in reality, three distinct, though connected, problems. First, should the provisional line of equidistance be regarded as inequitable, and therefore calling for adjustment, just because the coastal fronts of the two countries are of a different length? Second, should the provisional line of equidistance be regarded as inequitable, and therefore calling for adjustment, just because it gives the parties unequal maritime areas? Third, should the provisional line of equidistance be regarded as inequitable, and therefore calling for adjustment, just because it would leave the parties surface areas the ratio of which was not comparable to the ratio of their coastal lengths? The first problem raises the question of the legal relevance of considerations based on a comparison of coastal lengths; the second, the legal relevance of considerations based on the equality of surface areas, in other words the relationship between equity and equality; the third, the legal

[161] See pp. 65, 70-1, 75-9 above.

relevance of considerations drawn from a correlation between the ratio of coastal lengths and the ratio of surface areas. Strictly speaking, only the last problem merits the name of proportionality, even if it has become usual to give this generic description to all the questions just mentioned.

Although it has been firmly established since 1969 that equity does not imply equality of area, and that as a result equality is not a relevant circumstance,[162] the legal relevance of the comparison of coastal lengths *per se* and that of proportionality between the ratio of coastal lengths and the ratio of surface areas has been the object of some doubt, further aggravated by the fact that the judgments have not always clearly distinguished the different aspects of the problem.

It is on proportionality *stricto sensu* that the courts have taken their thinking the furthest, and this, therefore, is where it is easiest to get one's bearings. Although there is no question, say the courts, of proceeding to a delimitation by actively seeking a *proportion* between coastal lengths and the extent of maritime jurisdictions, an obvious and glaring *disproportion* between them should be avoided as unreasonable and inequitable. Proportionality thus conceived is not, however, understood as an ordinary relevant circumstance which comes directly into the assessment of the equity of the line of departure and the determination, if necessary, of the adjusted line. It is rather as a check which the courts use *a posteriori* to assure themselves that the provisional line (or the line resulting from its adjustment) does not involve an unreasonable disproportion between the ratio of the areas and that of the coastal lengths. The terminology of the judgments in this respect is significant. Proportionality is a "factor",[163] a "criterion",[164] an "element",[165] a "test",[166] an "aspect of equity",[167] indeed the "touchstone of equitableness".[168] It is not a relevant circumstance in the strict sense of the term.

The case-law seems settled on the question of proportionality properly speaking. It is less so on the legal relevance of coastal lengths as such. A careful examination of the judgments will show the

---

[162] Cf. pp. 256-7 below.

[163] *Anglo-French* award, paras. 99 and 101; *Libya/Malta*, para. 57.

[164] *Anglo-French* award, paras. 101 and 246; *Tunisia/Libya*, paras. 130 and 131; *Libya/Malta*, paras. 66, 75 and 78 ("auxiliary criterion" according to *Gulf of Maine*, para. 196).

[165] *Libya/Malta*, para. 58.

[166] *Ibid.*, para. 74.

[167] *Tunisia/Libya*, para. 131; *Libya/Malta*, para. 75.

[168] *Tunisia/Libya*, para. 108.

difficulty the courts have had in fixing the limits of these two theories and the connection between them.

In 1969, in the *North Sea* case, the parties were asked to take account of

> ... the element of a reasonable degree of proportionality which a delimitation effected according to equitable principles ought to bring about between the extent of the continental shelf appertaining to the States concerned and the lengths of their respective coastlines.[169]

It will be noted that the Court did not require an exact relationship, but a "reasonable" one. The purely approximate character of the required proportionality was further reinforced by the fact that the Court suggested referring not to the actual coastal lengths, but to their stylized lengths, measured according to the general direction of the two coasts.[170]

In turning this negotiating guidance into the law governing judicial and arbitral delimitations, the *Anglo-French* award at the same time developed it in terms to which the Court in *Libya/Malta* was to pay tribute.[171] For the Court of Arbitration, the problem of proportionality presents itself in the context of the theory of special geographical features. More precisely, the function of proportionality is to assess *a posteriori* the equity of an equidistance delimitation when a non-essential geographical feature causes the line to deviate. Too great a disproportion between the ratio of the surface areas and that of the coastal lengths will mean that the line is inequitable. Dealing with the concepts of "proportionality" and "a reasonable evaluation of natural features" together, the Court of Arbitration says:

> ... particular configurations of the coast or individual geographical features may, under certain conditions, distort the course of the boundary, and thus affect the attribution of continental shelf to each State, which would otherwise be indicated by the general configuration of their coasts. *The concept of "proportionality" merely expresses the criterion or factor by which it may be determined whether such a distortion results in an inequitable delimitation of the continental shelf as between the coastal States concerned.*
>
> ... it is *disproportion* rather than any general principle of proportionality which is the relevant criterion or factor.

---

[169] *North Sea*, para. 98.
[170] For the method of calculating coastal lengths, see pp. 76-7 above.
[171] *Libya/Malta*, para. 57.

Proportionality ... is to be used as a *criterion or factor relevant in evaluating the equities of certain geographical situations*, not as a general principle providing an independent source of rights to areas of continental shelf.

... "proportionality" is not in itself a source of title to the continental shelf, but is rather *a criterion for evaluating the equities of certain geographical situations*.

... "proportionality" ... being rather ... *a criterion to assess the distorting effects of particular geographical features and the extent of the resulting inequity*.[172]

Seen from this perspective, it may be noted in passing, there is no need for "nice calculations".[173] A rough overall assessment is enough. The courts have subsequently tried to clarify this theory, but not altogether successfully.

In *Tunisia/Libya* the proportionality factor was used without any reference to the equidistance line, which, as we know, the Court did not even envisage. What the Court eventually submitted to the proportionality test, conceived in the form of a verification of an approximate correlation between two arithmetical relationships, was the line it had arrived at by direct examination of the relevant circumstances. The arithmetical relationships were those between coastal lengths and the areas of maritime jurisdictions resulting from a line determined by other criteria.[174] Although, in the absence of a provisional equidistance line, it was not a question in this judgment of a correlation between the theory of proportionality and that of special geographical features, the *ex post* character of the factor of proportionality was clearly endorsed, as was its role of rejecting a possible disproportion rather than actively ensuring proportionality between the coastal length of each State and the extent of its maritime rights.

The *Gulf of Maine* judgment adopts an original approach on these problems, different in many respects from that of previous judgments. The line of equidistance suggested by Canada is regarded by the Chamber as inequitable because of the considerable difference between the length of the coastal fronts of the two States. "This difference in length", says the Chamber, "is a special circumstance of some weight, which ... justifies a correction of the equidistance

---

[172] *Anglo-French* award, paras. 100, 101, 246 and 250.

[173] *Ibid.*, paras. 27 and 250.

[174] The coastal lengths seemed to the Court to be in the ratio of about 31:69 or 34:66, according to the method used. The areas of continental shelf resulting from the proposed line were in the ratio 40:60 "approximately". "This result", the judgment says, "... seems ... to meet the requirements of the test of proportionality as an aspect of equity" (*Tunisia/Libya*, paras. 130-1).

line, or of any other line".[175] The Chamber makes the point that it "in no way intends to make an autonomous criterion or method of delimitation out of the concept of 'proportionality', *even if it be limited to the aspect of lengths of coastline*",[176] but nonetheless sees in the difference of coastal lengths of the two countries a "ground for correction" of the median line "more pressing even than others".[177] As a result, when it comes to drawing the second segment of the maritime boundary, the Chamber shifts the median line in such a way as to benefit the United States, whose maritime front in the Gulf of Maine is longer than that of Canada.[178] Although the *Gulf of Maine* judgment is opposed to any idea of making the purpose of the delimitation the attribution to each party of an area in direct proportion to the length of its shore-line,[179] nevertheless, for the first time, the comparison of coastal lengths is in itself treated as a relevant circumstance in the full sense of the term. As for the proportionality test properly speaking, i.e., the *a posteriori* check between the ratios of the areas and those of the coastal lengths, the *Gulf of Maine* judgment has no place for it.

Perhaps it was to put some order into these disparate approaches that, in *Libya/Malta*, the Court undertook what it called a "careful consideration"[180] of the concept of proportionality and seized the opportunity to make some important clarifications about its implementation.[181] Taking up the *Tunisia/Libya* formula, which defined proportionality as an "aspect of equity",[182] the Court starts from the *North Sea* judgment and the *Anglo-French* award, presenting the proportionality factor as linked to the correction of the deviation effect produced on an equidistance line by the very irregular or strongly concave or convex character of the coast.[183] This concept once confirmed, the Court, in an entirely new development, shows that the role of this factor within the second phase of the delimitation process is a double one. Referring to the lengths of the coasts, the Court says:

> . . . attention should be drawn to an important distinction . . . between the relevance of coastal lengths as a pertinent circumstance for a delimitation,

[175] *Gulf of Maine*, para. 184.
[176] *Ibid.*, para. 218.
[177] *Ibid.*, para. 185.
[178] *Ibid.*, paras. 221-2.
[179] *Ibid.*, para. 185.
[180] *Libya/Malta*, para. 55.
[181] *Ibid.*, paras. 55-9, 66-7 and 74-5.
[182] *Ibid.*, para. 75.
[183] *Ibid.*, para. 56.

and use of those lengths in assessing ratios of proportionality ... It is however one thing to employ proportionality calculations to check a result; it is another thing to take note, in the course of the delimitation process, of the existence of a very marked difference in coastal lengths, and to attribute the appropriate significance to that coastal relationship, without seeking to define it in quantitative terms which are only suited to the *ex post* assessment of relationships of coast to area ... Consideration of the comparability or otherwise of the coastal lengths is a part of the process of determining an equitable boundary on the basis of an initial median line; the test of a reasonable degree of proportionality, on the other hand, is one which can be applied to check the equitableness of any line, whatever the method used to arrive at that line.[184]

It emerges from this passage that the comparative length of coasts can come into the picture, in the first place, quite independently of any question of surface areas, as a relevant circumstance capable of justifying, by itself, a possible adjustment of the original line of equidistance. This is the case when there is "a very marked difference in the lengths of the relevant coasts", a "marked disparity", which need not, however, be defined in "quantitative" terms, an overall evaluation being sufficient:

Where a marked disparity requires to be taken into account as a relevant circumstance ... this rigorous definition is not essential and indeed not appropriate. If the disparity in question only emerges after scrupulous definition and comparison of coasts, it is *ex hypothesi* unlikely to be of such extent as to carry weight as a relevant circumstance.[185]

In other words, where a simple glance at the map will allow the court to see, without having to measure it, that there is a strong disparity between the coastal lengths of the two countries, *for that reason alone* it will have to make an adjustment of the equidistance line of departure favourable to the State which has the longer maritime front. This is what the Chamber did in *Gulf of Maine*. The Court proceeds in the same way here. Having envisaged a median line between Libya and Malta, the Court finds that the two coasts are so clearly different in length (192 miles for Libya, 24 for Malta) that this "considerable disparity"

... constitutes ... *a relevant circumstance* which should be reflected in the drawing of the delimitation line ... this difference is so great as to justify the adjustment of the median line so as to attribute a larger shelf area to Libya;

[184] *Ibid.*, para. 66.
[185] *Ibid.*, para. 67.

the degree of such adjustment does not depend upon a mathematical operation and remains to be examined.[186]

As we see, it is not a question of a disequilibrium between the ratio of the coastal lengths and the ratio of maritime areas. It is the difference between the coastal lengths of the two countries which, as in *Gulf of Maine*, is regarded as a relevant circumstance of nature justifying by itself a shift of the equidistance line in order to allot more maritime space to the State with the obviously longer coastline and less maritime space to the State with the clearly shorter coastline.

The role of the coastal lengths does not stop there, according to the *Libya/Malta* judgment. Once the median line has been shifted so as to increase the area of the State with the long coast and to decrease that of the State with the short coast, the ''proportionality test'' comes into effect in its classic form, that is to say, by a comparison of the ratio of the size of shelf allocated to each State by the median line thus shifted with the ratio of the coastal lengths.[187] At this second stage, it is a question of proportionality in the proper meaning of the word, and not consideration of the coastal lengths *per se*. The Court acknowledges that it is difficult to apply the proportionality test in this particular case because of the uncertainty affecting the determination of the relevant coasts and areas, and also because the Court confines its decision to areas not claimed by third States, so that the figures and ratios arrived at will probably be overthrown by future delimitations. The Court considers, however, that it is not necessary to ''achieve a predetermined arithmetical ratio in the relationship between the relevant coasts and . . . the areas generated by them''. Refraining from a calculation of the ratio of these areas, it considers it ''possible for it to make a broad assessment of the equitableness of the result, without seeking to define the equities in arithmetical terms''. The conclusion of the Court is that ''there is certainly no evident disproportion in the areas . . . attributed to each of the Parties respectively such that it could be said that the requirements of the test of proportionality as an aspect of equity were not satisfied''.[188] In contrast to what it had done in *Tunisia/Libya*, the Court contents itself here with finding that there is no flagrant disproportion between the ratio of the areas and the ratio of coastal lengths, without support from figures and without seeking to establish, even approximately, that these ratios are of the same order.

---

[186] *Ibid.*, para. 68.
[187] *Ibid.*, paras. 74-5.
[188] *Ibid.*, para. 75.

The distinction established by the judgment between the comparison of the coastal lengths themselves, on the one hand, and the "ratios between lengths of coast and areas of continental shelf"[189] on the other, comes out most strikingly in the *dispositif*, which cites separately, among the "circumstances and factors to be taken into account in achieving an equitable delimitation"

> . . .
>
> 2)   the disparity in the lengths of the relevant coasts of the Parties . . . ;
>
> 3)   the need to avoid in the delimitation any excessive disproportion between the extent of the continental shelf areas appertaining to the coastal State and the length of the relevant part of its coast, measured in the general direction of the coastlines.[190]

There are serious reservations about the double function given by the 1985 judgment to the coastal length within the second stage of the delimitation process.

It is true that a State with a long coast will normally have an area of maritime jurisdiction greater than if it had a short coastline. As Judge Schwebel has commented, "The base of a triangle is longer than the apex, and . . . correspondingly, there is a larger area lying off the base than is embraced by the apex".[191] But, as we have seen, that does not mean that there is a direct and automatic relationship between the length of the shore and the extent of the maritime area. The latter does not depend either directly or exclusively on the coastal length, but essentially on the configuration of the coasts and the points which geography designates as basepoints. Not having any specific role to play in respect of title, the coastal length ought not to play any in delimitation. The Court says, in the same *Libya/Malta* judgment, that it is "evident" that the only considerations which have a part to play in delimitation are those "that are pertinent to the institution" of the maritime jurisdiction concerned "as it has developed within the law". Since it rightly refuses[192] to accord any legal relevance to the physical facts of the seabed for the precise and decisive reason that this factor plays no role in respect of the legal title, it is hard to see why it accords legal relevance to the coastal length which has no more of a role to play in the legal basis of title than the physical structure of the seabed.

As a result, there is no legal reason why an equidistance line should be condemned as inequitable because the lengths of the two coasts are

---

[189] *Ibid.*, para. 66.

[190] *Ibid.*, para. 79B.

[191] *Ibid.*, Dissenting Opinion, p. 182.

[192] *Libya/Malta*, para. 40.

noticeably different. Otherwise, the comparative length of coasts would become a relevant circumstance capable of exercising a sort of veto, since, even where all the other relevant circumstances established the equitable character of the original equidistance delimitation, a substantial difference in the lengths of the coasts would suffice to neutralize this result and to condemn the equidistance line. The coastal length would then become the most decisive of the relevant circumstances, the one which, at the very least, must be the first to be taken into account, since on it will, in the end, depend the equitable character of the line. Such a concept would be unacceptable: the equality of coastal lengths cannot be regarded as the *sine qua non* of the equity of an equidistance line. An equidistance line is not equitable or inequitable simply because the maritime fronts of the two countries are or are not of the same length. The recognition in *Libya/Malta* that the comparison of coastal lengths is a relevant circumstance is incompatible with the doctrine professed in this same judgment on the link between title and delimitation, and with its definition of legal relevance. In this respect also, the *Libya/Malta* judgment would seem to be transitional, and to offer possibilities for ridding the law of maritime delimitation of the legal inconsistencies which still beset it.

As to proportionality *stricto sensu*, the *Libya/Malta* judgment confirms the low profile the courts at present unanimously accord it. In line with the principles set out in the *Anglo-French* award, the function of the proportionality test, which comes into play only at the very end of the delimitation process, consists less in ensuring proportionality, even approximate, between the ratio of the coastal lengths and that of the surface areas, than in avoiding a flagrant disproportion. According to the *Guinea/Guinea-Bissau* formula,

> . . . the rule of proportionality is not a mechanical rule based only on figures reflecting the length of the coastline. It must be used in a reasonable way, with due account being given to other circumstances in the case.[193]

The *Libya/Malta* judgment would not, therefore, depart from strict orthodoxy in not applying the criterion of proportionality in the absence of any deviation caused by a special geographical feature. In fact, the Court points out, in effect, that the space separating the two coasts "is clear of any complicating features".[194]

At all events, even for the most modest of purposes, the proportionality test has no legal basis. Neither the theory of coastal

---

[193] *Guinea/Guinea-Bissau*, para. 120.
[194] *Libya/Malta*, para. 70.

projections nor the concept of delimitation justifies the requirement of a relationship between the ratio of coastal lengths and that of areas. On a more practical basis, we have seen that the implementation of such a relationship, even if it were legally justified, runs into almost insuperable obstacles. Nothing is less objective than the idea of coastal length. What segments of the shoreline are to be taken into consideration? How are they to be measured? Nothing is less certain than the idea of surface area. What expanses are to be taken into account, especially when later delimitations with third States are likely to throw all the calculations, however rough they may be, back into the melting-pot? In short, there is nothing riskier than models of proportionality, which experience shows to be of such flexibility that they make it possible to prove, in an allegedly scientific way, almost anything one wants to. Theoretically unjustifiable, impossible to put into practice, the test of proportionality is, moreover, useless. Conceived basically as a sort of warning signal for detecting an inequitable deviation in the line of equidistance caused by a minor geographical feature, unreasonable disproportion between areas and coastal lengths can, as we shall see, today be replaced by a simpler indicator, the proximity of the equidistance line to the coast of the parties.

Whether it is in the context of a direct consideration of coastal lengths or, more modestly, of a last-minute proportionality test, the legal relevance of considerations of coastal length, surface areas and proportionality ought not to survive re-examination by the courts. Let us hope so.

Opposite and adjacent coasts

To what extent does the nature of the geographical relationship—opposition or adjacency—between the coasts of the two countries constitute a relevant circumstance? Although not as complex as that of proportionality, this problem is just as controversial.

The distinction, in various guises, has been a constant of the law of maritime delimitation since well before the emergence of the modern law of the sea. Going back no further than the 1930s, it will be recalled that, following the 1930 Hague Codification Conference, Gidel was already distinguishing the problem of the "delimitation of the territorial sea in straits" from that of the "lateral limits of the territorial sea between two adjacent States".[195] This distinction, which underlay the work of the International Law Commission and

---

[195] See pp. 135ff above.

was given expression in the provisions of the 1958 Geneva Conventions on the Territorial Sea and the Continental Shelf, was taken up by the Court in the *North Sea* case. In a well-known passage, the Court explained that the risks of inequity are less in the case of a median line between States with opposite coasts than an equidistance line between adjacent States. Between opposite coasts, the zones of overlap "can . . . only be delimited by means of a median line", which "must effect an equal division of the particular area involved". On the other hand, "[t]his type of case is . . . different from that of laterally adjacent States on the same coast with no immediately opposite coast in front of it, and does not give rise to the same kind of problem".[196]

The *North Sea* judgment thus endorsed the distinction for negotiated delimitations; the 1977 *Anglo-French* award was to carry it over into the law of maritime delimitation properly speaking and it has never since been challenged. The Court of Arbitration sees the 1969 judgment as having established a difference which was "clear", "sharp", "material".[197] Between opposite coasts, the median line is "in principle, the method applicable", which is not necessarily the case between adjacent coasts.[198] The distinction is made in the same terms in subsequent judgments,[199] and endorsed with particular force in *Libya/Malta*, which explains the "precise reason" it is necessary to distinguish between

> . . . the effect of an equidistance line between opposite coasts and the effect between adjacent coasts. In the latter situation, any distorting effect of a salient feature might well extend and increase through the entire course of the boundary; whilst in the former situation, the influence of one feature is normally quickly succeeded and corrected by the influence of another as the course of the line proceeds between more or less parallel coasts.[200]

It may be noted that, in line with this distinction, Article 6 of the Geneva Convention regulates situations of adjacency and opposition in two separate paragraphs, and that several judicial decisions have emphasized the necessity for terminology which rigorously distinguishes, as does Article 6, the "median line" between opposite

---

[196] *North Sea*, para. 57.
[197] *Anglo-French* award, paras. 85-6.
[198] *Ibid.*, paras. 87, 95 and 239.
[199] See, for example, *Tunisia/Libya*, para. 126; cf. paras. 78 and 109; *Gulf of Maine*, paras. 206 and 216-7; *Guinea/Guinea-Bissau*, paras. 91, 103 and 104.
[200] *Libya/Malta*, para. 70.

coasts from the "equidistance line", (or "lateral equidistance line") between adjacent coasts.[201]

Although the distinction seems firmly established, its reality and, even more, its legal relevance, are open to doubt.

Experience shows that the distinction is less obvious than one might think. In the first place, as several judgments have shown, coasts can be placed in a given relationship to one another over certain sections and in a different one over other sections,[202] without the precise point of transition always capable of being "objectively determined as a matter of fact".[203] The transition between a situation of opposition and one of adjacency (or vice versa) may be made gradually, with several intermediary stages, sometimes difficult to identify.[204] Secondly, besides the clear and indisputable relationships of opposition and adjacency there are less precise "partial relationships"[205] of "quasi-opposition"[206] and quasi-adjacency. For proof, one need only look at the uncertainties of the Anglo-French Court of Arbitration in respect of the situation in the Atlantic region,[207] or, again, the controversy caused by the description of the relationship between the American and Canadian coasts in the area of the Gulf of Maine. Canada had put forward mathematical criteria for distinguishing the relationship of adjacency from that of opposition,[208] but the judgment made the distinction without reference to them.[209] In *Guinea/Guinea-Bissau*, likewise, one of the parties saw a relationship of opposition where the other discerned adjacency. The Tribunal limited itself to the remark that "there is no reason why two States should not have coasts which are partially adjacent and partially opposite each other".[210]

The difficulty there may be in identifying the nature of the relationship between the coasts would not, however, be enough to put the soundness of the distinction in question, were it not that this distinction has a less decisive legal relevance than the weight of tradition might lead one to think.

---

[201] *North Sea*, para. 6; *Anglo-French* award, paras. 96, n. 1 and 97; *Gulf of Maine*, paras. 115 and 186.

[202] *Anglo-French* award, paras. 6, 94 and 206; *Tunisia/Libya*, para. 126; *Gulf of Maine*, para. 206.

[203] *Tunisia/Libya*, para. 123.

[204] Cf. *Gulf of Maine*, para. 187.

[205] *Ibid.*

[206] *Libya/Malta*, para. 43.

[207] *Anglo-French* award, paras. 204, 241-2 and 253.

[208] Canadian Counter-Memorial, paras. 110ff.

[209] *Gulf of Maine*, paras. 188-9.

[210] *Guinea/Guinea-Bissau*, para. 91.

It can, of course, be accepted as an indisputable fact that the effect of a concavity or a convexity, an islet or a salient, will be less pronounced as between opposite coasts than between adjacent. In the case of coasts facing one another, equidistance will present fewer "difficulties", to use the Court's word,[211] than in the case of adjacent coasts. But it is difficult to see the legal consequences of that. The technique of equidistance is the same, whether the relationship between the coasts is frontal, lateral or mixed. Its characteristics are the same in each case. And, above all, there is no difference between the two situations in the context of the delimitation process. Equidistance is legally required as the first step in delimitation in the one as in the other, for exactly the same reasons,[212] but it is not legally required, in either case, as the definitive line.[213] Equidistance is not always inequitable in a relationship of adjacency, any more than it is always equitable in a relationship of opposition. At the end of the day, the distinction is no more than a fragile and always debatable presumption.[214]

In these circumstances, it is understandable why, in 1953, on the technical plane, the Committee of Experts consulted by the International Law Commission should have decided on the same solution in both situations, for both the continental shelf and the territorial sea. The 1958 Geneva Conventions provided exactly the same rules for delimitation between adjacent coasts and delimitation between opposite coasts. Article 12 of the Convention on the Territorial Sea and the Contiguous Zone has the same provision for the two situations, and, although Article 6 of the Convention on the Continental Shelf has two separate paragraphs, it is clear, as the *Anglo-French* arbitral award pointed out, that "[t]he rules of delimitation laid down ... are essentially the same".[215] This identity of regime is endorsed by the 1982 Law of the Sea Convention, for the territorial sea (Article 15), as for the exclusive economic zone (Article 74) and the continental shelf (Article 83).

[211] *North Sea*, para. 57.

[212] It is difficult to explain, unless it was force of habit, why the Court should have been so cautious in *Libya/Malta*, where it justified taking the median line into account as a first step by implying that it ventured to do so only because it was a case of opposite coasts. (See, for example, *Libya/Malta*, paras. 44, 62 and 77).

[213] Judge Mosler took the view, however, that the median line is obligatory as the final outcome in the case of opposite coasts (*Libya/Malta*, Dissenting Opinion, p. 120).

[214] According to some, the distinction would be of interest outside the question of equidistance. Proportionality, it is maintained, has a role to play only between neighbouring coasts. It is irrelevant between opposite coasts. (Schwebel, *Libya/Malta*, Dissenting Opinion, p. 184; cf. Bowett [2], p. 164).

[215] *Anglo-French* award, para. 238.

Moreover, the courts have not attached as much importance to the distinction as they like to claim. The *Anglo-French* award, while emphasizing its significance, observes[216] that, in fact, "the answer to the question whether the effect of individual geographical features is to render an equidistance delimitation 'unjustified' or 'inequitable' cannot depend on whether the case is *legally* to be considered a delimitation between 'opposite' or 'adjacent' States". As a result, says the award, for delimitation purposes it is of little importance "to fix the precise legal classification" between opposite and adjacent coasts.[217] The *Gulf of Maine* judgment notes, in its turn, that the median line between coasts facing one another and the lateral equidistance line share "the same inspiration"[218] and are based on the "same technique".[219] The *Guinea/Guinea-Bissau* award says laconically that, in the face of disagreement between the parties as to the nature of their coastal relationship, "it is not necessary to linger over this circumstance".[220]

In short, although not totally lacking in legal relevance or interest, the distinction between adjacent and opposite coasts cannot be considered a relevant circumstance carrying any real weight.

The distance between the coasts

In *Libya/Malta*, the Court, for the first time, accorded the status of a relevant circumstance to another consideration which, like adjacency or opposition, also relates to the relationship between two coasts, namely, the distance between them. This factor, observes the Court

> . . . is an obviously important consideration when deciding whether, and by how much, a median line boundary can be shifted without ceasing to have an approximately median location, or approaching so near to one coast as to bring into play other factors such as security.[221]

The Court's idea would seem to be that the further the parties' coasts are from one another, the more room for manoeuvre it has for shifting the line of equidistance: "In the present case there is clearly

---

[216] *Ibid.*, para. 240 (italics in original).
[217] *Ibid.*, para. 242.
[218] *Gulf of Maine*, para. 187.
[219] *Ibid.*, para. 115; cf. para. 186.
[220] *Guinea/Guinea-Bissau*, para. 91.
[221] *Libya/Malta*, para. 73.

room for a significant adjustment, if it is found to be required for achieving an equitable result".[222]

But it must be recognized, as Judge Schwebel points out, that "the probative force of that consideration cannot actually be demonstrated".[223] As Judge Mbaye emphasizes, in sharp criticism, it is difficult to "understand by what process the distance between the coasts of the two States can instigate or justify the correction of the median line initially drawn by the Court as a provisional step in the delimitation" and why the correction is more necessary when the distance is "large" or "considerable" than when it is small. "If Malta", Judge Mbaye asks, "instead of lying at 183 miles from the Libyan coast, were separated from it by a distance of only 50 miles, would that make any difference?". Furthermore, the significance of taking this factor into account remains puzzling. Does the distance between the coasts justify a correction to the median line simply because it is large, or only when the distance from the coasts is accompanied by a disparity in their lengths? The first interpretation is absurd, and the second meaningless, Judge Mbaye concludes.[224]

The general geographical context

As already pointed out, although in principle only the area of delimitation and the coasts actually abutting on it should be taken into consideration, some tribunals have not resisted the temptation of a macrogeographical approach. The *Guinea/Guinea-Bissau* award is particularly interesting in this respect, when it takes "overall account of the shape of [the] coastline . . . [of] the whole of West Africa", and the general direction of the coast starting in one third country and finishing in another.[225] But it is to the *Libya/Malta* judgment that one owes a clear statement of the theory according to which, in order to reach an equitable delimitation, the Court

> . . . has . . . to look beyond the area concerned in the case, and consider the general geographical context in which the delimitation will have to effected.[226]

For this purpose, the judgment sees the delimitation between Malta and Libya from the wider perspective of a delimitation between "a

---

[222] *Ibid.*
[223] *Libya/Malta*, Dissenting Opinion, p. 182.
[224] *Libya/Malta*, Separate Opinion, pp. 99-103.
[225] *Guinea/Guinea-Bissau*, paras. 108-11.
[226] *Libya/Malta*, para. 69.

portion of the southern littoral and a portion of the northern littoral of the Central Mediterranean'', in which the Maltese islands ''appear as a minor feature''. This fact, according to the Court,

> ... constitutes a geographical feature which should be taken into account as a pertinent circumstance; its influence on the delimitation line must be weighed in order to arrive at an equitable result.[227]

As a result, the *dispositif* quotes their ''relationship to each other within the general geographical context'' among ''the circumstances and factors to be taken into account in achieving an equitable delimitation in the present case'',[228] in addition to the general configuration of the coasts of the parties and the disparity of their lengths.

Taking these statements of principle as its starting point, the Court reasons as follows. If the Maltese islands were part of Italian territory, their location to the south of the coast of Sicily, ''even if the minimum account were taken'' of them or of these islands, would cause the delimitation line between Italy and Libya to be drawn ''somewhat south of the median line between the Sicilian and Libyan coasts''. Since Malta is not a part of Italy but an independent State, ''it cannot be the case that, as regards continental shelf rights, it will be in a worse position because of its independence''. This means that ''it is reasonable to assume that an equitable boundary between Libya and Malta must be to the south of a notional median line between Libya and Sicily''. Since the median line between Libya and Malta (which lies at a latitude of about 34° 12′N) must be shifted northwards because of the ''great disparity in the lengths of the relevant coasts of the two Parties'' and the ''general geographical context in which the islands of Malta appear as a relatively small feature in a semi-enclosed sea'', the extreme limit of such an adjustment is marked by the median line between Italy and Libya (lying at about 34° 36′N, i.e. 24′ further north). The Court says it has ''concluded that a boundary line that represents a shift of around three-quarters of the distance between the two outer parameters ... achieves an equitable result in all the circumstances''. Consequently, ''the equitable boundary line is a line produced by transposing the median line [between Malta and Libya] northwards through 18′ of latitude''.[229] The definitive line will thus be situated at a latitude of about 34° 30′N, giving Libya, as a result of taking into combined

[227] *Ibid.*
[228] *Ibid.*, para. 79B.
[229] *Ibid.*, paras. 72-3.

consideration the disparity of coastal lengths and the overall geographical context, a bonus of 6,000 square kilometres of continental shelf.[230]

Consideration of the general geographical context runs up against serious objections. To start with, to describe the overall geographical context as a relevant circumstance seems unjustified in terms of the criteria of legal relevance set by the Court itself. It is difficult to see what the location of Malta to the south of Italy has to do with the ''institution of the continental shelf as established in law''. It is stated by the Court in the same judgment that ''the juridical link between the State's territorial sovereignty and its rights to certain adjacent maritime expanses is established by means of its coast''.[231] It is obvious that it is by the intermediary of its own coasts that the State projects its sovereignty seaward, and not by the intermediary of another State's coasts. By making the delimitation between Malta and Libya by reference to a delimitation between Libya and Italy, the Court introduced coasts other than those of Libya and Malta through which alone these two States can generate maritime jurisdictions. As Judge Sette-Camara notes, the Maltese coasts

> interrupt any possible relationship between the coasts of Libya and Italy. In opposite States it is the confrontation of coasts that plays the paramount role in the delimitation process, and there is no such confrontation between Libya and Sicily as long as the Maltese coasts are interposed between them.[232]

It is not without interest to recall once more that, in rejecting the French argument that the delimitation in the Atlantic region should be carried out by reference to the general direction of the coasts in the Channel, the Anglo-French Court of Arbitration said, as a matter of

[230] Figures given in Judge Schwebel's Dissenting Opinion, *Libya/Malta*, p. 183. It will be noted that the Court based its argument relating to the general geographical context essentially upon a hypothetical situation which Malta had thought, by a *reductio ad absurdum*, would show how unreasonable Libya's claim was and how reasonable was its own. How, Malta maintained, could one regard as equitable the line claimed by Libya north of the median line which might be drawn between Libya and Italy if Malta did not exist? And how could one regard as inequitable the median line between Malta and Libya claimed by Malta, which was scarcely any further south than the median line which might be drawn between Libya and Italy if Malta did not exist? (See CR 1984/25, pp. 75-6, 83; 1985/7, p. 80; 1985/8, pp. 20, 52). The Court made this *reductio ad absurdum* the substance of its argument, giving rise to criticism from some judges (Sette-Camara, *Libya/Malta*, Separate Opinion, p. 74; Ruda, Bedjaoui and Jiménez de Aréchaga, Joint Separate Opinion, p. 77, para. 3; Schwebel, Dissenting Opinion, pp. 180, 182).

[231] *Libya/Malta*, para. 49.

[232] *Ibid.*, Separate Opinion, pp. 74-5.

principle, that "the method of delimitation which it adopts for the Atlantic region must be one that has relation to the coasts of the Parties actually abutting on the continental shelf of that region".[233] The Court of Arbitration therefore rejected the extension of the problem to a wider geographical context. This principle, firmly anchored in the theory of coastal projections, prohibits, in so many words, looking beyond the area concerned. The macrogeographical approach of *Libya/Malta* contrasts with the detailed research the Court engaged in elsewhere in order to determine the relevant coasts and the delimitation area. Under cover of extending the area concerned to the overall geographical context, the Court eventually recognized as a relevant circumstance coasts which were completely foreign to the two countries in the case.

The concept of the general geographical context caused the Court to founder on another, still more serious, rock. By regarding the Maltese islands as a "minor geographical feature" of the northern coast of the Mediterranean which in itself justified a correction of the median line, the Court treated the very existence and locality of the Maltese State as sources of inequity. It saw the position of Malta in relation to the Italian coast as calling for a shift of the median line in the same way as the Anglo-French Court of Arbitration did the position of the Scillies in relation to the British coast. As Judge Schwebel says, the treatment of the Maltese islands "as if they were the anomalous dependent islands of a large mainland State" is difficult to reconcile with the principle of the sovereign equality of States.[234]

The general geographical context should have no more effect on the equitable nature of the original equidistance line than has the distance between the coasts. It is to be hoped that the courts will eventually eject these two factors from the list of relevant circumstances into which the *Libya/Malta* judgment pointlessly introduced them.

The interests of third States and other delimitations in the region

Although it is essentially an operation *inter partes*, judicial or arbitral delimitation cannot be carried out in a vacuum, cut off from the world around it and isolated from other delimitations already implemented, or still to be made, in the region. The Court thus recommended in the *North Sea* case that the Federal Republic of Germany, the Netherlands and Denmark take account of the

---

[233] *Anglo-French* award, para. 248; cf. pp. 71ff above.
[234] *Libya/Malta*, Dissenting Opinion, p. 182.

"effects, actual or prospective, of any other continental shelf delimitations between adjacent States in the same area".[235] But it was no more than an invitation to take account, in the negotiations, of delimitation agreements already concluded between States bordering on the North Sea. The Court did not regard itself as establishing a rule of law binding on the courts in any future delimitation.

In fact, the inclusion among the legally relevant circumstances, in a disputed delimitation between two States, of considerations relating to other delimitations and other States raises formidable problems. Can the principle of the consensual nature of judicial settlement allow the involvement of a third State in the proceedings, without its agreement or presence? Does not the principle of the relative effect of the matter adjudged render inoperative any position the courts may take vis-à-vis third parties? Apart from the difficulties of a procedural nature, there is a fundamental objection to the inclusion of the interests of third States in the category of relevant circumstances. Since only the coasts actually abutting on the area of delimitation whose projections may overlap are relevant to a delimitation, would it be conceivable for a court to widen its field of consideration to coasts which had nothing to do with the delimitation in question, and which might be situated far from the area of delimitation? Once again, we see, in another form, the need not to water down a delimitation in a macrogeographical context the flexibility of which would lend itself to subjective interpretation.

It is understandable why the courts began by taking a rigorous approach to the problem. Since they were opposed to an extension of the relevant coasts, it was logical for them to refuse to take any account of facts and interests outside the precise delimitation *sub judice*. This is why the Anglo-French Court of Arbitration refused to attach any weight to the fact that the line of delimitation it was called on to draw between France and the United Kingdom[236] ran the risk of cutting across the future delimitation line between the United Kingdom and Ireland. After hearing the views of the parties on this problem, the Court decided to make the delimitation between France and the United Kingdom without taking into account "conjectures" about a possible future line of delimitation between the United Kingdom and Ireland. It explained that the decision to be taken on the Anglo-French delimitation would not be binding on Ireland, for

---

[235] *North Sea*, para. 101D3.
[236] *Anglo-French* award, para. 25.

whom it would be *res inter alios acta*, and it would not in any way prejudge a future Anglo-Irish delimitation. The Court added:

> In so far as there may be a possibility that the two successive delimitations of continental shelf zones in this region, where the three States are neighbours abutting on the same continental shelf, may result in some overlapping of the zones, it is manifestly outside the competence of the Court to decide in advance and hypothetically the legal problem which may then arise. That problem would normally find its appropriate solution by negotiation directly between the three States concerned.[237]

This initial rigour, of a perfect legal orthodoxy, was not to survive the courts' trend towards more and more macrogeographical concepts. From the moment the courts considered it appropriate to rely on facts as broad as the general geographical context in which the delimitation was to take effect or the general configuration of the coast of a continent, it is hardly surprising that they should have extended their investigation of the facts of the situation to problems concerning third States and delimitations other than those upon which they were called to decide. This practice took some time to develop. It now seems to know scarcely any limit.

The Court began to distance itself from the rigour of the *Anglo-French* doctrine in *Tunisia/Libya*, where, in contrast to the 1977 award, the Court case expressly included among the relevant circumstances to be taken into consideration

> ... the existence and interests of other States in the area, and the existing or potential delimitations between each of the Parties and such States ....[238]

This is why it took no position on the length of the delimitation line towards the north-east, which was represented on the illustrative map by an arrow indicating the direction of the line, but not its end-point.[239]

It is in *Libya/Malta* that the question of the interests of third States was taken furthest. Italy, with pretensions to certain areas claimed by Malta and Libya, had sought the Court's permission to intervene in the proceedings between the two States. In its judgment of the *Application by Italy for permission to intervene*,[240] the Court did not content itself with pointing out that Italy's interests would be

---

[237] *Ibid.*, para. 28.
[238] *Tunisia/Libya*, para. 81.
[239] *Ibid.*, paras. 130 and 133C3.
[240] Judgment of 21 March 1984, ICJ *Reports*, 1984, p. 3.

protected by the principle of *res inter alios judicata*. It went further, saying that it "cannot wholly put aside the question of the legal interest of Italy as well as of other States of the Mediterranean region, and they will have to be taken into account, in the same way as was done for example in the Judgment of 24 February 1982" in *Tunisia/ Libya*. Therefore, "the Court will, in its future judgment in the case, take account, as a fact, of the existence of other States having claims in the region".[241] In its judgment on the merits of *Libya/Malta*, the Court acknowledged that the parties had invited it not to restrict the delimitation to the areas over which they were alone in making claims, but nonetheless chose the diametrically opposite path:

> The present decision must . . . be limited in geographical scope so as to leave the claims of Italy unaffected, that is to say that the decision of the Court must be confined to the area in which, as the Court has been informed by Italy, that State has no claims to continental shelf rights.[242]

One can track the course taken by the courts in the space of a few years. In 1977, the Court of Arbitration settled the whole of the Anglo-French litigation, simply reserving the rights of Ireland, as was natural, in conformity with the principle of *res inter alios judicata*. In *Tunisia/Libya*, the Court, in order to take account of future delimitations in the region, left a question mark, in the form of an arrow, as to where the maritime boundary between the two parties to the case should terminate. *Libya/Malta* settled the dispute between the two countries only in respect of the areas over which Italy had made no claim. Not only did the Court take account of the interests of third States, but the claims of a third State actually determined the extent and scope of the judicial function and set limits on the judicial settlement sought by the parties.[243]

[241] *Ibid.*, pp. 25-7, paras. 41-3.
[242] *Libya/Malta*, para. 21.
[243] In the *Frontier Dispute (Burkina Faso/Mali)* case (ICJ *Reports*, 1986, p. 554), the Chamber was faced with the same sort of problem over a land boundary. Could it draw the boundary right up to the point where the frontier of the two countries met that of Niger without also dealing with the question of the rights of Niger vis-à-vis each of the parties? The Chamber thought that Niger was adequately protected by Article 59 of the Statute. It added that the two parties could have agreed a boundary line between them up to this triple point, and what they could do by friendly means they could also do by judicial means, which are nothing but a substitute. In neither case would Niger be bound. The Chamber was obviously aware that it was thus rejecting the route taken in the *Libya/Malta* case and returning to that of the *Anglo-French* award. It also pointed out that "the process by which a court determines the line of a land boundary between two States can be clearly distinguished from the process by which it identifies the principles and rules applicable to the delimitation of the continental shelf" (*ibid.*, p. 578, para. 47).

Without going into the detail of this solution, which the Court dwelt on at length,[244] and which has been strongly criticized by Judge Schwebel,[245] it is to be noted that, as in *Tunisia/Libya*, the Court relies on the *interest of third States* to justify a *restriction of the judicial decision*. The idea in *Guinea/Guinea-Bissau* was quite different, in some respects even the opposite. In this case, which was decided a few months before *Libya/Malta*, the macrogeographical view led the Arbitration Tribunal to rely, not on the interests of third States, but on *the other delimitations in the region*—not the same thing—to justify, not the restriction of the geographical area of its decision, but, on the contrary, *the extension of its investigation* beyond just the coasts of the two parties before the Tribunal and even beyond the case itself. Starting with the concept of a "long coastline" which took in Sierra Leone and, still more, the general configuration of the western coast of Africa, the Tribunal sought a delimitation which, instead of being looked at on its own, would, in the words of the Tribunal, "be suitable for . . . integration into the existing delimitations of the West African region, as well as into future delimitations which would be reasonable to imagine from a consideration of equitable principles and the most likely assumptions".[246] As a result, the Tribunal did not limit itself to the delimitation between the two Guineas, but covered the situation from Senegal in the north to Sierra Leone and Liberia in the south.[247]

Taking account of delimitations affecting third States thus covers two concepts and two approaches which should be carefully distinguished. On the one hand, it may lead the court to limit its decision so as not to encroach upon future delimitations affecting States not party to the case. On the other hand, it may lead the court to extend its investigation to geographical facts falling outside the dispute before it. In the first case, it is the extent of the judicial function which is at issue. In the second, it is the determination of the relevant coasts and the area of delimitation. In neither case is the purpose of taking other delimitations into account to test the equidistance line. In short, therefore, it is not a relevant circumstance in the proper meaning of the term.

The equality of States

There is no doubt that the principle of the equality of States

---

[244] *Libya/Malta*, paras. 18-23.
[245] *Ibid.*, Dissenting Opinion, pp. 172ff.
[246] *Guinea/Guinea-Bissau*, para. 109.
[247] *Ibid.*, paras. 108-10.

occupies an important place in the law of maritime delimitation. It is because of this principle, as we have seen, that no legal discrimination is allowed between continental and island States, or according to the extent of the landmass. The principle has also played an important part in eliminating physical criteria in the delimitation of the continental shelf. And the equality of States lies at the root of the equal division of the area of overlap of coastal projections, and constitutes one of the justifications for the equidistance method.

Does this mean that the equality of States should be seen as a relevant circumstance for testing the equitableness of the line, in the sense that a line which left the parties with unequal areas would be regarded as inequitable, and therefore calling for correction? Certainly not. On this point, as already noted, the courts are unanimous. "Equity does not necessarily imply equality";[248] "[T]he function of equity ... is not to produce absolute equality of treatment";[249] "the existence of equal entitlement ... of coastal States, does not imply an equality of extent of shelf".[250] Since "equal treatment does not necessarily mean the attribution of equal shares",[251] the initial equidistance line cannot be regarded as inequitable simply because it does not give the parties equal areas of maritime jurisdiction. Nor does the final line have to ensure such equality in order to be regarded as equitable. As a result, "the doctrine of the equality of States ... cannot be considered as constituting [such] an equitable ground"[252] capable of leading to an adjustment of the provisional line.

The conduct of the parties

The *Tunisia/Libya* judgment was the first to acknowledge the conduct of the parties as a relevant circumstance.[253] The Court thought it necessary, in this case, to "take into account whatever indicia are available of the line or lines which the Parties themselves may have considered equitable or acted upon as such". As a result, it held as relevant the fact that a "*de facto* line" had been established between the two parties. In the same way it thought that "the presence of oil-wells in an area to be delimited ... may, depending on the facts, be an element to be taken into account ...".[254] The judgment

---

[248] *North Sea*, para. 91.
[249] *Anglo-French* award, para. 251.
[250] *Libya/Malta*, para. 54.
[251] Mosler, *ibid.*, Dissenting Opinion, p. 119.
[252] *Anglo-French* award, para. 195.
[253] *Tunisia/Libya*, paras. 81 and 117ff.
[254] *Ibid.*, paras. 107 and 118.

therefore prescribes a delimitation which respects the limits of the permits issued by Libya and Tunisia.[255]

As already noted,[256] to turn the conduct of the parties into a relevant circumstance capable of establishing the equity or inequity of a line of equidistance is to run the risk of making the law of maritime delimitation drift towards effectiveness as a criterion. It is perhaps significant that, apart from a discreet use of this concept in *Libya/Malta*,[257] the courts have not endorsed the *Tunisia/Libya* approach. Not only did the Chamber in *Gulf of Maine* reject the arguments of the parties based on their previous conduct, but it was careful to make it clear that equity did not require that present exploitation practices be maintained in the future.[258] This highly questionable relevant circumstance is likely, from now on, to come into play only very exceptionally.

Economic factors

At first sight, there are scarcely any considerations more closely linked to the institutions of the continental shelf and the exclusive economic zone than those relating to the economy. As the Court noted in 1969, ''[T]he natural resources of the subsoil of the sea in those parts which consist of continental shelf are the very object of the legal régime established subsequent to the Truman Proclamation''.[259] The same sort of remark could be made about superjacent waters in respect of the exclusive economic zone.

Although they are, in fact, the very object of the legal regime of the continental shelf and the exclusive economic zone, economic considerations do not come into play in respect of the legal basis of title. A State's title to marine and submarine areas adjacent to its coasts exists by virtue of State sovereignty, which extends a certain distance seawards by means of the coastal opening. Whether or not there are natural resources in these areas does not affect the existence of the title; nor does the fact that these resources are located within or beyond the distance prescribed by the law, or that they overlap the

---

[255] *Ibid.*, para. 133B2; cf. para. 121.

[256] See p. 92 above.

[257] *Guinea/Guinea-Bissau*, paras. 62 and 105.

[258] *Gulf of Maine*, paras. 126-54 and 236; cf. p. 261 n. 267 below.

[259] *North Sea*, para. 97. In the *North Sea* case, as Judge Jessup notes (Separate Opinion, p. 67), the parties remained remarkably discreet about ''the actuality of their basic interests'' in the matter of oil and natural gas. This makes it easier to understand why the judgment was silent about the location of hydrocarbon resources in the North Sea, on the drillings already made, and on the claims of the parties. On the role of economic factors in maritime delimitation, see Bowett [3].

limit resulting from this distance, affect the rights of the coastal State.

Since they have no role to play at the level of legal title, it is logical that considerations to do with the existence, importance and location of natural resources cannot be regarded as relevant for the purposes of delimitation. That is how the criterion of legal relevance stated in *Libya/Malta* normally works.

As a result, if the provisional line allocates all of a particular resource to one of the parties, equity does not require it to be shifted so as to allocate part of it to the other. Conversely, if the provisional line cuts across a resource, dividing it in two, this is not "anything more than a factual element which it is reasonable to take into consideration", but which does not require the line to be shifted. There are, suggests the Court, "possible ways of solving" the problem of the "unity of any deposits".[260] They consist, basically, in implementing the principle of cooperation on which Judge Jessup dwelt at length in a famous passage of his separate opinion in the *North Sea* case.[261] In short, resources are where they are, and the boundary is where it is.

State practice fully confirms this approach. Certainly, there are many delimitation agreements which take the location and sharing of resources into account in drawing the boundary line. Nothing prevents States from pursuing this goal just like any other, but still more numerous are the delimitation agreements which draw the boundary according to neutral criteria, such as equidistance, or a line of latitude or longitude, without taking any account of the existence and location of resources. These agreements often contain a clause providing for cooperation between the States should the same deposit extend both sides of the boundary. In addition, a few agreements set up, in various forms, joint development areas overlapping the line of delimitation.

When a court is asked to draw the line of a maritime boundary applying the principles and rules of international law, it will not regard as relevant the existence, importance or location of resources. There will therefore be no reason for adjusting the original equidistance line simply because an oil deposit or a fishery resource straddles this line, or because all the resources are to be found on one side of it and none on the other, or because there are more resources on one side than on the other. This accords with the principle that only those circumstances which play a role in the title are relevant to a delimitation, and makes all the more sense in that resources are not

---

[260] *North Sea*, para. 97.
[261] Jessup, *ibid.*, Separate Opinion, pp. 76ff.

always known or easy to determine. Oil may not be where one hopes, and can be where no-one expects it. Fish swim. In any case, products much in demand today may tomorrow fall into disrepute because of economic changes or developments in taste or technique. To draw a boundary on this basis would imply that, if these circumstances changed, the boundary would need to be reconsidered, which, quite apart from good sense, would be at odds with the principle of the permanence and stability of boundaries, maritime as much as land.[262] One understands why the courts should have excluded from the category of relevant circumstances, and thus of equitable principles, anything which might seem to relate to an apportionment of resources, a division of wealth, an allocation of shares.[263]

Although the courts have been unanimous, it cannot be excluded that, without saying so (or by implication), they may be tempted into including economic considerations in their assessment of equity. In *Gulf of Maine*, the issue was raised in a particularly sharp form. As the judgment notes, the "real subject of the dispute" was Georges Bank, because of the potential resources of its subsoil and, even more, its enormous fishery resources.[264] The United States sought to avoid any division of this bank, which it claimed in its totality. Canada asked for a line dividing the bank, located as far as possible to the west, but which would, on any hypothesis, give it the north-east corner, which has the greatest fishery stocks. The question of resources was accompanied by a socio-economic—i.e., human— aspect. The two parties, Canada more than the United States, claimed that the loss of the bank, especially the richer part, would ruin the economy of a region whose economy depended on the line the boundary took.

As noted previously,[265] the Chamber proceeded in three stages. It began by dividing the area of overlap into equal parts, then adjusted the line thus obtained according to purely geographical criteria; and finally, after drawing a line in the light of relevant circumstances which were not economic, checked that the socio-economic results of this line were not too serious. Factors relating to human and economic geography were not taken into account, the Chamber was careful to explain,[266] "as criteria to be applied in the delimitation process itself". Their role was simply to check, as a sort of appendix

---

[262] Cf. p. 94 above.
[263] Cf. p. 23 above.
[264] *Gulf of Maine*, para. 232.
[265] See pp. 195-6 above.
[266] *Gulf of Maine*, para. 232.

to the delimitation process, that the overall result reached on the basis of geographical considerations was not

> ... unexpectedly ... revealed as radically inequitable, that is to say, as likely to entail catastrophic repercussions for the livelihood and economic well-being of the population of the countries concerned.[267]

It was only when it was persuaded that no consequence of this nature was to be feared from a division of the bank in the way it envisaged that the Chamber regarded the line at which it had arrived as definitive.[268]

The Chamber went to considerable lengths to minimize the legal effect of economic factors on the delimitation process. These factors, it expressly states,[269] "cannot be taken into account as a relevant circumstance". They do not enter into the delimitation process properly speaking, which is carried out entirely on the basis of relevant circumstances of a geographical nature, the only ones to warrant the name, and when they do come into the picture, in the final stage of checking the "overall result", they can only justify a correction to this result in "exceptionally unusual circumstances", to avoid "catastrophic repercussions for the livelihood and economic well-being of the population".

By doing its best to maintain a low profile for socio-economic considerations, the Chamber certainly tried not to depart from the position previously taken by the courts. The principle established in 1969 remained intact: economic factors are not a relevant circumstance capable of justifying an adjustment to the initial line of delimitation. One cannot help asking oneself, however, whether, although it defends itself against the charge, the Chamber did not in fact treat socio-economic factors as a consideration which could not be ignored. Is there really any difference between taking separate

---

[267] *Ibid.*, para. 237. The judgment refuses "to ascribe any decisive weight ... to the ... continuity of fishing activities carried on in the past", limiting itself to current economic facts. It explains, however, that equity does not require that the two States maintain their present economic activities, just as they are, into the future. Delimitation *de jure* does not necessarily mean "each Party's enjoying an access to the regional fishing resources which will be equal to the access it previously enjoyed *de facto*" (*Gulf of Maine*, paras. 235-6). It is to be noted that, at the beginning of the century, the *Grisbadarna* award had taken a different position. Saying that "as far as possible, the state of affairs which has long existed *de facto* should not be altered", the award drew the line in such a way as to take account of the fishing practices of the nationals of the two parties (*UNRIAA*, vol. XI, p. 161).

[268] *Gulf of Maine*, para. 241.

[269] *Ibid.*, para. 237.

and successive account of geographical and economic factors, the latter to make any necessary corrections to the former, and doing it altogether, at once? The fragility of this distinction is reinforced by the remark, in the shape of an admission, that as regards possible "catastrophic repercussions" there is "[f]ortunately . . . no reason to fear that any such danger will arise . . . on account of the Chamber's choice of delimitation line".[270] This line, the Chamber explains, in practice gives each State the greater part of the fishery areas exploited by its nationals. As for the mineral resources of the sub-soil, both sides are left vast areas of exploration. The "tradition of friendly cooperation" between the two countries will do the rest.[271]

In short, although it was careful not to make any innovation of principle, the *Gulf of Maine* judgment did take some liberty over practice. But one has to ask whether it could have done otherwise. At least it was frank.

The question of the relevance of economic considerations sometimes comes up in a slightly different form of the location or distribution of resources. In certain cases, the State endowed with fewer natural resources, or less developed economically, has argued that equity requires that the delimitation should not aggravate, indeed should correct, this imbalance. Here, the courts have shown themselves particularly firm. The greater wealth of the one, the more conspicuous poverty of the other, especially in energy or fishery resources, are not factors which can have any influence on the assessment of the equity of the provisional line of equidistance, or of any other line.

The Court thus refused, in *Tunisia/Libya*, to take into account the relative poverty of Tunisia in natural resources, both agricultural and mineral, observing that

> They are *virtually extraneous factors, since they are variables* which unpredictable national fortune or calamity, as the case may be, might at any time cause to tilt the scale one way or the other. A country might be poor today and become rich tomorrow as the result of an event such as the discovery of a valuable economic resource.[272]

The same view, expressed slightly differently, is to be found in *Guinea/Guinea-Bissau*: economic factors cannot be regarded as relevant circumstances because a delimitation cannot be based on the

---

[270] *Ibid.*, para. 226.
[271] *Ibid.*, paras. 238-40.
[272] *Tunisia/Libya*, para. 107.

"evaluation of data which changes in relation to factors that are sometimes uncertain". The award adds that the Tribunal "does not have the power to compensate for the economic inequalities of the States concerned by modifying a delimitation which it considers is called for by objective and certain considerations". Having thus reaffirmed the traditional doctrine, the Tribunal seems perhaps to reduce its scope when it says that it "can nevertheless not completely lose sight of the legitimate claims by virtue of which economic circumstances are invoked, nor contest the right of the peoples concerned to a level of economic and social development which fully preserves their dignity".[273] The significance of this qualification should not, however, be exaggerated, since although it may have led the Tribunal to encourage the parties to a "mutually advantageous cooperation",[274] it does not seem to have had any influence on the delimitation itself.

In *Libya/Malta*, the Court confirmed its previous position, refusing to take account of the absence of energy resources on the island of Malta, its needs as a developing island country or the size of its fishing industry:

> The Court does not . . . consider that a delimitation should be influenced by the relative economic position of the two States in question, in such a way that the area of continental shelf regarded as appertaining to the less rich of the two States would be somewhat increased in order to compensate for its inferiority in economic resources. Such considerations are totally unrelated to the underlying intention of the applicable rules of international law. It is clear that *neither the rules determining the validity of legal entitlement to the continental shelf, nor those concerning delimitation between neighbouring countries, leave room for any considerations of economic development of the States in question.*[275]

To sum up, from 1969 to 1985, the rule remained immutable: economic factors are not circumstances which the courts can take into account in assessing the equitableness of an initial line of equidistance. At most, they may serve to check that the line reached when this initial line has been put to the test of legally relevant (and therefore non-economic) circumstances does not risk producing "catastrophic" socio-economic repercussions. Although this may be the principle repeatedly confirmed by the courts, one must assume that, in practice, economic considerations, whether to do with the location of resources or the respective wealth of the parties, have

[273] *Guinea/Guinea-Bissau*, paras. 122-3.
[274] *Ibid.*
[275] *Libya/Malta*, para. 50.

more than once been in the courts' mind. In theory, the sharing of resources has no part to play in the delimitation process, but in practice it cannot be ignored since it is in reality the heart of the matter. Economic considerations are a relevant circumstance which nobody dare (or rather, can) mention.[276]

Security considerations

Does equity require security considerations to be taken into account? Is it appropriate to rectify the provisional line in order to provide a better guarantee of the security of one or other of the parties?

While economic considerations are at the forefront of the concerns paraded by governments, political considerations, taken broadly, are, as already observed, rarely ignored. As far as the continental shelf is concerned, the Truman Proclamation as far back as 1945 stated that "self-protection compels the coastal nation to keep close watch over activities off its shores which are of the nature necessary for utilization of these resources". As Judge Jiménez de Aréchaga said,

> There was . . . an immediate and almost instinctive rejection by all coastal States of the possibility that foreign States, or foreign companies or individuals, might appear in front of their coasts, outside their territorial sea but at a short distance from their ports and coastal defences, in order to exploit the seabed and erect fixed installations for that purpose.[277]

Governments have had no hesitation in raising these concerns about sovereignty before the courts as relevant circumstances. Faced with this pressure, the courts at first reacted firmly, but gradually less and less so.

In the *Anglo-French* case, the Court of Arbitration rejected, as incapable of exercising a "decisive influence" on the drawing of the line, the "various equitable considerations invoked by the parties regarding their respective navigational, defence and security interest in the region". At the most, it said, these considerations can "support and strengthen" the conclusions it has reached by other means, but "cannot negative" them. This did not, however, stop the

---

[276] It is only in the *Jan Mayen* case that economic considerations have played a determining and admitted role, but there it was a conciliation process not intended to produce a legal solution (on this case, see p. 29 n. 26 and p. 131 above).

[277] *Tunisia/Libya*, Separate Opinion, p. 121, para. 72.

Court referring to the "predominant interest of the French Republic in the southern areas of the English Channel".[278]

In *Gulf of Maine*, the United States, as we have seen, put forward the argument that a maritime boundary too close to its shores would interpose Canadian maritime areas between those shores on the one hand and the high seas and Europe on the other.[279] The judgment, however, contained no echo of this highly political concern.

With *Guinea/Guinea-Bissau*, these scruples vanish. It may be true that the award mentions security only in the modest category of "additional circumstances", but it says, without any ambiguity, that this consideration "is not without interest". Going still further, it states forcefully:

> Its prime objective has been to avoid that either party . . . should see rights exercised opposite its coast or in the immediate vicinity thereof, which could . . . compromise its security.[280]

The International Court of Justice was to take this same route in *Libya/Malta*. Malta had emphasized the risk to its security of a continental shelf delimitation which would allow Libya to instal underwater exploration or exploitation platforms just a few miles from its shores. The Court admitted that:

> *Security considerations are of course not unrelated to the concept of the continental shelf.* They were referred to when this legal concept first emerged, particularly in the Truman Proclamation . . . in any event, the delimitation which will result from the application of the present Judgment is . . . not so near to the coast of either party as to make questions of security a particular consideration in the present case.[281]

These statements in *Guinea/Guinea-Bissau* and *Libya/Malta* are significant. They show that considerations of security, and, more generally, political considerations, are relevant in law for the assessment of the equitableness of a delimitation line. They also confirm the close link between these considerations and the spatial principle of non-encroachment. However, their main interest lies elsewhere. It is clear that at present it is for *political* reasons that the first-stage equidistance line is adjusted, and not because the equidistance method, on account of its inherent vices, in itself causes

[278] *Anglo-French* award, para. 188.

[279] Cf. pp. 93-4 above.

[280] *Guinea/Guinea-Bissau*, para. 124. Cf. the speech of the President of the Court, Judge Lachs, p. 61 above.

[281] *Libya/Malta*, para. 51.

inequity. The veil is lifted, and the truth revealed in all its clarity. The courts may consider it necessary to correct the equidistance line, but this is not in order to *take account* of the relevant circumstances of geography. On the contrary, it is to *rectify* them so as to cause the maritime boundary better to conform to the exigencies of politics, or, to put it more clearly, to place it less close to the shores of one of the parties than nature or geography would have it. Relevant circumstances of a political character, the principle of non-encroachment and the theory of non-essential geographical features, are thus three versions of one and the same vision of an equity called upon, not to remedy (as we have been in the habit of saying) the evil effects attributed to the equidistance method, but to mitigate the political consequences of the shape of the boundaries, and of the geographical reality of the coasts, which have been deemed undesirable.

Balancing the relevant circumstances: a false problem

As we have just seen, the courts have dealt with the identification of relevant circumstances in some detail. Even if the solutions reached have not all achieved their definitive form, even if there are still some uncertainties, even if, as we have noted, cases prior to *Libya/Malta* have to be treated with caution, it has, nonetheless, been possible to review a considerable number of circumstances, some of which the courts have accepted, some rejected.

In the light of this case-law, we need now to consider the balancing of the various circumstances regarded as relevant in a given case. As the Court said in 1969 in respect of a negotiated delimitation: "... more often than not it is the balancing-up of all such considerations that will produce this result [the equitable result] rather than reliance on one to the exclusion of all others".[282] In 1982, this time in reference to a judicial delimitation, the Court referred[283] to "... the process of weighing all relevant factors to achieve an

---

[282] *North Sea*, para. 93.

[283] *Tunisia/Libya*, para. 107. In the judgment on the *Application for Revision and Interpretation of the Judgment of 24 February 1982*, the Court noted that the method it had indicated in *Tunisia/Libya* for arriving at an equitable delimitation "derived in fact from a balance struck between a number of considerations, *a process which has always been regarded as inherent in the application of equity* ..." (ICJ *Reports*, 1984, p. 211, para. 35). The *Beagle Channel* award, as mentioned previously, listed "mixed factors of appurtenance, coastal configuration, equidistance, and also of convenience, navigability, and the desirability of enabling each party so far as possible to navigate in its own waters"(para. 110).

equitable result'' but it immediately explained that, although it had to ''balance up the various considerations which it regards as relevant . . . no rigid rules exist as to the exact weight to be attached to each element in the case''.[284] The Court took up the same theme in *Libya/Malta*: ''Weighing up these several considerations in the present kind of situation is not a process that can infallibly be reduced to a formula expressed in actual figures''.[285]

These images borrowed from the world of weights and measures[286] are indicative of the courts' approach. There is nothing to guarantee, *a priori*, that the circumstances considered relevant in law will always militate in the same direction, or appear on the same side of the scales. Some, it might be said, are seen as more relevant than others, weighing heavier in the scales. The ''problem of the relative weight''[287] can arise. Choices may have to be made. One certainly finds in the judgments expressions evoking circumstances as being ''of considerable relevance'', ''highly relevant'',[288] or, again, ''a valid ground for correction [which is] more pressing even than others''.[289] Nor is there any doubt that some decisions make a distinction between circumstances capable of directly influencing the drawing of the line and ''complementary'' or ''additional'' circumstances, used only to check the equity of the result.[290] It cannot be said, however, that the courts have ever tackled head-on the problem of the respective weight to be given various elements of fact, so much so that this apparently central problem of balancing the relevant circumstances remains, at present, unresolved.

Some of the explanations for this phenomenon are circumstantial and somewhat superficial. It might be thought, for example, that the reason the courts have managed to avoid this formidable problem is that, in the cases which have come before them so far, the many circumstances they have taken into consideration have, by happy chance, all seemed to lead to the same result. If this is the case, there can be no guarantee that the miracle will recur every time, and the possibility of a conflict between relevant circumstances, requiring the establishment of a hierarchy, cannot be excluded *a priori*. It might also be thought that a single ground of inequity will be enough to

---

[284] *Ibid.*, para. 71.
[285] *Libya/Malta*, para. 73.
[286] Cf. *Gulf of Maine*, para. 184.
[287] *North Sea*, para. 93.
[288] *Tunisia/Libya*, paras. 82 and 117.
[289] *Gulf of Maine*, para. 185.
[290] Cf. pp. 195ff above.

condemn a line. The fact that it is reasonable from some points of view, and in respect of some factual circumstances, cannot render equitable a line that is otherwise inequitable.

But, besides these rather facile explanations, there is perhaps a more fundamental and conclusive reason why the courts have always been able to avoid the difficult task of weighing up the equities. An analysis of the various circumstances so far considered by the courts as relevant shows that, once we exclude the false ones (the interests of third States and other delimitations in the region, for example) and those whose relevance is debatable and future not assured (such as the relationship of opposition or adjacency, the distance between coasts, the difference in coastal lengths, the general geographical context and the conduct of the parties), *the category of relevant circumstances*, at first sight so heterogenous, *boils down, at the end of the day, to just one: the distance of the delimitation line from the coasts*. It is by reference to this factor that a first-stage equidistance line will most often be judged. If this line comes too near to the coasts of one of the parties, it will call for correction. If it stays sufficiently far from the the coasts of both, it will become the definitive boundary. Whether one invokes the coastal geography or the principle of non-encroachment, or relies on the peculiarities attributed to the equidistance method, or resorts to considerations of security and economic development, it is always the same factor with which one ends up: the line will be adjudged equitable or inequitable by this single criterion. This brings us back to the observation made earlier about the leading role of political considerations in the theory of relevant circumstances and equitable principles. The problem of weighing up the equities simply does not exist.

B. *Possible Adjustment of the First-stage Line and the Definitive Boundary-line*

There are two possible outcomes when the line of equidistance is tested. It may be found to be either equitable or inequitable.

First possibility: the equidistance line turns out to be equitable

If it passes the test of confrontation with relevant circumstances successfully, the line of equidistance will become the boundary. The starting line will coincide with the finishing line.

In spite of their rather cautious attitude towards equidistance, the courts have never disputed that it can lead to an equitable result, not only *prima facie*, but definitively. As the Court said, as early as 1969, its "use . . . is indicated in a considerable number of cases".[291] The 1977 *Anglo-French* arbitral award resorted to it to draw the "primary boundary" in the Channel,[292] and commended the parties for choosing the equidistance solution for the greater part of the delimitation.[293] The *Tunisia/Libya* judgment of 1982, however unenthusiastic it may have been about equidistance, concedes[294] that in certain circumstances, in particular between opposite coasts, it can lead to an equitable solution. The *Gulf of Maine* judgment notes that equidistance "has rendered undeniable service in many concrete situations".[295] The *Libya/Malta* judgment declares that delimitation agreements are "impressive evidence that the equidistance method can in many different situations yield an equitable result".[296]

State practice fully confirms these statements.[297] The conclusion reached by writers who have studied this practice[298] is that in a very large number of cases—the majority—States have chosen strict or modified equidistance as being reasonable and equitable. It is not without interest to note that a number of agreements concluded by France, hardly *parti pris* in the matter of equidistance,[299] include the following phrase in their preamble:

> Whereas the application of the method of equidistance constitutes in this case an equitable means of delimitation.[300]

Despite the hostile position it took towards equidistance in *Gulf of Maine*, the United States has concluded several treaties with its neighbours adopting an equidistance line.[301] There is no escaping the fact that many governments consider equidistance as an equitable method, even for the definitive solution.

To this it may be added that during UNCLOS III the equidistance method was the only one to receive express mention in some of the

[291] *North Sea*, para. 22.
[292] *Anglo-French* award, para. 201.
[293] *Ibid.*, paras. 15, 22, 84-7, 103, 111, 120 and 146.
[294] *Tunisia/Libya*, paras. 109 and 126.
[295] *Gulf of Maine*, para. 107.
[296] *Libya/Malta*, para. 44.
[297] Cf. Sette-Camara, *Libya/Malta*, Separate Opinion, p. 61.
[298] For example, Conforti and Francalanci, p. XIII; Jagota [1], pp. 130-1 and [2], p. 121.
[299] At UNCLOS III, France was a member of the "equitable principles" group, and figured amongst the States who submitted the text known as NG7/10 to Working Group 7. Cf. Oda, *Tunisia/Libya*, Dissenting Opinion, pp. 223-4.
[300] For French practice, see Guillaume [1] and [2].
[301] See Feldman and Colson, p. 749.

negotiating texts. Although this mention disappeared in the final text of Articles 74 and 83 of the 1982 Convention, this was, as previously indicated, because these compromise texts, developed and adopted in haste on the eve of the closure of the Conference, simultaneously eliminated the two contenders in the long struggle which had taken place at the heart of the Conference.

The possibility of the transformation of the initial line of equidistance into the definitive delimitation is, one sees, far from being merely academic.

Second possibility: the equidistance line turns out to be inequitable

There are, however, cases where equidistance will not emerge from its confrontation with relevant circumstances as an equitable solution. Not every inequity, that is to say not every time the line goes too close to one of the coasts, justifies an adjustment to the line of equidistance. It has to be a blatant one. Only then will the courts intervene to modify the result by modifying the method. Only then will the question arise as to "how the continental shelf can be delimited when it is in fact the case that the equidistance principle does not provide an equitable solution".[302]

When two governments are faced with a situation of this sort in the context of a negotiated delimitation, the range of methods of adjustment which can be employed, either alone or in combination with one another, is very broad: a simple correction of the equidistance line, a line perpendicular to the coast or in a notional direction, one which follows a line of latitude or longitude, etc. Some agreements indicate the method or methods followed in place of equidistance; others, although silent on the subject, can nonetheless easily be interpreted; still others, in contrast, remain hermetically sealed as to the method followed, even for the most well-informed expert. This freedom of States, however, makes it the more noteworthy that in the majority of cases governments end up agreeing on a line based on equidistance; that is to say, a line in which, alongside other ingredients, equidistance occupies an important place, in larger or smaller doses. The *Anglo-French* award observed, in 1977, on the subject of continental shelf delimitation:

> ... State practice ... shows that up to date a large proportion of the delimitations of the continental shelf have been effected by the application either of the equidistance method or, not infrequently, of some variant of that method ... in a large proportion of the delimitations known to it, where

[302] *North Sea*, para. 21.

a particular geographical feature has influenced the course of a continental shelf boundary, the method of delimitation adopted has been some modification or variant of the equidistance principle rather than its total rejection.[303]

As for the courts, when called on to decide on the basis of law, is their discretionary power in correcting the line of equidistance such that they can resort to any method or combination of methods whatsoever in drawing the definitive line? Or is the possible adjustment of the provisional line and, therefore, the choice of the definitive line, subject to certain rules of law? In the first case, the role of the law would be exhausted with the drawing of the first-stage line of equidistance and the determination of the equitable principles and relevant circumstances; it would not extend to the drawing of the definitive line. In the second case, normativity would extend to the choice of methods of adjustment or to alternatives, and thus cover the whole of the delimitation process from beginning to end.

The courts have not so far given any precise answer to this question. This relative silence is probably explained by the fact that the two-stage delimitation process has not been clearly accepted in all the judgments. Indeed, in several cases, it has even been explicitly rejected, at least in principle. It goes without saying that when a court considers itself justified in proceeding directly to the choice of methods and the drawing of the line on the basis of the facts in the case, the question whether the correction of the initial equidistance line falls within its discretion does not arise.

In fact, only the *Anglo-French* award has really tackled this problem head-on, and it is no coincidence that it is this award which has most clearly adopted the two-stage process. The Court of Arbitration took the view that judges do not have total freedom at this final stage of the delimitation process any more than at the preceding stages. In a dictum to which we must return once more, the Court, while recognizing that the choice of definitive method and the final line is "very much a matter of appreciation",[304] does not regard itself as having "carte blanche to employ any method that it chooses in order to effect an equitable delimitation . . .".[305] In clarification of its thinking in this respect, the award states:

. . . it seems to the Court to be *in accord* not only *with the legal rules* . . . but also with State practice *to seek the solution in a method modifying or varying the*

[303] *Anglo-French* award, paras. 85 and 249. Cf. Jagota [2], p. 276.
[304] *Anglo-French* award, para. 70.
[305] *Ibid.*, para. 245.

equidistance method rather than to have recourse to a wholly different criterion of delimitation.[306]

Later judgments have been less demanding in this respect. Not only have the courts seen themselves as empowered to divide the line into as many segments, with as many methods, as the situation seems to them to require,[307] but they appear to adopt for each of these segments whatever method or combination of methods they deem appropriate for drawing a definitive line. This lack of certainty in the methods governing the drawing of the definitive line is, without doubt, the source of the accusation of judicial subjectivity sometimes laid against the courts. A little equidistance, more or less modified, here; a bit of a line of latitude or longitude there; a rounding-out here, a curtailment elsewhere; a slide eastwards in one place, a shift westwards in another; here a perpendicular, there an acute angle: such is the tangled, rather confused picture, which would emerge from a detailed list—if it were thought useful to compile one—of all the methods used by the courts. As with relevant circumstances, a more rigorous approach to the modalities of correction would no doubt represent a step forward which governments and lawyers would both welcome. It is encouraging that, although not put into practice, the views expressed in 1977 have never since been contradicted,[308] and that the Court should have spoken in *Libya/Malta* of "adjusting" the line of equidistance rather than of turning to an alternative method.

There is no lack of variations on equidistance capable of reducing or even effacing those consequences of this method which are considered unreasonable, without losing its advantages, that is, observing its spirit rather than the letter. Some of the methods of resolving the difficulties attributed to equidistance without destroying it have been proposed and studied by technical experts who have concentrated on the construction of lines of equidistance. The courts have described other correctives. Yet others have been suggested by the practice. A few examples will illustrate this idea of adjustment.

Instead of the strict or true line of equidistance which a computer would draw on the basis of all the points on the coastline, a so-called

---

[306] *Ibid.*, para. 249.

[307] See, for example, *Tunisia/Libya*, paras. 114-5; *Gulf of Maine*, paras. 205-7 and 224; *Guinea/Guinea-Bissau*, para. 111.

[308] In the *Beagle Channel* case, the Court of Arbitration, after listing the "mixed factors" it had taken into account, said that "*none of this has resulted in much deviation from the strict median line*", with the exception of the area around Gable Island where, as we have seen, the boundary was fixed along the navigation channel (para. 110).

simplified line can be used. The *Anglo-French* award defined such a line as

> one in which, in order to make the line less complicated, the number of its turning points is reduced by using straight lines between the principal points.[309]

It was on a line of this nature that France and the United Kingdom agreed before turning to the Court of Arbitration for certain sectors. The Court, after having the line thus obtained checked by an expert, accepted it as the "median delimitation ... indicated by the applicable law".[310] This method, avoiding too many changes of direction, is a standard practice. The Court added that:

> When this is done, an advantage to one State in one area is usually compensated by a roughly equivalent advantage to the other State in another area.[311]

This, in fact, is another method suggested by the practice: a line other than that of strict equidistance which evens out the gains and losses of the two parties. The Court alluded to this compensation method in its 1969 judgment.[312]

The attribution of *partial effect* is another way of correcting exaggerated distortions caused by special geographical features, including, in particular, islands. This method of correcting—but not rejecting—equidistance has been used and expounded by the courts on several occasions.[313] For islands, the *enclave* method is also a possibility.[314]

A correction can also be made by adjusting the *basepoints* rather than the method itself. To a certain extent, this is what the partial effect procedure already does. Playing with the basepoints makes it possible to modify the line to make it more equitable—that is, to move it further from the coast to which the court thinks it is too near—but without altering the technique of the construction of the

---

[309] *Anglo-French* award, para. 111, n. 1.

[310] *Ibid.*, para. 120.

[311] *Ibid.*

[312] *North Sea*, para. 89. A well-known example of this method is provided by the UK (Trinidad and Tobago)/Venezuela Agreement of 1942, relating to the Gulf of Paria and sometimes regarded as the ancestor and prototype of modern maritime delimitation agreements (*Limits in the Seas*, No. 11).

[313] Cf. pp. 230ff above. On the technique of the half-effect see Beazley [3].

[314] As in the *Anglo-French* case, for the Channel Islands, and in *Dubai/Sharjah*, for the island of Abu Musa.

line. In principle, a line of equidistance is drawn from the baseline of the territorial sea of the two States. This is the method prescribed in Article 6 of the Geneva Convention for the delimitation of the continental shelf. Between States which are not party to this Convention or for a delimitation other than of the continental shelf, the courts are left some room for manoeuvre and the baselines used for drawing the line of equidistance will not necessarily coincide with those used to establish the outer limit of the territorial sea.[315] Already in the *North Sea* case, the Court considered that the drawing of one or more straight baselines between the extreme ends of a coast which was strongly convex or concave "can play a useful part in eliminating or diminishing the distortions"[316] which the equidistance method risks producing. The Anglo-French Court of Arbitration, for its part, took the view that, even if the baseline for the territorial sea normally serves as baseline for the median line, the two ideas should be kept separate. This is why, although the arbitral agreement gave it no competence to decide the territorial sea basepoints, the Court nonetheless decided it had the power to determine the basepoints for calculating the line of equidistance.[317] In *Libya/Malta*, the Court confirmed that the baselines chosen by a coastal State for determining the outer limit of its territorial sea are not necessarily identical with those coastal points to be adopted for drawing the delimitation line. Although not expressing any opinion on the lawfulness of the inclusion of Filfla in the Maltese baselines, it refused to regard this deserted islet as a suitable basepoint for drawing the median line between Malta and Libya.[318]

The *transposition* of the median line, in other words, shifting it so as to move it further from one coast and nearer to the other, is a useful means of correction. In *Gulf of Maine*, the median line chosen as the second segment of the boundary between the opposite and parallel coasts of Massachusetts and Nova Scotia was shifted eastwards.[319] In *Libya/Malta*, the median line between the two countries was moved northwards.[320]

The *perpendicular* method can also, in certain cases, as already noted, be a useful variant for correcting the line of equidistance in the

---

[315] Cf. Oda, *Tunisia/Libya*, Dissenting Opinion, pp. 262-3, paras. 168-9.

[316] *North Sea*, para. 98.

[317] *Anglo-French* award, paras. 19, 139 and 144 (on the role of Eddystone Rock in drawing the median line).

[318] *Libya/Malta*, paras. 64 and 72.

[319] *Gulf of Maine*, para. 222.

[320] *Libya/Malta*, paras. 71-3.

case of adjacent coasts.[321] The two methods are closely related. A line of equidistance between two points is, by definition, the perpendicular bisecting the straight line between those two points, so a line of equidistance is simply a series of perpendiculars. It would scarcely be an exaggeration to say that the equidistance method is the scientific development of the perpendicular, which is a rather cruder method since it is "probably the oldest method to come to mind" for delimiting the territorial sea between neighbouring States.[322] In the case of a coast which is more or less straight, or the imaginary closing-line of a gulf, there is hardly any difference between a perpendicular bisecting the closing line and a line of equidistance.[323] The use of the perpendicular method is much more debatable in the case of a coast which is not altogether straight, for it presupposes a preliminary decision on the general direction of the coast between two points which have to be chosen. As we know, this is a particularly hazardous business, and it is easy to understand why the Committee of Experts consulted by the International Law Commission should, for this reason, have preferred the equidistance method to the perpendicular.[324] These reservations do not exclude the possibility that the perpendicular method may prove useful in particular cases, as, for example, in drawing a line which is almost but not quite equidistant. In *Tunisia/Libya*, for example, the Court mentioned it, but only for the segment nearest to the coast, on the grounds, it explained, that except in the rare case of a perfectly straight coast, "a line drawn perpendicular to the coast becomes, generally speaking, the less suitable as a line of delimitation the further it extends from the coast".[325] In *Gulf of Maine*, the Chamber chose, for the segment of the maritime boundary outside the Gulf, a perpendicular to the imaginary closing-line joining Cape Sable to Nantucket Island.[326] This perpendicular does not, however, cut the closing-line at its mid-point, but further to the east. It is the equivalent of an equidistance line controlled by two points at the far ends of the closing-line and shifted eastwards.

[321] Cf. p. 59 above.

[322] *Gulf of Maine*, para. 175.

[323] The Argentina/Uruguay Agreement (1973) (*Limits in the Seas,* No. 64) defines the delimitation line seawards of the Rio as an equidistance line; this line could equally well have been defined as a perpendicular to the imaginary line closing the Rio. Likewise, the Costa Rica/Panama delimitation (1980), defined by reference to equidistance, could, as observed in *Limits in the Seas,* No. 97, pp. 4-5, have been a perpendicular to the general direction of the coast.

[324] *ILCYB,* 1953, vol. II, pp. 78-9.

[325] *Tunisia/Libya*, para. 125.

[326] *Gulf of Maine*, paras. 224-5.

Another variant of equidistance is, in some cases, the *angle bisection* method. This method, as already mentioned, was used by the Chamber in *Gulf of Maine,* for the innermost sector of the Gulf, in preference to the equidistance method proper.[327]

The problem of adjusting the starting-line of equidistance remains largely unresolved, both because few judgments have clearly conceived delimitation as a two-stage process and because the very idea of a restriction on the discretionary power of the courts on this point has not really made any progress since it was proclaimed in 1977. It would be reasonable to expect the customary rule to develop towards a restriction of the power of correction to methods of adjustment which would move the definitive boundary as little as possible from the line of equidistance, and that it would only be in exceptional cases that the courts could, providing they gave reasons, use alternative methods. But it has to be accepted that there is no guarantee that the courts will move in this direction. Such a development would mark a new and decisive step towards the submission of maritime delimitation to the law, but it would also considerably reduce the courts' discretionary power.

[327] *Ibid.*, para. 213. It is not without interest that, basing itself on the inequity of the equidistance line claimed by Canada, the Chamber paradoxically drew a line more favourable to Canada (and therefore less favourable to the United States) than that claimed.

CONCLUSION

CONCLUSION

THIS long exploration of some aspects of the law of maritime delimitation has taken us not only across country already well-marked but also into more obscure areas where ordered presentation is difficult. The courts have managed, in less than twenty years, to clarify many of the issues, but there is still a long way to go before it will be possible to write a treatise on the law of maritime delimitation rather than simply indulge in a necessarily disjointed and fragmentary essay.

The acquis

The concept of maritime delimitation has been released from the naturalist dross which at one time threatened to smother it, and much refined. The search for the chimera of natural boundaries has been abandoned even in respect of the continental shelf, and the more so for other maritime areas, and delimitation is now a man-determined process related to the legal title of coastal States to maritime areas adjacent to their shores.

Delimitation is inextricably linked to title, being penetrated through and through by the theory of coastal projections which is the legal basis for the extension of territorial sovereignty seawards. This theory is perhaps in some ways regrettable: it restricts the benefit of maritime jurisdictions to States enjoying access to the sea; it means the outer contours of their jurisdictions depend on the shape of their coastline; and, as a result, it causes the inequalities due to the combined hazards of political history and nature to be extended to maritime spaces. But the theory is now so firmly established that it would be pointless to bemoan it. This is what States have wanted, and what States want is law. So, although all States are equal in law, some of them are more equal than others as far as maritime jurisdictions are concerned. At least (at any rate for the continental shelf) the abandonment of the theory of natural prolongation in favour of the distance criterion has eliminated an additional cause of discrimination, since from now on all maritime jurisdictions will be determined mathematically according to their distance from the shore.

This is the philosophy behind the theory of delimitation. The legal title of two neighbouring States being what it is, if there is not enough room for their coastal projections both to reach their full extent, they may enter into competition for the same space. Delimitation will consist in limiting the extension of each by drawing a line which, while cutting off a part of each State's projection, will guarantee both of them exclusive rights in the part they retain. If the States concerned are unable to reach agreement on this line, by what rules ought it to be determined? This is the purpose of the law of maritime delimitation, to impose on each some sacrifice but to guarantee them both space of their own.

The concept of maritime delimitation once stabilized, the problem of determining substantive rules for regulating it could be tackled in a noticeably uniform manner. This second achievement of the courts is no less significant than the first.

The delimitation of the continental shelf took over the monopoly of attention from its elder sister, the territorial sea, and almost systematically pursued an opposite course. Even though the 1958 Conventions subjected the two to identical rules, customary law—in other words, the courts—took the delimitation of the continental shelf up a largely different path. And since the law of the delimitation of the continental shelf threatened to draw that of the new-born exclusive economic zone in its wake, there was a risk of opening a great gulf between the rules governing the delimitation of the territorial sea on the one hand, and those governing the delimitation of the shelf and zone on the other. Substituting the distance criterion for the theory of natural prolongation in respect of both title to the continental shelf and its delimitation allowed this gulf to be filled.

But the unity was threatened not only by the originality of this star performer, as the delimitation of the continental shelf was for many years; there was also the decision of the International Court of Justice in 1969 to draw a sharp distinction between customary and treaty law, at least, once again, with respect to the continental shelf. Instead of elevating the 1958 conventional rules relating to the delimitation of the shelf into customary norms, the courts chose to develop a body of customary rules separate from the conventional: equitable principles for the former, equidistance for the latter—even though, paradoxically, they saw the conventional law as being made up of the same norms as the customary. But, by another paradox, the content of customary law is now tending to move towards that of the conventional system, so much so that, in this respect also, the original unity seems to be re-establishing itself.

In the end, the only delimitations to remain outside this common law are those freely negotiated by the interested governments, who are, theoretically, free of all constraints. However, to the extent that States tend to take their inspiration from legal guidelines, the single normative corpus being developed is likely, in practice if not law, to penetrate this reserved domain also.

The progress already made is reflected in the language of the law.[1] The vocabulary has been established and the concepts have acquired a more precise shape. *Delimitation* has been separated from the determination of outer *limits*, and its relationship with *title* has been refined. *Natural prolongation* is no longer the physical phenomenon justifying both title and delimitation, but has become simply the term for describing rights based on the theory of *coastal projections*. The logic of this theory leads to the use of a provisional line based on the legally required method of *equidistance*—legally required because it is inherent in the concept of delimitation; but this does not mean that the *equity* of the provisional line does not have to be checked before it is adopted as the definitive line. Conceived as an integral part of the law, equity lies in the fact that account is to be taken of *relevant circumstances*, assessed by the judge according to *equitable principles* (or, in some judgments, criteria or equitable factors). This assessment leads to the application of *methods* which must end in an *equitable result*, this result itself being confirmed by final *tests* (sometimes called criteria or factors) such as that of proportionality. Each concept thus has its place in the *process* (or *operation*) of delimitation, and for each one there is a clearly defined term.

Although the areas of certainty now established are by no means negligible, it has to be admitted that they are somewhat peripheral. As soon as we leave behind the outlines of the law of delimitation to look at its core, the certainties become blurred and give way to as many questions as answers. But important developments are taking place and, although it may still be far from clear how much normativity there is and what the rules are, there are rays of light.

4 *The normativity of the structure of the delimitation process*

The structure of the delimitation process is the area of greatest certainty. It is true that the judgments remain a little hesitant and that the courts have not defined the process with rigour or uniformity. Even *Libya/Malta*, which, of all the judgments, approached most closely a precise description of the process,

[1] Cf. Colliard.

preferred a pragmatic approach, free of any normative definition—
and thus of any general validity. However, by tying delimitation to
legal title and basing title to all maritime areas on distance, the courts
have blazed the trail for developments which should lead logically
to the "normativization" of the two-pronged process which the
courts have applied many times, but without so far according
it the obligatory character which alone can turn it into a rule of
law.

The structure of the delimitation process described here is more
than just a possibility. Although it is still at the embryonic stage, and
time will be needed for the existing elements to develop fully, it has
already become a fact. Let us remind ourselves, one last time, that
the process is extremely simple, and it is both surprising and regrettable that it has been obscured by so much pointless controversy.
First, the equidistance method is tried, not only because it is easy and
objective and can be regarded, *prima facie*, as equitable because it
divides the overlapping areas of the projections of the two coasts
almost equally, but also, above all, because it reflects the legal ideas
at the root of the title of States to maritime areas and expresses the
modern conception of maritime delimitation. Next, the equidistance
line is tested against the relevant circumstances of the case in
question in order to ensure that it does not, in practice, produce an
inequitable or unreasonable result, and, depending on the outcome,
is either retained as the definitive boundary or is adjusted.

In this way, the delimitation process satisfies simultaneously both
the legal considerations of title and the factual circumstances of the
actual situation. The given and the made both have their place in it.
The generality essential to any legal norm is safeguarded, but
without neglecting the need to adapt it to the diversity and
particularity of concrete situations. Relevant circumstances are
always present in the process but they never directly determine the
drawing of the line. The delimitation process thus maintains a
balance between the rigour of the law and the flexibility of equity,
between the general and the particular. Because it is rooted in title,
which is invariably precise, delimitation has the generality to protect
it from the risk of subjectivity. And the care taken to ensure it is
sufficiently individualized means the risk of blind automatism is
avoided and the demands of equity are met.

The normativity of equidistance as a first step

The courts' reluctance to accept clearly the two-pronged structure
is explained by the privileged place it gives to the equidistance

method. Although State practice has continued to use this method, at least as the point of departure in every negotiation, the courts (while recognizing it has some merits) turned away from it after 1969. Was this to preserve their total freedom to choose whatever method they prefer? Was it because they had fallen unconscious victims to the false antinomy, a matter of language rather than substance, between equidistance and equitable principles? At all events, the courts seem to have been permanently marked by the attempt made by Denmark and the Netherlands before the Court in 1969, to turn equidistance into a principle of law, and thus into a binding rule. No doubt the courts saw—and still see—in equidistance as a first step the spectre of automatic equidistance which was rejected in the *North Sea* case.

Once passions have cooled and serenity returned, things can fall back into place. Equidistance is indeed a method, but it is more than that. Under the combined influence of the correlation between title and delimitation, on the one hand, and the distance criterion dominating title and therefore also dominating delimitation, on the other, there can be no doubt that equidistance has the status of a legal principle. That is not to say that every delimitation must necessarily be equidistant: if that were so, there would never be any dispute to be brought before the courts since the solution would be predetermined and known in advance. What it does mean is that, legally, this method must have a place in delimitation, because it is inherent in the equitable division of the overlapping zones of two coastal projections of equal value, and equally inherent in the reciprocal and balanced cutting-off of the projection of each of the interested States. The courts, once they overcome their reluctance to accept that the law requires equidistance to be included in the delimitation process, will not thereby be condemned to the view that equidistance is a rule of universal application: the nuance is important and should reassure even those who are the least enthusiastic about equidistance. Once the obsession with equidistance as obligatory and automatic is out of the way, the legal truth will at last be able to emerge. With the *Libya/Malta* judgment, the moment is perhaps not far away when the two-pronged structure of the delimitation process will become part of the *acquis*.

The normativity of the verification of the equitable

Although the delimitation process must begin by taking the equidistant line into account, this first phase has to be followed by a test of the equity of the provisional result thus obtained and, if necessary, by its correction. These two requirements are not of the same order: it is legal logic which requires the use of equidistance as a first step; it is a customary rule, resulting from State practice and the will of the courts, which imposes equity as a corrective. The law could have stayed with the line of equidistance, which would then have become the legally binding rule, but it preferred to adopt a rule requiring a delimitation not only to reflect the distance criterion and the coastal geography, but also to be equitable. It is to this second legal rule that the verification of the equity of the provisional equidistance line relates, together with its corollary, the pursuit of an equitable result which is the goal of the second phase of the process.

The invasion of equity into the legal structure of the delimitation process certainly carries the risk of subjectivity and unpredictability. There can be no doubt that the risk has been fully calculated by those who have taken it. But the critical opinions of some judges and the reservations of many writers suggest that the courts have not always avoided the danger. It is true that the judgments give the impression that the judges do not see themselves as under any serious legal restraint in their assessment of equity. Were this impression well-founded, the long, slow structuring of the delimitation process would have been a waste of time, since, after a legally rigorous first phase, the operation would still end with an unconstrained assessment of equity. Subjectivity would be relegated to the second part of the process, and no longer dominate the whole of the delimitation, but the result would be practically the same. This means that, given the point which the development of the law of maritime delimitation has reached, jurists should now concentrate on the second phase of the process, since, in the last resort, this is what will determine the reality and effectiveness of the legal conquest of maritime delimitation.

Fortunately, this negative impression is a little misleading and, looked at more closely, the truth is more reassuring.

First, it is important to take proper account of the legal formulae integrating equity into the law. Even if they are partly a matter of rhetoric, they are also evidence of the intention to oppose the destructive myths of non-law and the ad hoc. But they go further. Declarations that equity is an integral part of the law mean that the assessment of equity can be "normativized" and subjected to the constraints inherent in legal normativity: generality, coherence, foreseeability, precision.

Moreover, reality is beginning to conform to intentions. The legalization of equitable principles and relevant circumstances has been a giant step forward in this process. Even if it is the courts which, in the silence of States, have been called on to define what, in law, it is appropriate to regard as equitable, and to determine what factors should be treated as relevant, the decision which they take in each case can no longer be seen as purely ad hoc, liable to fluctuate from one case to another at judicial whim. The decision which they take in each case *is a statement of the law*; it *makes the law*. No doubt future judgments will further clarify the content of the legal rules relating to equitable principles and relevant circumstances; after all, neither Rome nor the law was built in a day.

There has been more progress on this point than is often realized. We have seen that, behind the inchoate mass of relevant circumstances—"geographical or other", to adopt the all-embracing language of the *Anglo-French* award—lies an essentially simple reality. What the judge basically has to assess in the second phase of the delimitation process is whether or not the equidistant line seems to him to approach so close to the coast of one of the States as to compromise its political and economic interests. Equity here is nothing more and nothing less. Certainly, the very nature of the line of equidistance should ensure its reasonable distance from both the coasts. But the judge may think that geography has done things badly, and will then undertake the correction of the normal effect of nature. The provisional line of equidistance, originating in distance, will be tested against distance and, if necessary, adjusted by distance. The spatial parameter will have dominated the starting-line of equidistance; it will also dominate the definitive line which emerges from any adjustment of the provisional line. In the first, equidistant, phase, the spatial parameter will be applied to geography as it is; in the adjustment phase, it will be related to geography as corrected in the light of the judicial assessment of equity. This single, spatial, relevant circumstance comprises various elements including security and a sufficiently large area of economic resources for exploitation. But, beyond these acknowledged concepts, there is something more: the political, not to say geopolitical, idea (a little confused but very potent) that *maritime jurisdictions, just as territorial sovereignty, express themselves in spatial terms*. Behind the ostensibly technical analyses which dominate the matter lurks the gut concept of territory which is inherent in the idea of the State. Territory is power.

Finally, the last stage of the law's conquest of the delimitation process: the legal regulation of the adjustment of the starting line of equidistance. This final step is the least secure, and it will take time for the courts to implement the guidelines of the 1977 *Anglo-French* award, which favours a minimalist approach with any adjustment limited to a variant of equidistance and essential minor changes to the starting-line of equidistance.

But we should have no illusions. Even at its tightest, the normative net will always leave room for judicial assessment, an unassailable bastion of discretionary power. However great the legal conquest of maritime delimitation, the most refined of judicial reasoning will never lead automatically to a predetermined solution and the "gap", mentioned at the beginning of this study, between the legal argumentation of a judicial decision and the actual line, will never be completely closed. No matter how many legal rules there may be, the theory of relevant circumstances will always elude scientific definition: however much account the judge may take of circumstances, he will never be restricted to the passive discovery of the solution; he will always arrive at it through active intervention—a matter of appreciation in the words of the *Anglo-French* award.[2] And when all is said and done, it is "the judge's eye"[3] which would seem to be the instrument of last resort for assessing whether the line of equidistance stays sufficiently far from both coasts and, if it does not, for choosing an appropriate line. The words of the Anglo-French Court of Arbitration remain profoundly true:

> . . . it is never a question either of complete or of no freedom of choice as a method.[4]

A situation "regrettable but doubtless inevitable", the writers of the joint separate opinion in *Libya/Malta* say.[5] Inevitable, yes. Regrettable, no. In this matter as in every other, the judicial function includes an irreducible element of discretion which, in the eloquent language of this same opinion, constitutes the 'utmost, in all honour, that a judge can ... do''; this is both the difficulty and the importance of his task. Without this element, the law and the judicial function would be but slaves to the given when, in fact, they are and must remain the work of man.

In order, nonetheless, to reduce the irreducible, it has been suggested that the role of the International Court of Justice should be limited to indicating the applicable principles and rules. Except in the case of an explicit request for a judgment *ex aequo et bono*, the Court should refuse itself to make a real delimitation, that is, to decide the

---

[2] *Anglo-French* award, para. 70.

[3] Gros, *Gulf of Maine*, Dissenting Opinion, p. 386, para. 41.

[4] *Anglo-French* award, para. 84.

[5] Ruda, Bedjaoui and Jiménez de Aréchaga, *Libya/Malta*, Joint Separate Opinion, p. 90, para. 37.

actual line of the maritime boundary; this task, which is akin to that of a boundary commission, would be left to conciliation agencies.[6]

However attractive it may seem, this suggestion is unacceptable. It is one thing for the parties to be able to limit their request to an indication of the applicable principles and rules of international law, but to go on from there to say that they may not ask the Court to draw the boundary and that the Court should in any case decline such a task is quite another, and a totally inadmissible step. There is nothing abnormal or shocking in the fact that the line adopted by the Court, as by any other judge or arbitrator deciding on the basis of law, is not mathematically determined and that the Court chooses from amongst a number of lines, all equally acceptable legally, the one that will become *the* boundary. After all, no judge ever arrives at a decision determined in advance, whether he is decreeing a divorce, annulling a law or regulation, attributing responsibility or assessing damages. The courts have reacted healthily in declining, as we have seen, by a silence which speaks volumes if not actually by a formal refusal, all the attempts at quantification which the parties have suggested to it. Non-encroachment, coastal configuration, special geographical features, a relationship of opposition or adjacency, proportionality: none of the concepts making up the delimitation process has so far been the subject of any scientific, or even reasonably rigorous, definition; all depend, in various degrees, on the qualitative and therefore intuitive assessment of the judge.[7] ''I know it when I see it.''

---

[6] Conforti, pp. 324ff.

[7] The relations between the law of maritime delimitation and technique are complicated (cf. Weil [1]). The so-called envelope of arcs of circles (or tangential curve) method has been integrated into the law (see pp. 63ff above), but for fixing the outer limit, not delimitation. It is true that, in some respects, this technique has been a source of inspiration for the construction of lines of equidistance (cf. pp. 74ff above), but the legal status of the equidistance method and the legal regime of basepoints for the construction of lines of equidistance remain the subject of controversy. So far, no attempt to deal scientifically with any aspect of the law of maritime delimitation has succeeded. The abandonment of the theory of natural physical prolongation and, more generally, of the concept of the natural maritime boundary, has robbed the technical data relating to the geology and geophysics of the seabed or the ecology of superjacent maritime expanses of all interest. The United States' attempt to represent mathematically the encroachment effect it imputed to the equidistance method in the presence of certain special geographical features (see *Gulf of Maine*, United States Pleadings, C 1/CR 88/11, pp. 33ff: ''A Geometric Analysis of the Cut-off Effect'') was not reflected in the judgment. Nor was there any reaction to the Canadian attempt to present a mathematical definition of the distinction between adjacent and opposite coasts (see p. 246 above). There is a point, however, on which more precise

(Footnote continued on p. 288)

The law of maritime delimitation has acquired a bad reputation. It is sometimes said that despite all the talk of law there is really nothing the judge cannot do. There is no doubt that certain trends in the case-law have invited this criticism. But the courts, which are constantly groping their way forward, have made a good deal of progress and more is within reach. It would, however, be illusory to think that the day can come when the "power to judge", to adopt Montesquieu's formula, will be "in some way non-existent";[8] worse than that, it would be dangerous.

(Footnote continued from p. 287)
mathematical research could be useful: the concepts of overlapping zones and their division into (more or less) equal parts in relation to the equidistance technique (cf. pp. 58-9 above).

[8] *De l'esprit des lois*, Livre XI, 6.

LAW OF THE SEA CONVENTIONS, 1958 AND 1982: PROVISIONS RELATING TO DELIMITATION

1. Territorial Sea

Geneva Convention on the Territorial Sea and the Contiguous Zone, 1958, Article 12, paragraph 1:

1. Where the coasts of two States are opposite or adjacent to each other, neither of the two States is entitled, failing agreement between them to the contrary, to extend its territorial sea beyond the median line every point of which is equidistant from the nearest points on the baselines from which the breadth of the territorial seas of each of the two States is measured. The provisions of this paragraph shall not apply, however, where it is necessary by reason of historic title or other special circumstances to delimit the territorial seas of the two States in a way which is at variance with this provision.

United Nations Convention on the Law of the Sea, 1982, Article 15:

Where the coasts of two States are opposite or adjacent to each other, neither of the two States is entitled, failing agreement between them to the contrary, to extend its territorial sea beyond the median line every point of which is equidistant from the nearest points on the baselines from which the breadth of the territorial seas of each of the two States is measured. The above provision does not apply, however, where it is necessary by reason of historic title or other special circumstances to delimit the territorial seas of the two States in a way which is at variance therewith.

2. Contiguous Zone

Geneva Convention on the Territorial Sea and the Contiguous Zone, 1958, Article 24, paragraph 3:

3. Where the coasts of two States are opposite or adjacent to each other, neither of the two States is entitled, failing agreement between them to the contrary, to extend its contiguous zone beyond the median line every point of which is equidistant from the nearest points on the baselines from which the breadth of the territorial seas of the two States is measured.

3. Continental Shelf

Geneva Convention on the Continental Shelf, 1958, Article 6:

1. Where the same continental shelf is adjacent to the territories of two or more States whose coasts are opposite each other, the boundary of the continental shelf appertaining to such States shall be determined by agreement between them. In the absence of agreement, and unless another

boundary line is justified by special circumstances, the boundary is the median line, every point of which is equidistant from the nearest points of the baselines from which the breadth of the territorial sea of each State is measured.

2. Where the same continental shelf is adjacent to the territories of two adjacent States, the boundary of the continental shelf shall be determined by agreement between them. In the absence of agreement, and unless another boundary line is justified by special circumstances, the boundary shall be determined by application of the principle of equidistance from the nearest points of the baselines from which the breadth of the territorial sea of each State is measured.

United Nations Convention on the Law of the Sea, 1982, Article 83, paragraph 1:

1. The delimitation of the continental shelf between States with opposite or adjacent coasts shall be effected by agreement on the basis of international law, as referred to in Article 38 of the Statute of the International Court of Justice, in order to achieve an equitable solution.

4. Exclusive Economic Zone

United Nations Convention on the Law of the Sea, 1982, Article 74, paragraph 1:

1. The delimitation of the exclusive economic zone between States with opposite or adjacent coasts shall be effected by agreement on the basis of international law, as referred to in Article 38 of the Statute of the International Court of Justice, in order to achieve an equitable solution.

BIBLIOGRAPHY

The bibliography which follows is devoted in the main to those principal works and articles treating the legal problems raised by judicial or arbitral delimitation of which the full titles and references are not given in the text or footnotes. It also includes some studies dealing with the techniques of delimitation and delimitation agreements already concluded. Studies relating to delimitations being made or still to be made have been omitted. General works on the law of the sea are cited only in so far as they include significant discussion of the problems raised in the present book.

Adede, A.O., "Toward the Formulation of the Rule of Delimitation of Sea Boundaries between States with Adjacent or Opposite Coasts", 19 *Virg. J* (1979), 207.

Alexander, L.M. [1], "Special Circumstances: Semi-Enclosed Seas", in Gamble and Pontecorvo (eds), *Law of the Sea: The Emerging Regime of the Oceans*, Cambridge, Mass., Ballinger (1974), p. 201.

Alexander, L.M. [2], "Baseline Delimitation and Maritime Boundaries", 23 *Virg. J* (1982-83), 503.

Allott, P., "Power Sharing in the Law of the Sea", 77 *AJIL* (1983), 1.

American Society of International Law, "ICJ Decision in the Libya-Tunisia Continental Shelf Case", *Proceedings of the 76th Annual Meeting*, Washington (1982), p. 150.

Apollis, G. [1], *Les frontières maritimes en droit international. Mutations et perspectives*, Paris, Publications du Centre National pour l'exploitation des océans (CNEXO), 7 Rapports économiques et juridiques (1979).

Apollis, G. [2], *L'emprise maritime de l'Etat côtier*, Paris, Pedone (1981).

Auburn, F.M., "The North Sea Continental Shelf Boundary Settlement", 16 *Archiv des Völkerrechts* (1973), 28, 80.

Azcarraga, J.L. de [1], "La sentencia del Tribunal internacional de Justicia sobre los casos de la plataforma continental del mar del Norte", 22 *Revista española de derecho internacional* (1969), 529.

Azcarraga, J.L. de [2], "España suscribe, con Francia e Italia, dos convenios sobre delimitación de sus plataformas submarinas comunes", 28 *Revista española de derecho internacional* (1975), 131.

Beazley, P.B. [1], "Territorial Sea Baselines", 48 *International Hydrographic Review* (1971), 143.

Beazley, P.B. [2], *Maritime Limits and Baselines: A Guide to their Delimitation*, London, The Hydrographic Society, 2nd ed., (1978).

Beazley, P.B. [3], "Half-Effect Applied to Equidistance Lines", 56 *International Hydrographic Review* (1979), 153.

Beazley, P.B. [4], "Maritime Boundaries", 59 *International Hydrographic Review* (1982), 149.

Ben Achour, Y., "L'affaire du plateau continental tuniso-libyen (analyse empirique)", 110 *JDI* (1983), 247.

Blecher, M.D., "Equitable Delimitation of the Continental Shelf", 73 *AJIL* (1979), 60.

Boggs, S.W. [1], "Delimitation of the Territorial Sea", 24 *AJIL* (1930), 541.

Boggs, S.W. [2], "Problems of Water Boundary Definition: Median Lines and
  International Boundaries Through Territorial Waters", 27 *Geographical
  Review* (1937), 445.
Boggs, S.W. [3], *International Boundaries, A Study of Boundary Functions and
  Problems*, New York, Columbia University Press (1940).
Boggs, S.W. [4], "Delimitation of Seaward Areas under National
  Jurisdiction", 45 *AJIL* (1951), 240.
Bowett, D.W. [1], "The Arbitration between the United Kingdom and France
  Concerning the Continental Shelf in the English Channel and South-western
  Approaches", 49 *BYIL* (1978), 1.
Bowett, D.W. [2], *The Legal Regime of Islands in International Law*, Dobbs Ferry,
  New York, Oceana (1979).
Bowett, D.W. [3], "The Economic Factor in Maritime Delimitation Cases",
  in *Etudes en l'honneur de Roberto Ago* (vol. II), Milan, Giuffrè (1987), p. 45.
Brown, E.D. [1], "The North Sea Continental Shelf Cases", 23 *Current Legal
  Problems* (1970), 187.
Brown, E.D. [2], "The Continental Shelf and the Exclusive Economic Zone:
  The Problem of Delimitation at UNCLOS III", 4 *Maritime Policy and
  Management* (1977), 377.
Brown, E.D. [3], "The Anglo-French Continental Shelf Case", *The Year Book
  of World Affairs* (1979), 304.
Brown, E.D. [4], "Delimitation of Offshore Areas: Hard Labour and Bitter
  Fruits at UNCLOS III", 5 *Marine Policy* (1981), 172.
Brown, E.D. [5], "The Tunisia-Libya Continental Shelf Case. A Missed
  Opportunity", 7 *Marine Policy* (1983), 142.
Burmester, H., "The Torres Strait Treaty: Ocean Boundary Delimitation by
  Agreement", 76 *AJIL* (1982), 321.

Caflisch, L. [1], "Les zones maritimes sous juridiction nationale, leurs limites
  et leur délimitation", 84 *RGDIP* (1980), 68.
Caflisch, L. [2], "Les zones maritimes sous juridiction nationale, leurs limites
  et leur délimitation", in Bardonnet and Virally (eds), *Le nouveau droit
  international de la mer*, Paris, Pedone (1983), p. 34.
Caflisch, L. [3], "La délimitation des espaces marins entre Etats dont les côtes
  se font face ou sont adjacentes", in Dupuy and Vignes (eds), *Traité du nouveau
  droit de la mer*, Paris, Economica et Bruxelles, Bruylant (1985), p. 374.
Charney, J.I. [1], "The Delimitation of Lateral Seaward Boundaries in a
  Domestic Context", 75 *AJIL* (1981), 28.
Charney, J.I. [2], "Ocean Boundaries between Nations: A Theory for
  Progress", 78 *AJIL* (1984), 582.
Chiu, H., "Some Problems Concerning the Application of the Delimitation of
  Maritime Boundary Provisions in the 1982 United Nations Convention on
  the Law of the Sea Between Adjacent and Opposite States", 9 *Maryland
  Journal of International Law and Trade* (1985), 1.
Christie, D.R., "From the Shoals of Ras Kaboudia to the Shores of Tripoli:
  The Tunisia/Libya Boundary Delimitation", 13 *Georgia Journal of
  International and Comparative Law* (1983), 12.
Churchill, R.R., "Maritime Delimitation in the Jan Mayen Area", 9 *Marine
  Policy* (1985), 26.

Clain, L.E., "Gulf of Maine: A Disappointing First in the Delimitation of a Single Maritime Boundary", 25 *Virg. J* (1985), 521.

Colliard, C.A., "Principes et règles de droit international applicables en matière de délimitation maritime. Analyse de la 'jurisprudence' de la Cour internationale de Justice", in *Etudes en l'honneur de Roberto Ago* (vol. II), Milan, Giuffrè (1987), p. 87.

Collins, E. and Rogoff, M.A., "The Gulf of Maine Case and the Future of Ocean Boundary Delimitation", 38 *Maine Law Review* (1986), 1.

Colson, D.A., "The United Kingdom-France Continental Shelf Arbitration", 72 *AJIL* (1978), 95.

Combacau, J., *Le droit international de la mer*, Paris, Presses Universitaires de France, Coll. "Que sais-je?" (1985).

Conforti, B. [1], "La delimitazione della piattaforma continentale del Mare del Nord", 52 *Rivista di diritto internazionale* (1969), 509.

Conforti, B. [2], "L'arrêt de la Cour internationale de Justice dans l'affaire de la délimitation du plateau continental entre la Libye et Malte", 90 *RGDIP* (1986), 313.

Conforti, B. and Francalanci, G., *Atlante dei confini sottomarini—Atlas of the Seabed Boundaries*, Milan, Giuffrè (1979).

Cooper, J., "Delimitation of the Maritime Boundary in the Gulf of Maine Area", 16 *Ocean Development and International Law* (1986), 59.

David, E., "La sentence arbitrale du 14 février 1985 sur la délimitation de la frontière maritime Guinée/Guinée-Bissau", *AFDI* (1985), 350.

Decaux, E. [1], "L'arrêt de la Cour internationale de Justice dans l'affaire du plateau continental (Tunisie/Libye)", *AFDI* (1982), 357.

Decaux, E. [2], "L'arrêt de la Chambre de la Cour internationale de Justice sur l'affaire de la délimitation de la frontière maritime dans le golfe du Maine", *AFDI* (1984), 304.

Decaux, E. [3], "L'arrêt de la Cour internationale de Justice dans l'affaire du plateau continental (Libye/Malte)", *AFDI* (1985), 294.

Degan, V.D., "'Equitable Principles' in Maritime Delimitations", in *Etudes en l'honneur de Roberto Ago* (vol. II), Milan, Giuffrè (1987), p. 107.

Delin, L., "Shall Islands Be Taken into Account when Drawing the Median Line According to Art. 6 of the Convention on the Continental Shelf?" 41 *NTIR* (1971), 205.

Dipla, H., *Le régime juridique des îles dans le droit international de la mer*, Paris, Presses Universitaires de France (1984).

Dupuy, P.M., "Note sur la disparition récente de deux groupements insulaires en Méditerranée orientale", 7 *Annuaire de droit maritime et aérien* (1983), 209.

Durante, F., "Norme generali e regole convenzionali per la delimitazione della piattaforma continentale", 53 *Rivista di diritto internazionale* (1970), 5.

Ely, N., "Seabed Boundaries Between Coastal States: The Effect to be Given Islets as 'Special Circumstances'", 6 *International Lawyer* (1972), 219.

Eustache, F., "L'affaire du plateau continental de la Mer du Nord devant la Cour internationale de Justice", 74 *RGDIP* (1970), 590.

Evensen, J. [1], "La délimitation entre la Norvège et l'Islande du plateau continental dans le secteur de Jan Mayen", *AFDI* (1981), 711.

Evensen, J. [2], "The Delimitation of the Exclusive Economic Zone as Highlighted by the International Court of Justice", in Rozakis and Stephanou (eds), *The New Law of the Sea*, Athens and Amsterdam, North Holland (1983), p. 107.

Feldman, M.B. and Colson, D., "The Maritime Boundaries of the United States", 75 *AJIL* (1981), 729.
Feldman, M.B., "The Tunisia-Libya Continental Shelf Case: Geographic Justice or Judicial Compromise?", 77 *AJIL* (1983), 219.
Feulner, G.R., "Delimitation of Continental Shelf Jurisdiction Between States: The Effect of Physical Irregularities in the Natural Continental Shelf", 17 *Virginia Law Journal* (1976), 77.
Foighel, I., "The North Sea Continental Shelf Case", 39 *NTIR* (1969), 109.
Friedmann, W., "The North Sea Continental Shelf Cases—A Critique", 64 *AJIL* (1970), 229.

Galindo Pohl, R., "Comentarios sobre el caso relativo a la plataforma continental entre Libia y Tunez", *Anuario juridico interamericano* (1984), 95.
Gherari, M., "Délimitation du plateau continental tuniso-libyen", *Revue politique africaine* (1984), 39.
Gidel, G., *Le droit international de la mer*, 3 volumes, Paris, Sirey (1932-1934).
Goldie, L.F.E. [1], "The North Sea Continental Shelf Cases: A Ray of Hope for the International Court?", 16 *New York Law Forum* (1970), 325.
Goldie, L.F.E. [2], "The North Sea Continental Shelf Cases: A Postscript", 18 *New York Law Forum* (1972), 411.
Goldie, L.F.E. [3], "A Lexicographical Controversy: The Word 'Adjacent' in Article 1 of the Continental Shelf Convention", 66 *AJIL* (1972), 829.
Goldie, L.F.E. [4], "The International Court of Justice's 'Natural Prolongation' and the Continental Shelf Problem of Islands", 4 *Netherlands Yearbook of International Law* (1973), 237.
Gounaris, E. [1], "The Delimitation of the Continental Shelf of Islands: Some Observations", 33 *Revue hellénique de droit international* (1980), 111.
Gounaris, E. [2], "The Delimitation of the Continental Shelf of Jan Mayen", 21 *Archiv des Völkerrechts* (1983), 492.
Grisel, E., "The Lateral Boundaries of the Continental Shelf and the Judgment of the International Court of Justice in the North Sea Continental Shelf Case", 64 *AJIL* (1970), 562.
Gros Espiell, H., "Le traité relatif au 'Rio de la Plata' et sa façade maritime", *AFDI* (1975), 241.
Guillaume, G. [1], "La pratique française en matière de délimitation maritime", in *Propos sur le nouveau droit de la mer*, Colloque de l'Académie diplomatique internationale (Paris, 1983), Paris, Pedone (1985), p. 71.
Guillaume, G. [2], "Les accords de délimitation maritime passés par la France", in *Perspectives du droit de la mer à l'issue de la troisième Conférence des Nations Unies*, Colloque de la Société française pour le droit international (Rouen, 1983), Paris, Pedone (1984), p. 276.
Gutteridge, J.A.C., "The 1958 Geneva Convention on the Continental Shelf", 35 *BYIL* (1959), 102.

Herman, L., "The Court Giveth and the Court Taketh Away: An Analysis of the Tunisia-Libya Continental Shelf Case", 33 *ICLQ* (1984), 825.

Hodgson, D.C., "The Tunisia-Libya Continental Shelf Case", 16 *Case Western Reserve Journal of International Law* (1984), 1.

Hodgson, R.D. [1], "Islands: Normal and Special Circumstances", in Gamble and Pontecorvo (eds), *Law of the Sea: The Emerging Regime of the Oceans*, Cambridge, Mass., Ballinger (1974), p. 137.

Hodgson, R.D. [2], "The Delimitation of Maritime Boundaries between Opposite and Adjacent States through the Economic Zone and the Continental Shelf: Selected State Practice", in *Law of the Sea: State Practice in Zones of Special Jurisdiction*, Proceedings of the Law of the Sea Institute (1979), Honolulu (1982), p. 280.

Hodgson, R.D. and Cooper, J., "The Technical Delimitation of a Modern Equidistant Boundary", 3 *Ocean Development and International Law Journal* (1976), 361.

Hodgson, R.D. and Smith, R.W. [1], "The Informal Single Negotiating Text (Committee II): A Geographical Perspective", 3 *Ocean Development and International Law Journal* (1976), 225.

Hodgson, R.D. and Smith, R.W. [2], "Boundary Issues Created by Extended National Marine Jurisdictions", 69 *Geographic Review* (1979), 422.

Hutchinson, D.N., "The Seaward Limit to Continental Shelf Jurisdiction in International Law", 56 *BYIL* (1985), 111.

Irwin, P.C., "Settlement of Maritime Boundaries Disputes: An Analysis of the Law of the Sea Negotiations", 8 *Ocean Development and International Law Journal* (1979), 105.

Jagota, S.P. [1], "Maritime Boundary", 171 *Recueil des Cours de l'Académie de droit international* (1981-II), 83.

Jagota, S.P. [2], *Maritime Boundary*, The Hague, Nijhoff (1985).

Jennings, R.Y., "The Limits of Continental Shelf Jurisdiction: Some Possible Implications of the North Sea Case Judgment", 18 *ICLQ* (1969), 819.

Jewett, M., "The Evolution of the Legal Regime of the Continental Shelf", *CYIL*, vol. 22 (1984), p. 153 and vol. 23 (1985), p. 201.

Jiménez de Aréchaga, E., "The Conception of Equity in Maritime Delimitation", in *Études en l'honneur de Roberto Ago* (vol. II), Milan, Giuffrè (1987), p. 229.

Johnson, D.H.N., "The North Sea Continental Shelf Cases", 3 *International Relations* (1969), 522.

Kamto, M., "L'affaire de la délimitation maritime Guinée/Guinée-Bissau", 41 *Revue égyptienne de droit international* (1985), 73.

Karl, D.E., "Islands and the Delimitation of the Continental Shelf: A Framework for Analysis", 71 *AJIL* (1977), 642.

Kingue, N., "La sentence du 14 février 1985 du Tribunal d'arbitrage dans l'affaire de la délimitation de la frontière maritime entre la Guinée et la Guinée-Bissau", 91 *RGDIP* (1987), 45.

Klemm, U.D., "Allgemeine Abgrenzungsprobleme verschiedener seerechtlich definierter Räume", 38 *ZaöRV* (1978), 512

Lagoni, R., "Interim Measures Pending Maritime Delimitation Agreements", 78 *AJIL* (1984), 345.

Lang, J., *Le plateau continental de la Mer du Nord*, Paris, Librairie Générale de Droit et de Jurisprudence (1970).

Langeraar, W. [1], "Maritime Delimitation: The Equiratio Method: A New Approach", 10 *Marine Policy* (1986), 3.

Langeraar, W. [2], "Delimitation of Continental Shelf Areas: A New Approach", 17 *Journal of Maritime Law and Commerce* (1986), 389.

Lapidoth, R., "Equity in International Law", 22 *Israel Law Review* (1987), 161.

Laveissière, J., "Les îles et la détermination des frontières maritimes", in 14 *National and International Boundaries, Thesaurus Acroasium* (Session 1983), Institute of Public International Law and International Relations, Thessaloniki (1985), p. 79.

Legault, L.H., "A Line for All Uses: the Gulf of Maine Boundary Revisited", 40 *International Journal* (Toronto) (1985), 461.

Legault, L.H. and Hankey, B., "From Sea to Seabed: The Single Maritime Boundary in the Gulf of Maine Case", 79 *AJIL* (1985), 961.

Legault, L.H. and McRae, D., "The Gulf of Maine Case", 22 *CYIL* (1984), 267.

Lucchini, L. and Voelckel, M., *Les Etats et la mer. Le nationalisme maritime*, Paris, La Documentation française (1978).

Lumb, R.D., "The Delimitation of Maritime Boundaries in the Timor Sea", 7 *Australian Year Book of International Law* (1976-77), 72.

McDorman, T.L., "The Libya-Malta Case: Opposite States Confront the Court", 24 *CYIL* (1986), 335.

McDorman, T.L., Saunders, P.M. and Vander Zwaag, D.L., "The Gulf of Maine Boundary: Dropping Anchor or Setting a Course?", 9 *Marine Policy* (1985), 90. McHugh, P., "Delimitation of Maritime Boundaries", 25 *Natural Resources Journal* (1985), 1025.

McRae, D.M., "Proportionality and the Gulf of Maine Maritime Boundary Dispute", 19 *CYIL* (1981), 287.

Manner, E.J., "Settlement of Sea Boundary Disputes According to the Provisions of the 1982 Law of the Sea Convention", in *Etudes de droit international en l'honneur du juge Manfred Lachs*, The Hague, Nijhoff (1984), p. 625.

Marek, F., "Le problème des sources de droit international d'après l'arrêt de la Cour internationale de Justice du 20 février 1969 concernant la mer du Nord", 6 *Revue belge de droit international* (1970), 44.

Marín López, A., "El régimen de las islas en el actual derecho del mar", 38 *Revista española de derecho internacional* (1986), 151.

Marsh, J.E., "The Boundary Provisions of the New United Nations Convention on the Law of the Sea", in 14 *National and International Boundaries, Thesaurus Acroasium* (Session 1983), Institute of Public International Law and International Relations, Thessaloniki (1985), p. 229.

Monconduit, F., "Affaire du plateau continental de la Mer du Nord", *AFDI* (1969), 213.

Münch, F. [1], *Die technischen Fragen des Küstenmeers*, Kiel (1934).

Münch, F. [2], "Das Urteil des Internationalen Gerichtshofes vom 20. Februar 1969 über den deutschen Anteil am Festlandsockel in den Nordsee", 29 *ZaöRV* (1969), 455.

Nelson, L.D.M., "Equity and the Delimitation of Maritime Boundaries", *Revue iranienne de relations internationales* (1978), 197.

Nordquist *et al.* (eds), *New Directions in the Law of the Sea*, published by The British Institute of International and Comparative Law, 10 vols, Dobbs Ferry, New York, Oceana (1973-1980).

O'Connell, D.P., *The International Law of the Sea*, edited by Shearer, I.A., 2 volumes, Oxford, Clarendon Press, (1982 and 1984).

Oda, S. [1], "Boundary of the Continental Shelf", *The Japanese Annual of International Law* (1968), 264.

Oda, S. [2], *The International Law of the Ocean Development. Basic Documents*, 2 vol., Leiden, Sijthoff (1976).

Oda, S. [3], "Delimitation of a Single Maritime Boundary. The Contribution of Equidistance to Geographical Equity in the Interrelated Domains of the Continental Shelf and the Exclusive Economic Zone", in *Etudes en l'honneur de Roberto Ago* (vol. II), Milan, Giuffrè (1987), p. 349.

Oellers-Frahm, K., "Die Entscheidung des Internationalen Gerichtshofes zur Abgrenzung des Festlandsockels zwischen Tunisien und Libyen", 42 *ZaöRV* (1982), 804.

Orrego Vicuna, F., "La zone économique exclusive: régime et nature juridique dans le droit international", 199 *Recueil des Cours de l'Académie de droit international* (1986-IV), 9.

Padwa, D.J., "Submarine Boundaries", 9 *ICLQ* (1960), 628.

Pazarci, H., *La délimitation du plateau continental des îles*, Ankara, Publication de la Faculté des Sciences Politiques de l'Université d'Ankara (1982).

Pharand, D., "Delimitation of Maritime Boundaries: Continental Shelf and Exclusive Economic Zone in Light of the Gulf of Maine Case", 16 *Revue générale de droit* (Ottawa) (1985), 363.

Prescott, J.R.V., *Maritime Political Boundaries of the World*, London, Methuen (1985).

Quéneudec, J.P., "L'affaire de la délimitation du plateau continental entre la France et le Royaume-Uni", 83 *RGDIP* (1979), 53.

Reuter, P., "Une ligne unique de délimitation des espaces maritimes?", in *Mélanges Georges Perrin*, Lausanne, Payot (1984), p. 251.

Reynaud, A. [1], *Le différend du plateau continental de la Mer du Nord devant la Cour internationale de Justice*, Paris, Librairie Générale de Droit et de Jurisprudence, (1975).

Reynaud, A. [2], *Le plateau continental de la France*, Paris, Librairie Générale de Droit et de Jurisprudence (1984).

Rhee, S.M., "Sea Boundary Delimitation between States Before World War II", 76 *AJIL* (1982), 555.

Richardson, E.L., "Jan Mayen in Perspective", 82 *AJIL* (1988), 443.

Rigaldies, F. [1], "La délimitation du plateau continental entre Etats voisins", 14 *CYIL* (1976), 116.

Rigaldies, F. [2], "L'affaire de la délimitation du plateau continental entre la République française et le Royaume-Uni de Grande-Bretagne et d'Irlande du Nord", 106 *JDI* (1979), 506.

Rodríguez Carrión, A., "La sentencia arbitral de 30 de junio de 1977", 30 *Revista española de derecho internacional* (1977), 423.

Rothpfeffer, T., "Equity in the North Sea Continental Shelf Cases", 42 *NTIR* (1972), 81.

Rüster, B. [1], *Verträge und Deklarationen über den Festlandsockel*, Frankfurt, Metzner (1975).

Rüster, B. [2], *Die Rechtsordnung des Festlandsockels*, Berlin, Duncker & Humblot (1977).

Sanchez Rodríguez, L.I., "La sentencia del Tribunal internacional de Justicia de 24 de Febrero de 1982, en el asunto relativo a la plataforma continental entre Tunez y la Jamahiriya Arabe Libia", 35 *Revista española de derecho internacional* (1983), 61.

Scelle, G., "Plateau continental et droit international", 68 *RGDIP* (1955), 5.

Schneider, J., "The Gulf of Maine Case: The Nature of an Equitable Result", 79 *AJIL* (1985), 539.

Shalowitz, A.L., *Shore and Sea Boundaries*, Washington, Department of Commerce, 2 volumes (1962-1964).

Smith, R.W. [1], "The Maritime Boundaries of the United States", 71 *Geographical Review* (1981), 395.

Smith, R.W. [2], "A Geographical Primer to Maritime Boundary Making", 12 *Ocean Development and International Law* (1982), 1.

Smith, R.W. [3], *Exclusive Economic Zone Claims: An Analysis and Primary Documents*, The Hague, Nijhoff (1986).

Symonides, J., "Delimitation of Maritime Areas between States with Opposite or Adjacent Coasts", 12 *Polish Yearbook of International Law Journal* (1984), 19.

Symmons, C.R., *The Maritime Zones of Islands in International Law*, The Hague, Nijhoff (1979).

Tullio, L., "L'accordo italo-jugoslavo per la delimitazione della piattaforma continentale d'ell'Adriatico", 35 *Rivista del diritto della navigazione* (1969), 300.

US Department of State, Office of the Geographer, *Limits in the Seas*: since 1970, a number of maritime delimitation agreements, among other documents, together with maps and commentaries, have been published under this title.

Usman, A., "The Timor Gap in the Delimitation of the Continental Shelf Boundary Between Indonesia and Australia", 14 *The Indonesian Quarterly* (1986), 375.

Vallée, Ch., *Le plateau continental dans le droit positif actuel*, Paris, Pedone (1971).

Villani, U., "La delimitazione della piattaforma continentale e della zona economica esclusiva ai sensi della Convenzione delle Nazioni Unite sul diritto del mare", 68 *Rivista di diritto internazionale* (1985), 261.

Virally, M., "L'équité dans le droit. A propos des problèmes de délimitation maritime", in *Etudes en l'honneur de Roberto Ago* (vol. II), Milan, Giuffrè (1987), p. 523.

Visscher, C. de, *Problèmes de Confins en Droit International Public,* Paris, Pedone (1969).

Voelckel, M. [1], "Les lignes de base dans la Convention de Genève sur la mer territoriale", *AFDI* (1973), 820.

Voelckel, M. [2], "Aperçu de quelques problèmes techniques concernant la délimitation des frontières maritimes", *AFDI* (1979), 693.

Vukas, B., "The Law of the Sea Convention and Sea Boundaries Delimitation", in *Essays on the New Law of the Sea*, Zagreb (1985), p. 147.

Waldock, H.M., "The International Court and the Law of the Sea", TMC Asser Institute, Cornelis von Vollenhoven First Memorial Lecture, 22 March 1979.

Weil, P. [1], "La technique 'comme partie intégrante du droit international': à propos des méthodes de délimitation des juridictions maritimes", in *Etudes offertes à Claude-Albert Colliard*, Paris, Pedone (1984), p. 347.

Weil, P. [2], "A propos du droit coutumier en matière de délimitation maritime", in *Etudes en l'honneur de Roberto Ago* (vol. II), Milan, Giuffrè (1987), p. 535.

Wengler, W., "Der Internationale Gerichtshof und die Abgrenzung des Meeresbodens im Mittelmeer", 35 *Neue Juristische Wochenschrift* (1982), p. 1198.

Whiteman, M.M. [1], *Digest of International Law* (vol. 4), Washington, Department of State (1965), Chapters IX and XI.

Whiteman, M.M. [2], "Conference on the Law of the Sea: Convention on the Continental Shelf", 52 *AJIL* (1958), 629.

Willis, L.A., "From Precedent to Precedent: The Triumph of Pragmatism in the Law of Maritime Boundaries", 24 *CYIL* (1986), 3.

Wlosowicz, Z., "The Malta/Libya Case: Shelf Delimitation by the Distance Principle and How to Influence Decisions Without Intervening", 44 *CLJ* (1985), 341.

Young, R., "Equitable Solutions for Offshore Boundaries: The 1968 Saudi-Arabian-Iran Agreement", 64 *AJIL* (1970), 152.

Zoller, E. [1], "L'affaire de la délimitation du plateau continental entre la République française et le Royaume-Uni de Grande-Bretagne et d'Irlande du Nord", *AFDI* (1977), 359.

Zoller, E. [2], "Recherche sur les méthodes de délimitation du plateau continental: à propos de l'affaire Tunisie-Libye", 86 *RGDIP* (1982), 645.

INDEX